WORKBOOK

Auto Brakes 》

Fifth Edition

Chris Johanson
ASE Certified Master Technician

Martin T. Stockel
Automotive Writer

Publisher
The Goodheart-Willcox Company, Inc.
Tinley Park, Illinois
www.g-w.com

Copyright © 2021
by
The Goodheart-Willcox Company, Inc.

Previous editions copyright 2015, 2008, 2004, 2000

All rights reserved. No part of this work may be reproduced, stored, or transmitted
in any form or by any electronic or mechanical means, including information storage
and retrieval systems, without the prior written permission of
The Goodheart-Willcox Company, Inc.

Manufactured in the United States of America.

ISBN 978-1-64564-077-6

4 5 6 7 8 9 – 21 – 24 23 22

The Goodheart-Willcox Company, Inc. Brand Disclaimer: Brand names, company names, and illustrations for products and services included in this text are provided for educational purposes only and do not represent or imply endorsement or recommendation by the author or the publisher.

The Goodheart-Willcox Company, Inc. Safety Notice: The reader is expressly advised to carefully read, understand, and apply all safety precautions and warnings described in this book or that might also be indicated in undertaking the activities and exercises described herein to minimize risk of personal injury or injury to others. Common sense and good judgment should also be exercised and applied to help avoid all potential hazards. The reader should always refer to the appropriate manufacturer's technical information, directions, and recommendations; then proceed with care to follow specific equipment operating instructions. The reader should understand these notices and cautions are not exhaustive.

The publisher makes no warranty or representation whatsoever, either expressed or implied, including but not limited to equipment, procedures, and applications described or referred to herein, their quality, performance, merchantability, or fitness for a particular purpose. The publisher assumes no responsibility for any changes, errors, or omissions in this book. The publisher specifically disclaims any liability whatsoever, including any direct, indirect, incidental, consequential, special, or exemplary damages resulting, in whole or in part, from the reader's use or reliance upon the information, instructions, procedures, warnings, cautions, applications, or other matter contained in this book. The publisher assumes no responsibility for the activities of the reader.

The Goodheart-Willcox Company, Inc. Internet Disclaimer: The Internet resources and listings in this Goodheart-Willcox Publisher product are provided solely as a convenience to you. These resources and listings were reviewed at the time of publication to provide you with accurate, safe, and appropriate information. Goodheart-Willcox Publisher has no control over the referenced websites and, due to the dynamic nature of the Internet, is not responsible or liable for the content, products, or performance of links to other websites or resources. Goodheart-Willcox Publisher makes no representation, either expressed or implied, regarding the content of these websites, and such references do not constitute an endorsement or recommendation of the information or content presented. It is your responsibility to take all protective measures to guard against inappropriate content, viruses, or other destructive elements.

Cover Image Credit. socrates471/Shutterstock.com

Table of Contents

Copyright Goodheart-Willcox Co., Inc.
May not be reproduced or posted to a publicly accessible website

Copyright Goodheart-Willcox Co., Inc.
May not be reproduced or posted to a publicly accessible website

Introduction

The **Workbook for Auto Brakes** is a supplemental text designed to reinforce your understanding of the important information supplied in the textbook. To accomplish this task, the workbook utilizes several types of questions to highlight key aspects relating to the operation, construction, design, maintenance, troubleshooting, and repair of brake systems.

As with the textbook, a list of objectives is provided at the beginning of each chapter of the workbook to summarize what should be learned. Each question in every workbook chapter is presented in a manner that measures your comprehension and knowledge of the important topics.

The workbook units correlate to those in the textbook. The order of the questions follows the sequence of the textbook material. This will make it easier for you to find information in the text and also to check your answers. It is recommended that you study the **Auto Brakes** textbook before you attempt to answer questions in this workbook. After studying the textbook, try to answer as many of the workbook questions as possible without referring to the text. Answer any remaining questions by referring to the appropriate areas in the textbook chapter.

The basic purpose of the **Auto Brakes** textbook is to help you become a successful brake technician. The basic function of the workbook is to provide a study guide that reinforces your knowledge and understanding of the important information contained in the textbook.

Chris Johanson
Martin T. Stockel

Copyright Goodheart-Willcox Co., Inc.
May not be reproduced or posted to a publicly accessible website

Instructions for Answering Workbook Questions

Each chapter in this workbook directly correlates to the same chapter in the text. Before answering the questions in the workbook, study the assigned chapter in the text and answer the end-of-chapter review questions. Then, review the objectives at the beginning of each workbook chapter. This will help you review the important concepts presented in the chapter. Try to complete as many workbook questions as possible without referring to the textbook. Then, use the text to complete the remaining questions.

A variety of questions are used in the workbook including multiple choice, identification, completion, and short answer. These questions should be answered in the following manner:

Multiple Choice

Select the best answer and write the correct answer in the blank.

1. Most parking brakes are operated by a _____.
   (A) push button
   (B) foot pedal
   (C) computer
   (D) None of the above.

1. _B_____

Completion

In the blank provided, write the word or words that best complete the statement.

2. Brake lines should never be cut with a _____.

2. _hacksaw_____

Copyright Goodheart-Willcox Co., Inc.
May not be reproduced or posted to a publicly accessible website

Identification

Identify the components indicated on the illustration or photograph accompanying the question.

3. Identify the parts of the disc brake assembly illustrated below.

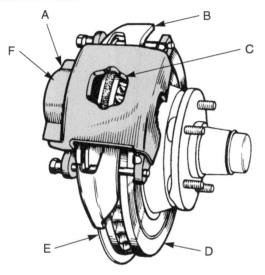

3. (A) Floating caliper

(B) Anchor plate

(C) Inspection hole

(D) Rotor

(E) Splash shield

(F) Piston housing

Short Answer

Provide complete responses to the statements.

4. Why is it important to keep hand tools free of oil and grease?

To prevent slippage that can cause injury; to have a professional appearance.

Other Types of Questions

When other types of workbook questions are presented, follow the specific instructions that accompany the problem.

Copyright Goodheart-Willcox Co., Inc.
May not be reproduced or posted to a publicly accessible website

Copyright Goodheart-Willcox Co., Inc.
May not be reproduced or posted to a publicly accessible website

Chapter 1

Introduction to Brake Systems

After studying this chapter, you will be able to:
- ❏ Identify the purpose of automotive brakes.
- ❏ Compare holding and stopping brakes.
- ❏ Describe the development of modern brake systems.
- ❏ Describe basic brake system hydraulic components.
- ❏ Describe basic brake system friction components.
- ❏ Describe power brake components and state their purpose.
- ❏ Describe parking brake components and state their purpose.
- ❏ State the purpose and major types of wheel bearings.
- ❏ Define the purpose of anti-lock brakes and traction control systems.
- ❏ Explain the operation of regenerative brake systems.
- ❏ Describe basic brake system operation.

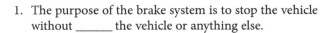

1. The purpose of the brake system is to stop the vehicle without _____ the vehicle or anything else.

1. _____

2. Identify the brake components listed in the illustration below.

2. (A)_____

(B)_____

(C)_____

(D)_____

(E)_____

(F)_____

(G)_____

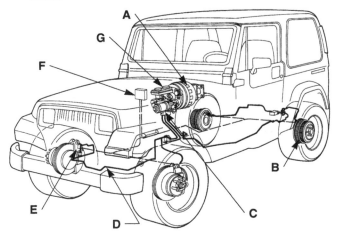

Copyright Goodheart-Willcox Co., Inc.
May not be reproduced or posted to a publicly accessible website

3. The holding brake is applied when the vehicle is _____.

4. The stopping brake is applied when the vehicle is _____.

5. When the brake friction elements become so hot they can no longer stop the vehicle, the vehicle is experiencing brake _____.

6. The first automotive brakes were operated by _____ between the brake pedal and wheel brakes. _____ brakes replaced the linkage operating method.

7. All of the following were used as early brakes, EXCEPT:
   (A) wheel hole and stick.
   (B) disc brake.
   (C) snubbing chain.
   (D) rim brake.

8. All of the following were used as friction material in early brake systems, EXCEPT:
   (A) brass.
   (B) leather.
   (C) camel hair
   (D) kevlar.

9. In what year did federal law require dual master cylinders?

10. Dual master cylinders have two separate _____ in one housing.
    (A) power boosters
    (B) proportioning valves
    (C) pistons
    (D) brake pedals

11. The brake pedal is connected to the _____ through a pushrod.

12. Identify the power brake components listed in the illustration below.

3. _____

4. _____

5. _____

6. _____
   _____

7. _____

8. _____

9. _____

10. _____

11. _____

12. (A)_____

(B)_____

(C)_____

(D)_____

(E)_____

(F)_____

(G)_____

(H)_____

Name _____

13. If one side of a dual master cylinder loses its pressure, the
_____ will illuminate a dashboard warning light.

13. _____

14. A(n) _____, sometimes called a(n) _____, is installed
between the master cylinder and firewall.

14. _____

_____

15. Most power boosters are powered by _____ or _____.

15. _____

_____

16. Technician A says steel brake lines are used to connect
hydraulic parts that move. Technician B says brake hoses
are used to connect hydraulic parts that do not move.
Who is right?
(A) A only.
(B) B only.
(C) Both A and B.
(D) Neither A nor B.

16. _____

17. Match the part with its function or description.
(A) Limits pressure to rear wheels.
(B) Type of pressure cylinder.
(C) Transmits hydraulic pressure.
(D) Reduces pedal effort.
(E) A combination of two valves.
(F) Limits pressure to front wheels.

17. _D_ Power brake booster

_C_ Brake hoses

_F_ Metering valve

_A_ Proportioning valve

_B_ Caliper

18. _____ are pressure cylinders with pistons on each end.

18. _____

19. Technician A says that brake friction materials must
resist heat. Technician B says that modern brake friction
materials are made of asbestos. Who is right?
(A) A only.
(B) B only.
(C) Both A and B.
(D) Neither A nor B.

19. _____

20. It has been determined that brake linings made with
asbestos can cause _____.

20. _____

21. Contact with the stationary disc brake pads and the spin-
ning _____ slows the vehicle.

21. _____

22. Most drums and rotors are made of what metal?
(A) Aluminum.
(B) Cast iron.
(C) Brass.
(D) Copper.

22. _____

23. Wheel cylinders push the brake shoes into contact with the:
(A) parking brake.
(B) pedal linkage.
(C) rotor.
(D) drum.

23. _____

Copyright Goodheart-Willcox Co., Inc.
May not be reproduced or posted to a publicly accessible website

24. What are the three types of antifriction bearings?

_____

_____

_____

25. Which antifriction bearing is adjustable?   25. _____

26. *True or False?* Parking brakes are usually installed on the   26. _____
    rear wheels.

27. The _____ operates only during hard braking when   27. _____
    skidding is likely.

28. In drum brake systems, _____ release the shoes.   28. _____

29. *True or False?* The caliper piston is pulled away from the   29. _____
    rotor by springs.

30. What happens to the extra brake fluid in the hydraulic system when the brake pedal is released?

_____

_____

_____

_____

_____

31. Regenerative braking is used on hybrid gas/electric vehi-   31. _____
    cles to recover the _____ lost while braking.

Copyright Goodheart-Willcox Co., Inc.
May not be reproduced or posted to a publicly accessible website

Chapter 2

Shop Safety and Environmental Protection

After studying this chapter, you will be able to:
- ❑ Identify the major causes of accidents.
- ❑ Identify brake dust hazards.
- ❑ Explain how to avoid exposure to brake dust.
- ❑ List ways to maintain a safe workplace.
- ❑ List safe work procedures.
- ❑ Identify types of environmental damage caused by improper auto shop practices.
- ❑ Identify ways to prevent environmental damage.

1. *True or False?* Some accidents are inevitable.

2. If the following injuries or illnesses are the result of an accident, mark them with an "A". If they are the result of long-term bodily exposure, mark them with a "B".

1. _____

2. Cancer _____

   Electric shock _____

   Falling _____

   Lung damage _____

   Skin disorders _____

   Hand injury _____

   Poisoning _____

Copyright Goodheart-Willcox Co., Inc.
May not be reproduced or posted to a publicly accessible website

3. Whenever a technician is cutting or grinding, he or she should wear a(n) _____.

3. _____

4. _____ is nothing more than friction material, mixed with road dirt.

4. _____

5. A buildup of asbestos or other fibers in the lungs is called _____.
(A) asbestosis
(B) black lung
(C) cancer
(D) tuberculosis

5. _____

6. Asbestos was used in which of the following parts?
(A) Brake shoes.
(B) Transmission clutches.
(C) Seat cushions.
(D) Both A and B.

6. _____

7. What two factors are responsible for most accidents?

7. _____

_____

8. Technician A says you should always know what types of chemicals are stored in the shop. Technician B says there is an SDS for every piece of equipment in the shop. Who is right?
(A) A only.
(B) B only.
(C) Both A and B.
(D) Neither A nor B.

8. _____

9. You should never use extension cords to operate _____ electrical devices.

9. _____

10. Technician A says that fire extinguishers are permanently charged and do not require periodic service. Technician B says that the fire extinguisher used should be compatible for fighting the type of fire. Who is right?
(A) A only.
(B) B only.
(C) Both A and B.
(D) Neither A nor B.

10. _____

11. *True or False?* A cigarette can ignite oily rags.

11. _____

12. All of the following statements about carbon monoxide are true, EXCEPT:
(A) carbon monoxide is odorless.
(B) carbon monoxide is colorless.
(C) carbon monoxide is harmless.
(D) carbon monoxide can build up quickly.

12. _____

13. *True or False?* Never reach between moving engine parts.

13. _____

14. Parts and scrap materials should be _____ whenever possible.

14. _____

15. Liquids sink into the ground and could contaminate the local source of _____ water.

15. _____

16. Some used engine oil is burned by _____.

16. _____

Copyright Goodheart-Willcox Co., Inc.
May not be reproduced or posted to a publicly accessible website

Name _____

17. Used oil or antifreeze could contain poisonous _____ or heavy _____.

17. _____

_____

18. Changing an engine thermostat could affect vehicle _____.

18. _____

19. In addition to federal laws, _____ may have additional emissions laws.

19. _____

20. The Environmental Protection Agency (EPA) enforces which of the following laws?
    (A) Federal shop safety laws.
    (B) Federal wage and hour laws.
    (C) Federal vehicle emissions laws.
    (D) State laws.

20. _____

21. Automobile repair shops are inherently dangerous. However, many areas in the automotive shop have extra dangers. These areas are designated as _____, or areas where extra alertness and safety precautions are needed.

21. _____

22. Technician A says that it is important to know the quickest route to exit the shop during an emergency. Technician B says that all shops should have clearly marked exits and exit pathways. Who is right?
    (A) A only.
    (B) B only.
    (C) Both A and B.
    (D) Neither A nor B.

22. _____

23. When workplace debris, such as a liquid or dirt, gets into the eyes, it is important that it be removed as soon as possible. Technician A says that this is done by flushing the eye at an eyewash station. Technician B says that the eyewash station should not be blocked by vehicles, boxes, parts, or anything else that prevents easy access. Who is right?
    (A) A only.
    (B) B only.
    (C) Both A and B.
    (D) Neither A nor B.

23. _____

24. Technician A says that electrical systems on older vehicles operated on vehicle battery power and technicians did not have to worry about electrical injury. Technician B says that modern vehicles have various electrical systems using high voltages and amperages that can cause injury or even death. Who is right?
    (A) A only.
    (B) B only.
    (C) Both A and B.
    (D) Neither A nor B.

24. _____

25. *True or False?* Do not assume that a dead high-voltage battery is safe. A high-voltage battery that will no longer operate a vehicle may still produce several hundred volts.

25. _____

Copyright Goodheart-Willcox Co., Inc.
May not be reproduced or posted to a publicly accessible website

26. All of the following statements about working on hybrid
    vehicle voltage circuits are true, EXCEPT:
    (A) Wear insulated rubber gloves when near any of the
        high-voltage electrical components.
    (B) Hybrid vehicle batteries develop hundreds of
        amperes at as much as 600 volts.
    (C) A dead high-voltage battery is safe.
    (D) Before beginning work on hybrid vehicle voltage
        circuits, check the manufacturer's service informa-
        tion for exact procedures.

26. _____

27. All of the following statements about servicing vehicles
    equipped with Supplemental Restraint Systems (SRS), or
    Air Bag Systems are true, EXCEPT:
    (A) When there is a chance of electrical power
        entering any air bag electrical component,
        disconnect or remove the air bag module before
        servicing the vehicle.
    (B) Once out of the vehicle, an air bag is so safe that
        you can literally jump on it. There is no danger of
        it deploying because it is no longer connected to
        the battery.
    (C) Always carry a live (undeployed) inflator module
        securely with both hands and ensure that the bag
        (trim cover side) is pointed away from your body.
    (D) Always place a live module on a bench or other
        surface with the bag and trim cover
        facing up.

27. _____

28. *True or False?* When servicing a brake system on a
    vehicle equipped with Anti-Lock Brakes (ABS) or trac-
    tion control (TCS), these systems must be depressurized
    before loosening bleeder valves or hydraulic lines. If this
    is not done, brake fluid could spray out with great force.

28. _____

Copyright Goodheart-Willcox Co., Inc.
May not be reproduced or posted to a publicly accessible website

Chapter 3

Brake Tools, Shop Equipment, and Service Information

After studying this chapter, you will be able to:
- ❏ Identify common specialty brake tools and explain their use.
- ❏ Identify brake system measuring tools and explain their use.
- ❏ Identify power tools and equipment used in brake service and explain their use.
- ❏ List general rules for the correct use and storage of tools.
- ❏ Identify tool safety rules where they apply.
- ❏ Select the proper tool for the job at hand.

1. Flare-nut wrenches are used to remove tubing _____.

1. _____

2. Technician A says brake spring removal tools are used on drum brakes. Technician B says spring removal tools are used to service disc brake components. Who is right?
   (A) A only.
   (B) B only.
   (C) Both A and B.
   (D) Neither A nor B.

2. _____

3. What are the only two kinds of tubing flares that should be formed on the ends of brake lines?

3. _____
   _____

4. The _____ is the tool used to adjust the brake shoes.

4. _____

5. What type of fastener is shown in the following illustration?

5. _____

Copyright Goodheart-Willcox Co., Inc.
May not be reproduced or posted to a publicly accessible website

6. A wheel cylinder that cannot be cleaned up by honing should be _____.

6. _____

7. Under what conditions would a painter's mask be acceptable for filtering brake dust particles?
    (A) When it is thoroughly wetted with water.
    (B) When it is thoroughly wetted with brake fluid.
    (C) When it is thoroughly wetted with transmission fluid.
    (D) Never.

7. _____

8. _____ resemble steel gauges, but can be identified by their distinct yellow color.

8. _____

9. Proper use of a(n) _____ can prevent the reinstallation of a drum or rotor that is too thin.

9. _____

10. Overtightening a micrometer can cause what two problems?

10. _____

11. A shoe and drum gauge is used to _____ the brake shoes before the _____ is installed.

11. _____

_____

12. *True or False?* A dial indicator can measure rotor thickness.

12. _____

13. The _____ is used to measure the amount of foot pressure needed to apply the brakes.

13. _____

14. The tool in the following picture is used to test the condition of what part of the brake system?
    (A) Brake system fluid.
    (B) Brake hydraulic system.
    (C) Brake friction system.
    (D) Brake pedal effort.

14. _____

15. When installing a new dust boot or seal, use an installer to fully _____ the new part without damaging it.

15. _____

16. A(n) _____ can be used to install a bearing race.

16. _____

17. All of the following tools are used to service the brake hydraulic system, EXCEPT:
    (A) syringe.
    (B) hose and jar.
    (C) spanner.
    (D) siphon.

17. _____

Copyright Goodheart-Willcox Co., Inc.
May not be reproduced or posted to a publicly accessible website

Name _____

18. *True or False?* A jumper wire can be used to energize any electrical circuit.

18. _____

19. _____ can be powered or non-powered.

19. _____

20. Ohmmeters are used to measure electrical _____. Ammeters are used to check _____ flow in a circuit. Voltmeters can measure voltage _____ between two places in a circuit.

20. _____

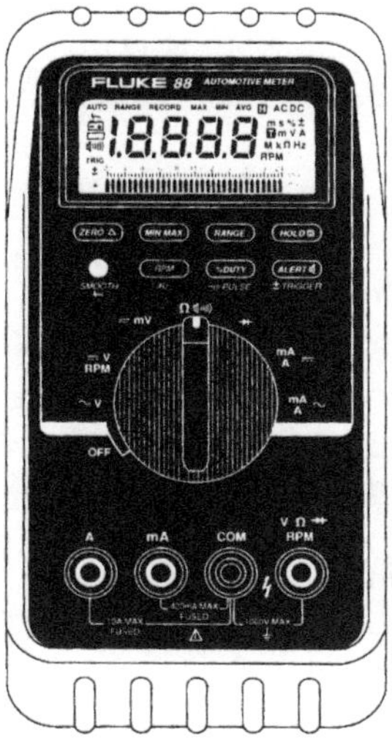

_____

_____

21. The electrical tester shown above contains all of the following meters, EXCEPT:
    (A) voltmeter.
    (B) ammeter.
    (C) ohmmeter.
    (D) scan tool.

21. _____

22. Waveform meters are used to test components of the _____ system.

22. _____

23. To diagnose some early anti-lock brake (ABS) systems, a multimeter was used with a(n) _____ box.

23. _____

24. A scan tool may have all of the following components, EXCEPT:
    (A) a pressure gauge.
    (B) a backup battery.
    (C) a display screen.
    (D) a mass storage cartridge.

24. _____

25. Do not attempt to monitor a scan tool display screen while _____.

25. _____

26. When referring to shop filters, what does HEPA stand for?

26. _____

27. The process of removing the glazed and scored outer layer from a brake drum or rotor is called _____.

27. _____

28. Burnishing the rotor means to _____ its surface.

28. _____

Copyright Goodheart-Willcox Co., Inc.
May not be reproduced or posted to a publicly accessible website

29. Using a pressure bleeder eliminates the need for what?

_____

30. Even simple procedures on modern vehicles require complex _____.

30. _____

31. The three major types of service information are:

31. _____

_____

_____

32. In order to prevent damage to a customer's vehicle, all of the following protective items are installed by a technician before starting service, EXCEPT:
    (A) a seat cover.
    (B) window curtain panels.
    (C) a paper floor mat.
    (D) fender covers.

32. _____

33. All of the following statements about general manuals are true, EXCEPT:
    (A) general manuals contain service information about many makes of vehicles.
    (B) general manuals contain service information about one kind of vehicle system.
    (C) general manuals may be divided into car and truck editions.
    (D) general manuals contain information about preventive maintenance.

33. _____

34. Technician A says a troubleshooting chart shows the flow of energy through a system. Technician B says a troubleshooting chart is a summary of troubleshooting information. Who is right?
    (A) A only.
    (B) B only.
    (C) Both A and B.
    (D) Neither A nor B.

34. _____

35. Dealership technicians have access to manufacturer-issued _____ for newer vehicles, which include descriptions of new service procedures and repair information to correct unusual or frequently occurring problems.
    (A) schematics
    (B) vehicle warranty documents
    (C) safety reports
    (D) technical service bulletins

35. _____

Copyright Goodheart-Willcox Co., Inc.
May not be reproduced or posted to a publicly accessible website

Name _____

Date _____ Class _____→ 5

Chapter 4

Hydraulic System Fundamentals

After studying this chapter, you will be able to:
- ❏ Explain the use of hydraulic pressure in braking systems.
- ❏ Explain the incompressibility of liquids as the basis of hydraulic system operation.
- ❏ Describe how movement is transferred by way of liquids.
- ❏ Explain how cylinder size changes hydraulic force and distance traveled.
- ❏ Explain Pascal's law.
- ❏ Identify the components of a simple brake hydraulic system.
- ❏ Identify the qualities of brake fluid and fluid classifications.
- ❏ Recognize the importance of using the proper brake fluid.
- ❏ Describe how to check for various types of fluid contamination.

1. The study of liquids and how they work is called _____.

1. _____

2. Technician A says that gases cannot be compressed. Technician B says that liquids cannot be compressed. Who is right?
   (A) A only.
   (B) B only.
   (C) Both A and B.
   (D) Neither A nor B.

2. _____

Note: Read This Section before Answering Questions 3-7:
Two cylinder and piston assemblies are connected by tubing and completely filled with a liquid. The surface of one piston is one square inch. The surface of the other piston is three square inches. Use the system described to answer the following questions.

3. A force of 10 pounds (44.5 N) is placed on the one-inch piston. How much force will the three-inch piston exert?

3. _____30_____

Copyright Goodheart-Willcox Co., Inc.
May not be reproduced or posted to a publicly accessible website

4. When force is placed on the one-inch piston, it moves 1″ (25.4 mm). How far would the three-inch piston move?

4. _____ 3″ _____

5. A force of 40 pounds (178 N) is placed on the one-inch piston. How much force will the three-inch piston exert?

5. _____ 120 pounds _____

6. When force is placed on the one-inch piston, it moves 0.25″ (6.35 mm). How far would the three-inch piston move?

6. _____ .75″ _____

7. When force is placed on the three-inch piston, it moves 1″ (25.4 mm). How far would the one-inch piston move?

7. _____

8. Modern master cylinders have _____ pistons.

8. _____ 2 _____

9. Match the brake hydraulic valve with the type of wheel hydraulic unit that it controls.
   (A) rear wheel cylinders
   (B) front calipers
   (C) front and rear brake units

9. _B_ Metering valve
   _C_ Proportioning valve
   _A_ Residual pressure valve
   _C_ Pressure differential valve

10. The _____ will not open until pressure builds up in the front hydraulic system.
    (A) metering valve
    (B) proportioning valve
    (C) residual pressure valve
    (D) pressure differential valve

10. _____

11. The _____ will close when pressure becomes too high in the rear hydraulic system.
    (A) metering valve
    (B) proportioning valve
    (C) residual pressure valve
    (D) pressure differential valve

11. _____

12. Two or more control valves are often combined into a single assembly called a _____.
    (A) metering valve.
    (B) proportioning valve.
    (C) residual pressure valve.
    (D) combination valve.

12. _____

13. All of the following statements about anti-lock brake (ABS) systems are true, EXCEPT:
    (A) to work properly, the ABS system must sometimes increase pressure.
    (B) to work properly, the ABS system must sometimes reduce pressure.
    (C) some ABS systems have no input from the vehicle electrical system.
    (D) some ABS systems dump fluid into the master cylinder or reservoir.

13. _____

14. *True or False?* Several organizations have developed brake fluid standards.

14. _____

Copyright Goodheart-Willcox Co., Inc.
May not be reproduced or posted to a publicly accessible website

Name _____

15. Brake fluid must resist _____ at high temperatures, and
    must be able to absorb _____.

15. _____

    _____

16. Technician A says DOT 3 brake fluid is glycol based.
    Technician B says DOT 4 brake fluid is silicone based.
    Who is right?
    (A) A only.
    (B) B only.
    (C) Both A and B.
    (D) Neither A nor B.

16. _____

17. Technician A says that DOT 3 and DOT 5 brake fluids
    cannot be mixed. Technician B says that DOT 4 and
    DOT 5 brake fluids cannot be mixed. Who is right?
    (A) A only.
    (B) B only.
    (C) Both A and B.
    (D) Neither A nor B.

17. _____

18. *True or False?* Glycol and silicone brake fluids are not
    compatible.

18. _____

19. *True or False?* One of the jobs of brake fluid is to
    lubricate moving parts.

19. _____

20. The above figure shows a technician checking a brake
    fluid sample for excess:
    (A) cloudiness.
    (B) water.
    (C) oil.
    (D) alcohol loss.

20. _____

21. Brake fluid may be contaminated with copper. Copper in
    the brake fluid can be detected by using _____.

21. _____

Copyright Goodheart-Willcox Co., Inc.
May not be reproduced or posted to a publicly accessible website

Copyright Goodheart-Willcox Co., Inc.
May not be reproduced or posted to a publicly accessible website

Chapter 5

Master Cylinders, Calipers, and Wheel Cylinders

After studying this chapter, you will be able to:
- ❑ Describe the purpose and operation of brake pedal linkage.
- ❑ Explain the operation of dual master cylinders.
- ❑ Explain the operation of quick take-up master cylinders.
- ❑ Describe the operation of disc brake calipers.
- ❑ Identify the kinds of calipers.
- ❑ Describe the operation of drum brake wheel cylinders.
- ❑ Explain the purpose of bleeder screws.

1. The brake pedal linkage increases braking pressure by what process?

1. _____

2. All of the following switches may be attached to the brake pedal linkage, EXCEPT:
   (A) stoplight switch.
   (B) brake warning light switch.
   (C) ABS control switch.
   (D) cruise control switch.

2. _____

3. The function of the master cylinder is to change pedal movement into _____ pressure.

3. _____

4. Modern master cylinders have two _____, which move inside of one _____.

4. _____
   _____

5. Technician A says the rear master cylinder piston usually applies pressure to one front brake and the rear brake diagonal to it. Technician B says the front master cylinder piston only operates if the rear piston fails. Who is right?
   (A) A only.
   (B) B only.
   (C) Both A and B.
   (D) Neither A nor B.

5. _____

Copyright Goodheart-Willcox Co., Inc.
May not be reproduced or posted to a publicly accessible website

6. Modern master cylinders are usually made of _____.

    6. _____

7. On either piston, the _____ piston cup is used to ensure the piston develops hydraulic pressure.

    7. _____

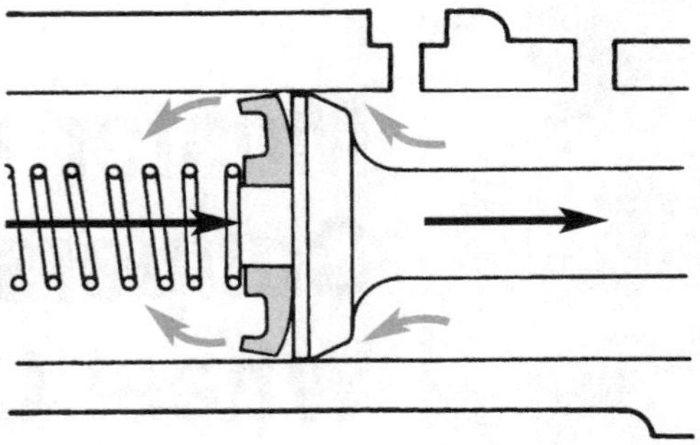

8. The illustration above shows a primary cup seal in operation as the brakes are:
   (A) being applied easily.
   (B) being applied hard.
   (C) being released.
   (D) at the rest position.

    8. _____

9. What is the purpose of the compensating port?

_____

_____

_____

10. Pressure development in the master cylinder is being discussed. Technician A says a pressure increase in the rear chamber will push on the front piston. Technician B says a pressure increase in the rear chamber will cause the secondary piston seal to close the compensating port. Who is right?
    (A) A only.
    (B) B only.
    (C) Both A and B.
    (D) Neither A nor B.

    10. _____

11. Which port allows the pressure chamber to be refilled from the reservoir?

    11. _____

12. A residual pressure valve is used on systems with _____ brakes.

    12. _____

Copyright Goodheart-Willcox Co., Inc.
May not be reproduced or posted to a publicly accessible website

Name _____

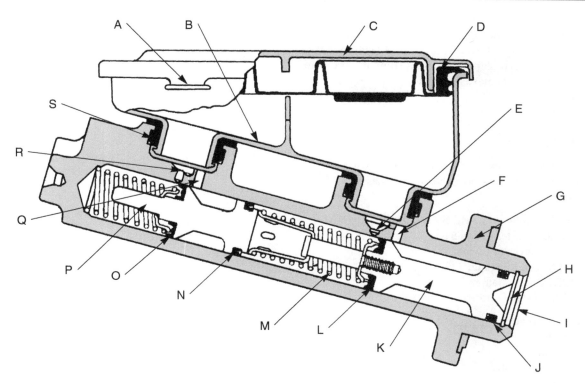

13. Identify the parts on the master cylinder shown above.

(A) _____   (K) _____

(B) _____   (L) _____

(C) _____   (M) _____

(D) _____   (N) _____

(E) _____   (O) _____

(F) _____   (P) _____

(G) _____   (Q) _____

(H) _____   (R) _____

(I) _____   (S) _____

(J) _____

14. Technician A says the master cylinder reservoir
    diaphragm is vented. Technician B says the master
    cylinder reservoir cover is vented. Who is right?
    (A) A only.
    (B) B only.
    (C) Both A and B.
    (D) Neither A nor B.

14. _____

15. On a dual master cylinder hydraulic system, the front brakes
    lose all hydraulic pressure due to a broken hose. Which of
    the following is the driver *least likely* to experience?
    (A) A hard pedal.
    (B) A low pedal.
    (C) Warning light illumination.
    (D) Loss of braking power.

15. _____

Copyright Goodheart-Willcox Co., Inc.
May not be reproduced or posted to a publicly accessible website

16. Technician A says the quick take-up master cylinder is used with no-drag calipers. Technician B says the quick take-up master cylinder produces much higher pressure than a conventional master cylinder. Who is right?
    (A) A only.
    (B) B only.
    (C) Both A and B.
    (D) Neither A nor B.

16. _____

17. *True or False?* Master cylinders used with most anti-lock brake systems work the same way as non-ABS master cylinders.

17. _____

18. Which of the following vehicles is *most likely* to have a single piston master cylinder?
    (A) 1966 Chevrolet Impala.
    (B) 1976 Ford Mustang.
    (C) 1986 Toyota Camry.
    (D) 1998 Dodge Durango.

18. _____

19. Calipers are made of _____.
    (A) cast iron
    (B) aluminum
    (C) phenolic plastic
    (D) Both A & B.

19. _____

20. How many pistons do floating calipers have?

20. _____

21. How many pistons do fixed calipers have?

21. _____

22. The piston of a single piston caliper is *always* located:
    (A) at the front of the rotor.
    (B) at the rear of the rotor.
    (C) inboard of the rotor.
    (D) outboard of the rotor.

22. _____

23. All of the following statements about disc brake calipers are true, EXCEPT:
    (A) calipers can be fixed or floating.
    (B) calipers can have one, two, or four pistons.
    (C) calipers apply force to one side of the rotor.
    (D) caliper seals return the caliper piston to the released position.

23. _____

24. How many pistons do wheel cylinders have?

24. _____

25. Hydraulic pressure forces the wheel cylinder pistons in what direction?
    (A) Outward.
    (B) Inward.
    (C) The pistons do not move.
    (D) None of the above.

25. _____

26. A small _____ keeps the wheel cylinder cups against the pistons.

26. _____

Copyright Goodheart-Willcox Co., Inc.
May not be reproduced or posted to a publicly accessible website

Name _____

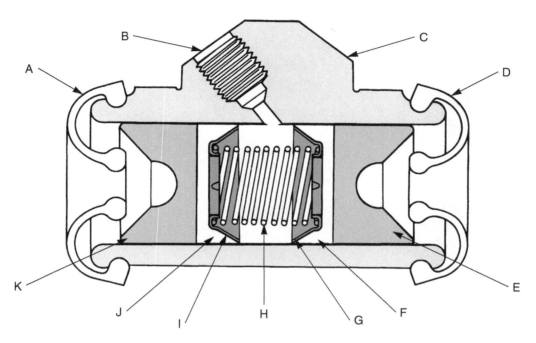

27. Identify the parts of the wheel cylinder shown above.

(A) _____

(B) _____

(C) _____

(D) _____

(E) _____

(F) _____

(G) _____

(H) _____

(I) _____

(J) _____

(K) _____

28. Which of the following devices causes the wheel cylinders to retract when hydraulic pressure is removed?
 (A) An internal wheel cylinder spring.
 (B) Rotation and vibration of the brake drum.
 (C) Hydraulic pressure back waves.
 (D) The brake shoe return springs.

28. _____

29. To remove air from the brake hydraulic system, _____ are used.

29. _____

30. Technician A says that the bleeder screw is always located at the bottom of the caliper or wheel cylinder bore to make sure that any sludge or water can be removed along with the air. Technician B says that the bleeder screw is always located at the top of the caliper or wheel cylinder bore since air is lighter than brake fluid. Who is right?
 (A) A only.
 (B) B only.
 (C) Both A and B.
 (D) Neither A nor B.

30. _____

Copyright Goodheart-Willcox Co., Inc.
May not be reproduced or posted to a publicly accessible website

Copyright Goodheart-Willcox Co., Inc.
May not be reproduced or posted to a publicly accessible website

Chapter 6

Master Cylinder, Caliper, and Wheel Cylinder Service

After studying this chapter, you will be able to:
- ❑ Check master cylinder condition.
- ❑ Remove, overhaul, and install master cylinders.
- ❑ Check disc brake caliper condition.
- ❑ Remove, overhaul, and install disc brake calipers.
- ❑ Check wheel cylinder condition.
- ❑ Remove, overhaul, and replace wheel cylinders.
- ❑ Bleed air from the hydraulic system.

1. If fluid disappears from a master cylinder with no visible sign of a leak, it may be entering the engine through the _____.

1. _____

2. What is the most common sign of an internal master cylinder leak?

_____

3. Why is failure of the master cylinder internal seals difficult to detect?

_____

_____

4. Pedal travel on most vehicles is about:
   (A) 1/4" (6.3 mm)
   (B) 1/2" (12.7 mm)
   (C) 1" (25.4 mm)
   (D) 1/8" (3.1 mm)

4. _____

5. Oil in the master cylinder may cause the pistons to _____.

5. _____

Copyright Goodheart-Willcox Co., Inc.
May not be reproduced or posted to a publicly accessible website

6. If the reservoir is part of the master cylinder body, do not remove the _____ while removing the master cylinder from the vehicle.
   (A) hydraulic lines
   (B) reservoir cover
   (C) electrical connectors
   (D) All the above.

6. _____

7. All of the following statements about master cylinder overhaul are true, EXCEPT:
   (A) while removing the snap ring, keep pressure on the rear piston. ✓
   (B) if a bolt is used to hold the front piston in place, it may need to be removed before or after removing the snap ring. ✓
   (C) if the quick take-up valve is defective, replace the entire master cylinder. ✓
   (D) cast iron master cylinders should be thoroughly washed out with tap water.

7. _____

8. Brake fluid can damage vehicle _____.

8. _____

9. Under what conditions can brake fluid be reused?

_____

10. Most master cylinder pistons are held in the master cylinder bore with a(n) _____.

10. _____

11. All aluminum master cylinder bores have a(n) _____ coating.

11. _____

12. If the aluminum bore of a master cylinder is scored, the master cylinder should be _____.

12. _____

13. To obtain parts for a master cylinder you may have to find out all of the following, EXCEPT:
    (A) master cylinder manufacturer.
    (B) vehicle identification number (VIN).
    (C) vehicle engine type. ✓
    (D) code stamp or tag on the master cylinder body.

13. _____

14. Master cylinder seals should be lightly _____ before installation.

14. _____

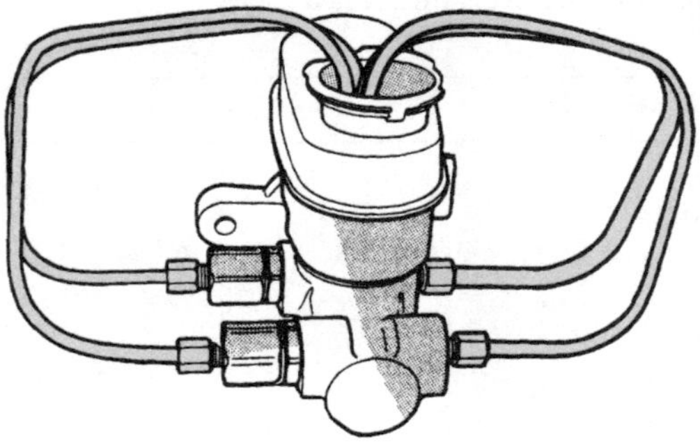

15. The illustration shown above shows a master cylinder being _____.

15. _____

Copyright Goodheart-Willcox Co., Inc.
May not be reproduced or posted to a publicly accessible website

Name _____

16. *True or False?* If a caliper piston sticks, the wheel brake might not apply.

16. _____

17. A(n) _____ should be used to push in the caliper piston.

17. _____

18. *True or False?* Air pressure should never be used to remove a caliper piston.

18. _____

19. An aluminum caliper's bore has an anodized coating. It should not be:
    (A) honed.
    (B) rebuilt.
    (C) replaced.
    (D) cleaned.

19. _____

20. A caliper piston should be reinstalled in its bore using only:
    (A) air pressure.
    (B) a C-clamp.
    (C) a hammer and drift.
    (D) hand pressure.

20. _____

21. Some rear calipers have a(n) _____.

21. _____

22. *True* or *False?* If many caliper parts are needed, it is cheaper to get a new caliper.

22. _____

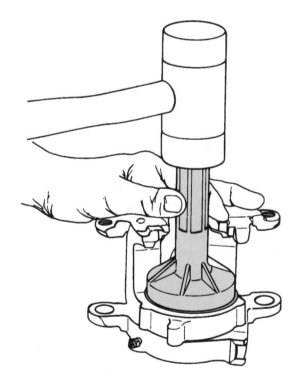

23. Technician A says the figure above shows a dust boot being removed. Technician B says the figure above shows a dust boot being installed. Who is right?
    (A) A only.
    (B) B only.
    (C) Both A and B.
    (D) Neither A nor B.

23. _____

Copyright Goodheart-Willcox Co., Inc.
May not be reproduced or posted to a publicly accessible website

24. A wheel cylinder just starting to leak will show fluid
    under the _____.

24. _____

25. Technician A says excessive wear on one brake shoe is a
    sign a wheel cylinder piston is sticking. Technician B says a
    sticking wheel cylinder should be tapped with a hammer
    to free it up. Who is right?
    (A) A only.
    (B) B only.
    (C) Both A and B.
    (D) Neither A nor B.

25. _____

26. Sometimes a wheel cylinder can be _____ without
    removing it from the vehicle.

26. _____

27. Explain how you would remove the internal parts of a wheel cylinder.

   _____

   _____

   _____

28. Before rebuilding the wheel cylinder, check the replacement
    parts, especially the size of the piston _____.

28. _____

29. The wheel cylinder bore can be honed if it is made
    of _____.

29. _____

30. All wheel cylinder parts can be installed through _____
    of the cylinder.

30. _____

31. Both wheel cylinder cups should face toward the _____
    of the wheel cylinder.

31. _____

32. No air or brake fluid is exiting from one brake bleeder
    screw during a bleeding operation. The other bleeders are
    operating normally. What is the *most likely* cause?
    (A) Defective master cylinder.
    (B) Air leak at the wheel hydraulic unit.
    (C) Disconnected pedal linkage.
    (D) Clogged bleeder screw.

32. _____

33. When using a pressure bleeder, what is the maximum pres-
    sure that should be placed on a plastic master cylinder?
    (A) 0 psi (0 kPa).
    (B) 5 psi (34.5 kPa).
    (C) 10 psi (69 kPa).
    (D) 15 psi (103.5 kPa).

33. _____

34. Allowing the brake system to bleed itself is called _____
    bleeding.

34. _____

35. Brake hydraulic system flushing is being discussed.
    Technician A says flushing is similar to bleeding, but
    removes old fluid instead of air. Technician B says when
    fluid begins to exit the bleeder screw, flushing is
    complete. Who is right?
    (A) A only.
    (B) B only.
    (C) Both A and B.
    (D) Neither A nor B.

35. _____

Copyright Goodheart-Willcox Co., Inc.
May not be reproduced or posted to a publicly accessible website

Name _____
Date 2-22-23   Class   —→ 7.8
2 ~~15~~ ~~22~~ ~~23~~

Chapter 7

Power Assist Units

After studying this chapter, you will be able to:
- ❏ Explain the purpose of brake power assist units.
- ❏ Identify vacuum and hydraulic power assist units.
- ❏ Explain how vacuum power assist units operate.
- ❏ Identify the components of vacuum power assist units.
- ❏ Identify the power sources and safety provisions of vacuum power assist units.
- ❏ Explain how hydraulic power assist units operate.
- ❏ Identify the components of hydraulic power assist units.
- ❏ Identify the power sources and safety provisions of hydraulic power assist units.

1. Technician A says disc brakes require more pedal effort than drum brakes. Technician B says vacuum power assist units are installed between the brake pedal and firewall. Who is right?
   (A) A only.
   (B) B only.
   (C) Both A and B.
   (D) Neither A nor B.

   1. _____

2. *True or False?* Vacuum power assists were first developed during the 1990s.

   2. _____

3. All vacuum power assists operate by creating a(n) _____.

   3. _____

4. *True or False?* The brake pedal pushrod goes completely through the vacuum assist housing.

   4. _____

5. The most common vacuum brake assist is the _____ diaphragm type.

   5. _____

6. What operates the control valve of a vacuum assist unit?

_____

Copyright Goodheart-Willcox Co., Inc.
May not be reproduced or posted to a publicly accessible website

7. Technician A says the vacuum check valve is sometimes located on the vacuum assist housing. Technician B says the vacuum check valve is sometimes located in the hose to the vacuum assist housing. Who is right?
   (A) A only.
   (B) B only.
   (C) Both A and B.
   (D) Neither A nor B.

7. _____

8. The two types of reaction assemblies are the _____ and the _____.

8. _____
   _____

9. When is the vacuum on each side of a single diaphragm vacuum booster the same?
   (A) Before the brakes are applied.
   (B) When the brakes are being applied.
   (C) At the midpoint of brake application.
   (D) When the brakes are being released.

9. _____

10. All of the following statements about vacuum are true, EXCEPT:
    (A) the downward movement of the pistons in the engine creates vacuum.
    (B) vacuum is a condition of greater than atmospheric pressure.
    (C) an extra vacuum pump is often needed on vehicles with small engines.
    (D) heavy engine loads reduce available vacuum.

10. _____

11. When the check valve is operating properly, will air be drawn in or out of the vacuum assist unit?

11. _____

12. When the brakes are applied, the passage between the front and rear vacuum chambers is _____.

12. _____

13. When the brakes are released, the passage between the front and rear vacuum chambers is _____.

13. _____

14. Technician A says that the vacuum check valve saves enough extra vacuum for 2–3 stops if the engine dies. Technician B says that the accumulator saves enough extra hydraulic pressure for 2–3 stops if the engine dies. Who is right?
    (A) A only.
    (B) B only.
    (C) Both A and B.
    (D) Neither A nor B.

14. _____

15. If vacuum is lost, the brakes will still work but pedal effort will be _____.

15. _____

16. The three kinds of vacuum pump drive methods are:

16. _____
    _____
    _____

17. Vacuum pump motors on modern vehicles are controlled by _____.

17. _____

Copyright Goodheart-Willcox Co., Inc.
May not be reproduced or posted to a publicly accessible website

Name _____

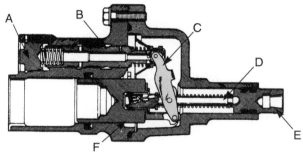

18. Identify the parts in the illustration shown above.

(A) _____   (D) _____

(B) _____   (E) _____

(C) _____   (F) _____

19. The _____ is a piston in a bore, attached to the   19. _____
Hydro-boost assembly.

20. Match the Hydro-boost hydraulic power assist unit with   20. _____ Spool valve
its function.
(A) Pushes in master cylinder pushrod.   _____ Power piston
(B) Stores pressure for emergencies.
(C) Creates pressurized fluid.   _____ Accumulator
(D) Controls fluid flow.

21. The Hydro-boost power assist unit uses pressurized fluid   21. _____
created by the _____ system.

22. In a Hydro-boost system at rest, the spool valve _____.   22. _____
(A) restricts the diameter of fluid passages to increase
fluid velocity
(B) blocks completely all fluid inlets and outlets
(C) allows unpressurized fluid to enter from and exit to
the power steering pump
(D) compresses a container of nitrogen gas to slow the
vehicle's speed

23. During brake application in a Hydro-boost system, what   23. _____
moves the spool valve?
(A) Exhaust system backpressure.
(B) Brake pedal pressure creating pushrod movement of
the lever assembly.
(C) Brake pedal pressure causing the tightening of a
worm screw setup.
(D) Brake pedal pressure initiating an accumulator
release into the valve body.

24. *True or False?* The moment that hydraulic pressure is lost   24. _____
in a Hydro-boost system, the driver is immediately left
without any degree of power brake assist.

25. Power brake assist in an anti-lock brake system involves   25. _____
the use of _____.
(A) a hybrid vacuum and Hydro-boost brake booster unit
(B) either a turbocharger or supercharger
(C) specialized drum brake assemblies at all of the
vehicle's wheels
(D) either a vacuum booster or electric vacuum pump

Copyright Goodheart-Willcox Co., Inc.
May not be reproduced or posted to a publicly accessible website

Copyright Goodheart-Willcox Co., Inc.
May not be reproduced or posted to a publicly accessible website

Name _____
Date __3-1-23__ Class ____—›9____

Chapter 8

Power Assist Unit Service

After studying this chapter, you will be able to:
- ❑ Check and adjust brake pedal free travel.
- ❑ Diagnose problems in a vacuum power assist unit.
- ❑ Check vacuum power assist unit for leaks.
- ❑ Inspect vacuum hoses and check valves.
- ❑ Check electrical and mechanical vacuum pumps.
- ❑ Remove and replace a vacuum assist unit.
- ❑ Overhaul a vacuum assist unit.
- ❑ Diagnose problems in a Hydro-boost power assist unit.
- ❑ Overhaul a Hydro-boost power assist unit.
- ❑ Flush and bleed a Hydro-boost unit and related components.

1. Before deciding that a brake power assist unit is defective, what should you check?

   _____

   _____

2. Before disassembling a brake power assist unit, what should you check?

   _____

   _____

3. During a brake system test, the brake pedal does not go down when the engine is started. Technician A says this may be caused by a defective check valve. Technician B says engine vacuum may be low. Who is right?
   (A) A only.
   (B) B only.
   (C) Both A and B.
   (D) Neither A nor B.

   3. _____

4. A hissing noise from the brake power assist unit is a sign of an internal vacuum _____.

   4. _____

Copyright Goodheart-Willcox Co., Inc.
May not be reproduced or posted to a publicly accessible website

5. If the power assist unit loses all vacuum as soon as the engine is stopped, the problems is probably a defective vacuum _____.

5.

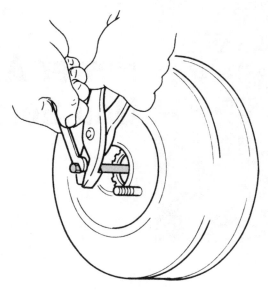

6. What is being performed in the above illustration?

_____

7. A height gauge is needed to check the _____ adjustment.

7. _____

8. In some cases, it may be possible to move the _____ far enough to remove the vacuum booster.

8. _____

9. Removing the brake assist unit may cause what electrical problem?

_____

_____

10. The following are steps in disassembling a vacuum brake assist unit. Which of these steps should the technician do *first*?
    (A) Rotate the housing clockwise to loosen the locking tabs.
    (B) Rotate the housing counterclockwise to remove rust from the locking tabs.
    (C) Loosen the tabs.
    (D) Scribe match marks on the two halves of the housing.

10. _____

11. Separating the two halves of a vacuum assist housing requires the use of a(n) _____ wrench.

11. _____

12. A vacuum power brake assist should always be placed in a holding fixture before disassembly because the assist unit contains a large _____.

12. _____

Copyright Goodheart-Willcox Co., Inc.
May not be reproduced or posted to a publicly accessible website

Name _____

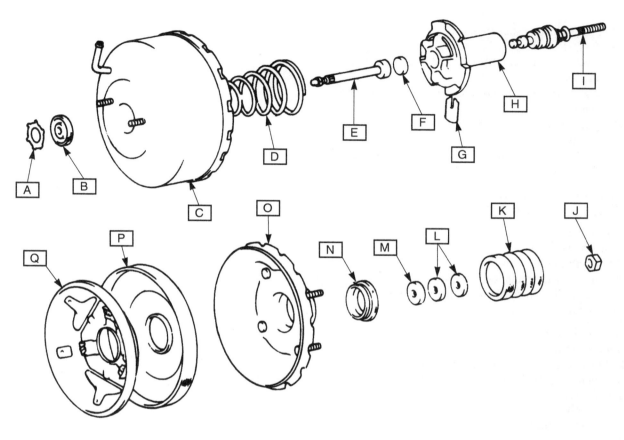

13. Identify the parts indicated in the disassembled vacuum brake assist unit shown.

(A) _____   (J) _____

(B) _____   (K) _____

(C) _____   (L) _____

(D) _____   (M) _____

(E) _____   (N) _____

(F) _____   (O) _____

(G) _____   (P) _____

(H) _____   (Q) _____

(I) _____

14. _____ inside a vacuum booster indicates a leaking
    master cylinder.

14. _____

15. Use _____ to polish minor corrosion from vacuum
    booster parts.
    (A) bead blasting
    (B) sand blasting
    (C) a wire wheel
    (D) crocus cloth

15. _____

Copyright Goodheart-Willcox Co., Inc.
May not be reproduced or posted to a publicly accessible website

16. All of the following statements about vacuum pumps are true, EXCEPT:

    (A) electric pumps can be mounted in many places on the vehicle.

    ✓(B) a gear-driven pump is often driven by the crankshaft.

    (C) gear-driven pumps are often mounted in place of the distributor.

    (D) the belt must be adjusted after replacing a belt-driven pump.

16. _____

17. Before working on any Hydro-boost system, always remove all _____ by pressing the brake pedal at least 30 times.

17. _____

18. What could be the cause of slow brake pedal return in a Hydro-boost system?

    (A) No fluid in Hydro-boost unit.

    (B) Internal accumulator leak.

    (C) Restriction in power steering return line.

    (D) System contamination.

18. _____

19. The power steering belt of a vehicle with a Hydro-boost brake assist squeals when the brakes are applied. Technician A says the accumulator may be defective. Technician B says the belt may be too tight. Who is right?

    (A) A only.

    (B) B only.

    (C) Both A and B.

    (D) Neither A nor B.

19. _____

20. A Hydro-boost accumulator is being disassembled. What should you *always* do before removing the accumulator snap ring?

    _____

    _____

21. If a Hydro-boost's spool valve or power piston shows deep scratching or scoring upon disassembly, what action should an automotive technician take?

    (A) Install a new spool valve and power piston that are half the size in diameter.

    (B) Equip a new power steering pump with two in-line fluid filters.

    (C) Replace the whole Hydro-boost assembly.

    (D) Use a lathe to knurl a pattern in the old spool valve and power piston.

21. _____

22. To begin the Hydro-boost flushing procedure, remove the large _____ pressure hose from the power steering pump.

22. _____

23. If the power steering fluid is _____, the system must be bled.

23. _____

Copyright Goodheart-Willcox Co., Inc.
May not be reproduced or posted to a publicly accessible website

Name _____

24. If a Hydro-boost system cannot be successfully flushed, what should you do next?
    (A) Replace all system parts.
    (B) Remove and manually clean all system parts.
    (C) Replace the system hoses.
    (D) Return the vehicle to service.

24. _____

25. What is the first step in bleeding a Hydro-boost system?
    (A) Perform two sharp turns in each direction and five full panic stops during a test-drive.
    (B) Fill the power steering fluid reservoir to the full mark.
    (C) Disconnect the brake hose from each caliper and/or wheel cylinder.
    (D) Mix engine oil with the power steering fluid to increase its viscosity.

25. _____

Copyright Goodheart-Willcox Co., Inc.
May not be reproduced or posted to a publicly accessible website

Copyright Goodheart-Willcox Co., Inc.
May not be reproduced or posted to a publicly accessible website

Name _____

Date _3-8-23_ Class _____

9+10

Chapter 9

Hydraulic Valves, Switches, Lines, and Hoses

After studying this chapter, you will be able to:
- ❏ Explain how metering valves operate.
- ❏ Explain the purpose and construction of a proportioning valve.
- ❏ Discuss the reason load-sensing proportioning valves are used.
- ❏ Explain the purpose and construction of a residual pressure valve.
- ❏ Describe the operation of a pressure differential valve and switch.
- ❏ Explain the purpose and construction of a low brake fluid switch.
- ❏ Explain the purpose and construction of a brake light switch.
- ❏ Recall the reasons for using steel hydraulic lines.
- ❏ Identify types of brake line flares.
- ❏ Recognize why flexible hoses are used to connect some brake parts.
- ❏ Identify various types of brake fittings and explain their function.

1. If the front brakes apply before the rear brakes, the vehicle could _____.

1. ___skid_____

2. The _____ valve delays front brake application.

2. _____

3. Metering valves are installed in the _____.
   (A) master cylinder
   (B) combination valve
   (C) brake lines
   (D) All of the above.

3. _____

4. The _____ valve keeps rear wheel hydraulic pressure from increasing past a certain point.

4. _____

Copyright Goodheart-Willcox Co., Inc.
May not be reproduced or posted to a publicly accessible website

5. All of the following statements about hydraulic brake
control valves are true, EXCEPT:
   (A) metering valves may have an external plunger to
       make brake bleeding easier.
   (B) diagonally split braking systems have two propor-
       tioning valves.
   (C) metering valves do not allow pressure to increase
       beyond a set value.
   (D) metering and proportioning valves both help to
       prevent skids.

5. _____

6. In a proportioning valve, a(n) _____ holds the valve
away from the opening to the rear brakes.

6. _____

7. The _____ can be thought of as a proportioning
valve with a mechanism which controls rear brake pressure.

7. _____

8. *True or False?* A load-sensing proportioning valve is the
same as a ride height sensor?

8. _____

9. Which of the following valves is *not* used on a vehicle
with four-wheel disc brakes?
   (A) Metering valve.
   (B) Proportioning valve.
   (C) Residual pressure valve.
   (D) Pressure differential valve.

9. _____

10. All vehicles with drum brakes have a(n) _____.

10. _____

11. Most residual pressure valves are located on or in what
hydraulic system component?

11. _____

12. What is the purpose of the residual pressure valve? _____
_____

13. A pressure differential valve is used in all _____ brake
systems.

13. _____

14. The pressure differential valve is used as a(n) _____
device.

14. _____

15. How many individual brake system valves can be
combined into a single combination valve?

15. _____

16. Technician A says the low brake fluid switch is some-
times installed in the combination valve. Technician B
says the only purpose of the low brake fluid switch is to
illuminate a dashboard warning light. Who is right?
   (A) A only.
   (B) B only.
   (C) Both A and B.
   (D) Neither A nor B.

16. _____

17. One end of a plunger type brake light switch is located
on the vehicle body. The other end contacts the _____.

17. _____

18. When the brake switch contacts close, an electrical
circuit is completed between the _____ and the _____.

18. _____
_____

Copyright Goodheart-Willcox Co., Inc.
May not be reproduced or posted to a publicly accessible website

Name _____

19. Brake lines are sometimes referred to as brake _____. 19. _____

20. Double-wall construction means the line has two _____ of steel. 20. _____

21. What materials are sometimes used to coat steel brake lines? _____

_____

_____

_____

22. Steel wire is coiled around standard brake lines to make _____ lines. 22. _____

23. Factory brake lines are usually _____ to fit the vehicle and frame. 23. _____

24. Where would a flexible brake hose be *most likely* to be used? 24. _____
(A) Between the master cylinder and the pressure differential valve.
(B) Between the master cylinder and the metering valve.
(C) Between the metering valve and the front brake caliper.
(D) Between the pressure differential valve and the proportioning valve.

25. Flexible hoses are always securely mounted at each _____. 25. _____

26. Brake hoses are made from _____ rubber. 26. _____

27. Identify the following types of flare fittings in the illustration: 27. (A) _____
(B) _____

A

B

28. Which of the above types of flares makes use of an interference angle as a sealing device? 28. _____

Copyright Goodheart-Willcox Co., Inc.
May not be reproduced or posted to a publicly accessible website

29. Elbows, unions, and tees are types of brake _____.

29. _____

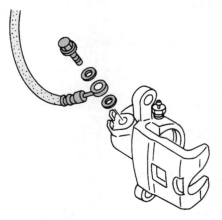

30. Technician A says the type of fitting shown in the above
    illustration is a banjo fitting. Technician B says the type
    of fitting shown in the above illustration is a union.
    Who is right?
    (A) A only.
    (B) B only.
    (C) Both A and B.
    (D) Neither A nor B.

30. _____

Copyright Goodheart-Willcox Co., Inc.
May not be reproduced or posted to a publicly accessible website

Chapter 10

Hydraulic Valve, Switch, Line, and Hose Service

After studying this chapter, you will be able to:
- ❑ Diagnose braking problems caused by hydraulic system valves.
- ❑ Test the operation of hydraulic system valves.
- ❑ Test the operation of low brake fluid switches.
- ❑ Test the operation of brake light switches.
- ❑ Remove and replace valves and switches.
- ❑ Check steel hydraulic lines, hoses, and fittings for defects.
- ❑ Bend, cut, and flare replacement steel hydraulic lines.
- ❑ Replace flexible hoses.
- ❑ Replace brake fittings.

1. The brake system valve that causes the most driver complaints is the pressure differential valve. Why?

   _____

   _____

2. If the metering valve sticks closed, the front wheel brakes will not _____.

   2. _____

3. Technician A says rear wheel skidding could be caused by a metering valve that is stuck closed. Technician B says rear wheel skidding could be caused by a metering valve that is stuck open. Who is right?
   (A) A only.
   (B) B only.
   (C) Both A and B.
   (D) Neither A nor B.

   3. _____

4. If a brake hydraulic valve holds pressure in the brake lines, the front or rear brakes may _____.

   4. _____

Copyright Goodheart-Willcox Co., Inc.
May not be reproduced or posted to a publicly accessible website

5. The wheel cylinders on a vehicle are leaking. This could
   be caused by a defective _____.
   (A) residual pressure valve
   (B) brake hose
   (C) master cylinder
   (D) pressure differential valve

5. _____

6. If the proportioning valve sticks open, the rear wheels
   could _____.

6. _____

7. If fluid squirts out of a front bleeder screw as soon as the
   brake pedal is pressed, the metering valve is:
   (A) operating normally.
   (B) stuck closed.
   (C) stuck open.
   (D) the metering valve cannot be tested this way.

7. _____

8. Some _____ valves are adjustable.

8. _____

9. The best place to adjust a load-sensing proportioning
   valve is on a(n) _____.

9. _____

10. The ignition switch is in the *on* position, a bleeder screw is opened, and the brake pedal is pressed. What should the
    dashboard brake warning light do?

    _____

    _____

11. All of the following statements about pressure testing
    hydraulic brake valves are true, EXCEPT:
    (A) when the gauge on the input side of a metering
        valve reaches a certain value, the gauge on the
        output side should begin to rise.
    (B) if residual pressure drops to 7–10 psi (48–69 kPa) but
        no lower, the residual pressure valve is stuck closed.
    (C) the proportioning valve should keep rear brake
        pressure from rising above a set value.
    (D) if the brake pedal is pressed hard, the propor-
        tioning valve outlet pressure will be lower than the
        input pressure.

11. _____

12. When testing metering valves, at what input pressure
    should the output pressure begin to rise?

12. _____

13. Typical proportioning valve cutoff pressure ranges
    from _____.

13. _____

14. If the low brake fluid light does not come on when the
    float is at its lowest position, which of the following
    could be the problem?
    (A) The float is sinking.
    (B) The switch is shorted.
    (C) The light fuse is blown.
    (D) The fluid level is low.

14. _____

15. If no rear brake lights come on when the brake pedal is
    depressed, begin by checking for electrical power at
    the _____.

15. _____

16. If the brake lights are out on only one side, begin by
    checking the _____.

16. _____

Copyright Goodheart-Willcox Co., Inc.
May not be reproduced or posted to a publicly accessible website

Name _____

17. Technician A says defective brake hydraulic valves are replaced instead of being repaired. Technician B says the hydraulic system must be bled after hydraulic valves are replaced. Who is right?
    (A) A only.
    (B) B only.
    (C) Both A and B.
    (D) Neither A nor B.

17. _____

18. Always _____ damaged brake lines or hoses.

18. _____

19. When is it permissible to repair a stripped brake line fitting with an oversized nut?

19. _____

20. It is important to bend new brake lines with a special tool to prevent _____.

20. _____

21. Special tools used to bend tubing are the _____.
    (A) coil spring bender
    (B) gear or lever bender
    (C) vise and pliers
    (D) Both A and B.

21. _____

22. *True or False?* Double-lap and Bubble (ISO) flares will interchange.

22. _____

23. *True or False?* A single-lap flare should never be used on any brake line.

23. _____

24. *True or False?* Making a double-lap flare is a two-step process.

24. _____

25. *True or False?* Double-lap and Bubble (ISO) flares can be formed using the same flaring tool.

25. _____

Copyright Goodheart-Willcox Co., Inc.
May not be reproduced or posted to a publicly accessible website

Copyright Goodheart-Willcox Co., Inc.
May not be reproduced or posted to a publicly accessible website

Name _____

Date __3-22-23__ Class __→ 12613__

Chapter 11

Friction Brake Theory

After studying this chapter, you will be able to:
- ❑ Define friction.
- ❑ Explain the relationship of weight and speed to kinetic energy.
- ❑ Define coefficient of friction.
- ❑ Define static and kinetic friction.
- ❑ Define brake fade.
- ❑ Explain the relationship of friction to heat development.
- ❑ Identify and describe the factors affecting stopping power.
- ❑ Identify outside factors affecting coefficient of friction.
- ❑ Describe brake lining materials and construction.

1. Friction is the resistance to movement by two objects _____ against each other.

1. _____

2. Name some situations where friction is a good thing.

_____

_____

_____

3. Momentum is a combination of what two things?

3. _____

_____

Copyright Goodheart-Willcox Co., Inc.
May not be reproduced or posted to a publicly accessible website

4. All of the following statements about kinetic energy are true, EXCEPT:
   (A) kinetic energy increases exponentially with an increase in weight.
   (B) kinetic energy increases exponentially with an increase in speed.
   (C) the terms momentum and kinetic energy both refer to a combination of the vehicle's weight and speed.
   (D) speed has more effect on kinetic energy than weight does.

4. _____

Solve the following coefficient of friction problems involving a block pulled across a surface.

5. A 4 pound block moved by a force of 2 pounds.

5. _____

$$\frac{2}{4} = \frac{1}{2} \text{ or } .5$$

6. A 20 pound block moved by a force of 5 pounds.

6. _____

$$\frac{5}{20} = \frac{1}{4} \text{ or } .25$$

7. A 5 pound block moved by a force of 5 pounds.

7. _____

$$\frac{5}{5} = 1$$

8. An 18 pound block moved by a force of 9 pounds.

8. _____

$$\frac{9}{18} = \frac{1}{2} \text{ or } .5$$

Copyright Goodheart-Willcox Co., Inc.
May not be reproduced or posted to a publicly accessible website

Name _____

9. Technician A says the coefficient of friction is always a
    number greater than one. Technician B says a vehicle
    must be able to stop in shorter distance than it takes to
    accelerate. Who is right?
    (A) A only.
    (B) B only.
    (C) Both A and B.
    (D) Neither A nor B.

9. _____

10. Define *static friction*.

    _____

    _____

11. Define *kinetic friction*.

    _____

    _____

12. Which of the above types of friction produces heat?

12. _____

13. Which of the following braking situations would generate
    the *most heat* in the brake system? Assume all vehicles stop
    in the same distance without skidding.
    (A) 60 mph to 0 (96–0 kph), 4000 pound (1814 kg)
         vehicle.
    (B) 60 mph to 0 (96–0 kph), 2000 pound (907 kg)
         vehicle.
    (C) 30 mph to 0 (48–0 kph), 4000 pound (1814 kg)
         vehicle.
    (D) 30 mph to 0 (48–0 kph), 2000 pound (907 kg)
         vehicle.

13. _____

14. Will the changes in braking factors in the right column
    result in more or less friction in the brake system? Select
    the letter that applies.
    (A) Friction increases
    (B) Friction decreases

14. __B__ The friction materials get hotter.

     __A__ Friction material contact area increases.

→   __B__ Less pressure applied to the friction
            materials.

     __B__ The friction material contact areas get
            smoother.

     __A__ The coefficient of friction of the friction
            material increases.

15. Heat generated by the braking system is directly related
    to the amount of _____ developed to stop the vehicle.

15. _____

16. In your own words, explain why brake linings are designed to fade.

    _____

    _____

    _____

17. Heat generated by the brake system passes directly to
    the _____.

17. _____

Copyright Goodheart-Willcox Co., Inc.
May not be reproduced or posted to a publicly accessible website

18. To absorb and transfer heat, most brake rotors and   18. _____
    drums are made of what metal?
    (A) Cast iron.
    (B) Stainless steel.
    (C) Plastic.
    (D) Rubber.

19. The purpose of fins on some rotors and drums is to: 19. _____
    (A) reduce weight.
    (B) strengthen the rotor or drum.
    (C) throw off water and dirt.
    (D) remove more heat.

20. As much as 80% of vehicle weight is over the   20. _____
    _____ wheels.

21. Because of weight transfer, the front brake friction mate- 21. _____
    rials must have a(n) _____ area.

22. Skidding occurs when the tire of a moving vehicle   22. _____
    stops _____.

23. Which type of brake, drum or disc, dries off quickest   23. _____
    after driving through deep water?

24. The amount of engine braking developed by a vehicle   24. _____
    depends on all of the following factors, EXCEPT:
    (A) rear axle ratio.
    (B) drum and/or rotor size.
    (C) type of transmission.
    (D) engine compression ratio.

25. What must modern brake linings be able to do? List five characteristics.

    _____

    _____

    _____

26. List the three types of brake lining materials.   26. _____

                                                                 _____

                                                                 _____

27. Of the two methods of attaching linings to backing   27. _____
    plates, which would be *more likely* to be used on a
    smaller car?

28. Why are the friction surfaces of rotors and drums machined smooth?

    _____

29. The extra thickness of rotor and drum friction surfaces 29. _____
    allow the rotors or drums to be _____ if they become
    worn or damaged.

30. Why are the rotors and drums heavy?

    _____

    _____

Copyright Goodheart-Willcox Co., Inc.
May not be reproduced or posted to a publicly accessible website

Name _____

Date 3-22-28   Class 12 & 13

Chapter 12

Disc Brake System Components and Operation

After studying this chapter, you will be able to:
- ❑ Identify the components of a disc brake.
- ❑ Identify the two main types of rotors.
- ❑ Identify the three types of front caliper piston arrangements.
- ❑ Identify and explain the operation of fixed and floating calipers.
- ❑ Identify floating caliper mounting methods.
- ❑ Identify and explain the operation of rear calipers.
- ❑ Identify brake pad materials and construction.

1. The rotor surface must be _____ where it contacts the disc brake pads.

1. _____

2. All stock disc brake rotors are made of what metal?

2. _____

3. *True or False?* A rotor's thickness can vary throughout its diameter.

3. _____

4. Which of the following rotors provides the most braking area?
   (A) 8 inch (20 cm) ventilated.
   (B) 9 inch (23 cm) non-ventilated.
   (C) 10 inch (25 cm) ventilated.
   (D) 11 inch (28 cm) ventilated.

4. _____

5. Technician A says the minimum rotor thickness is stamped on the machined area of the rotor. Technician B says rotor thickness affects heat absorption. Who is right?
   (A) A only.
   (B) B only.
   (C) Both A and B.
   (D) Neither A nor B.

5. _____

Copyright Goodheart-Willcox Co., Inc.
May not be reproduced or posted to a publicly accessible website

6. Identify the following disc brake components.

(A) _____   (G) _____

(B) _____   (H) _____

(C) _____   (I) _____

(D) _____   (J) _____

(E) _____   (K) _____

(F) _____   (L) _____

7. Ventilated rotors have internal fins between the two
   _____ surfaces.

   7. _____

8. Which of the following vehicles would be *most likely* to
   use vented rotors?
   (A) Subcompact car.
   (B) Large pickup truck.
   (C) Small pickup truck.
   (D) Medium size car.

   8. _____

9. Cross-drilled rotors are used on what types of vehicles?

   9. _____

10. If the rotor is not accurately attached to the _____, it
    may wobble.

    10. _____

11. The wheel hub is attached to the spindle or axle
    through _____.

    11. _____

12. What is an integral rotor and hub?

_____

_____

Copyright Goodheart-Willcox Co., Inc.
May not be reproduced or posted to a publicly accessible website

Name _____

13. The splash shield keeps water and debris from the rotor's _____ surface.

13. _____

14. Calipers have a(n) _____ over every piston.

14. _____

15. Increases in hydraulic pressure always cause the caliper piston to move _____ in relation to the housing.

15. _____

16. What retracts the caliper piston when hydraulic pressure is removed?

16. _____

17. Since they have no _____ action, disc brakes require _____ brake pedal pressure than drum brakes to get the same braking effect.

17. _____

_____

18. Low-drag calipers have as much as _____ clearance when the brakes are released.

18. _____

19. Floating calipers use _____ piston(s).

19. _____

20. All of the following statements about caliper types are true, EXCEPT:
(A) floating calipers may have two pistons.
(B) floating calipers must move in and out in relation to the center of the vehicle.
(C) fixed calipers may have four pistons.
(D) fixed calipers apply pressure to only one side of the rotor.

20. _____

21. Explain, in your own words, how the disc brake pad and rotor clearance is automatically adjusted.

_____

_____

_____

22. Today, fixed calipers are primarily used on _____ vehicles.

22. _____

23. Most rear brake calipers are _____ designs.

23. _____

24. All of the following are parking brake designs used in rear disc brake calipers, EXCEPT:
(A) screw type.
(B) servo type.
(C) ball-and-ramp type.
(D) cam-type.

24. _____

25. A disc brake pad may be grooved for what four purposes?

_____

_____

_____

26. Linings may be attached to the shoe by _____ or _____.

26. _____

_____

Copyright Goodheart-Willcox Co., Inc.
May not be reproduced or posted to a publicly accessible website

27. What is the purpose of the shoe portion of a disc brake
    assembly?
    (A) To provide a smooth braking surface.
    (B) Support the lining.
    (C) Reduce noise.
    (D) Increase smoothness.

27. _____

28. Springs, clips, and insulators are often used to reduce
    brake _____.

28. _____

29. Anti-squeak compounds are installed on the _____ of
    the brake pad assembly.

29. _____

30. Technician A says a metal brake wear indicator makes
    noise when the brakes are not applied. Technician B says
    some brake wear indicators illuminate a dashboard light
    when the brakes are not applied. Who is right?
    (A) A only.
    (B) B only.
    (C) Both A and B.
    (D) Neither A nor B.

30. _____

Copyright Goodheart-Willcox Co., Inc.
May not be reproduced or posted to a publicly accessible website

Chapter 13

Disc Brake Service

After studying this chapter, you will be able to:
- ❑ Identify common disc brake problems.
- ❑ Diagnose disc brake problems.
- ❑ Remove and replace front disc brake calipers.
- ❑ Remove and replace rear disc brake calipers.
- ❑ Remove and replace disc brake pads.
- ❑ Refinish disc brake rotors.

1. Match the disc brake problem with its *most likely* symptom.
   (A) Power booster problem.
   (B) Pads worn to metal.
   (C) Glazed linings.
   (D) Pad wear sensor contacting rotor.
   (E) Caliper misaligned.

   C̶A̶ Squeal only when brakes are applied.

   _D_ Squeal only when brakes are released.

   _E_ Inboard pad worn more than outboard.

   _B_ Grinding noise when brakes are applied.

2. Pulsation is usually caused by a problem in the brake system _____.

   2. _____

3. Technician A says ABS or TCS systems complicate even the simplest brake repairs. Technician B says a non-ABS brake hose should never be used on the hydraulic system of an ABS-equipped vehicle. Who is right?
   (A) A only.
   (B) B only.
   (C) Both A and B.
   (D) Neither A nor B.

   3. _____

Copyright Goodheart-Willcox Co., Inc.
May not be reproduced or posted to a publicly accessible website

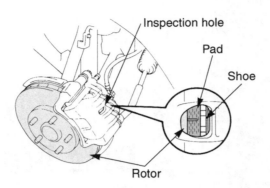

4. This figure shows a method of checking which of the
   following disc brake conditions?
   (A) Rotor runout.
   (B) Rotor thickness.
   (C) Pad thickness.
   (D) Shoe overheating.

4. _____

5. The easiest and quickest way to determine disc brake
   condition is to visually observe the pad _____ and the
   rotor _____.

5. _____
   _____

6. Pushing the _____ away from the rotor makes caliper
   removal easier.

6. _____

7. Some manufacturers recommend loosening the _____
   before pushing the piston.

7. _____

8. Some _____ are threaded into the caliper and slide on
   the spindle.

8. _____

9. Always suspend the removed caliper with a(n) _____.

9. _____

10. A loaded caliper is sold complete with which of the
    following components?
    (A) Rotor.
    (B) Pads.
    (C) Fluid.
    (D) Hose.

10. _____

11. What is a C-clamp used for during disc brake pad replacement?

   _____

   _____

12. Anti-squeal compound, when used, should be placed on
    the _____ of the brake pads.

12. _____

13. Why should wheel bearing grease or chassis lube never be used to lubricate the disc brake sliding surfaces?

   _____

   _____

14. All of the following statements about caliper installation
    are true, EXCEPT:
    (A) do not force the caliper over the rotor.
    (B) some calipers must be installed straight onto the rotor.
    (C) some calipers must be installed on one end first.
    (D) scraping noises when the rotor is turned indicate
        proper pad contact.

14. _____

Copyright Goodheart-Willcox Co., Inc.
May not be reproduced or posted to a publicly accessible website

Name _____

15. _____ must be performed on some vehicles to keep the outer pad from moving.

15. _____

16. List the three common disc parking brake designs.

16. _____

_____

_____

17. When the parking brake is built into the rear caliper, most rear disc brake pistons are retracted into the caliper by _____ them.

17. _____

18. A(n) _____ is sometimes used to adjust rear disc parking brakes.

18. _____

19. Deep cuts or ridges in the rotor surface is called _____.

19. _____

20. Heat damage to the rotor is called _____ or _____.

20. _____

_____

21. Rotor defects can sometimes be removed by _____ the rotor.

21. _____

22. To accurately measure rotor thickness, the technician must use a(n) _____.

22. _____

23. In this illustration, the technician is using a(n) _____ to check for _____.

23. _____

_____

24. When measured, a rotor has runout of about .005" (.127 mm). The rotor surface is otherwise in good condition and has never been turned. Technician A says the rotor must be turned. Technician B says the rotor must be replaced. Who is right?
(A) A only.
(B) B only.
(C) Both A and B.
(D) Neither A nor B.

24. _____

Copyright Goodheart-Willcox Co., Inc.
May not be reproduced or posted to a publicly accessible website

25. Technician A says some rotors are held to the hub by fasteners. Technician B says some rotors are held to the hub by the wheel nuts. Who is right?
    (A) A only.
    (B) B only.
    (C) Both A and B.
    (D) Neither A nor B.

25. _____

26. Some hubs can only be removed with a(n) _____.

26. _____

27. Before installing the rotor in the arbor, check the arbor and _____ it if necessary.

27. _____

28. The rotor will have a "wood grain" finish if the _____ is not installed before turning.

28. _____

29. To make a rough cut, the feed speed should be set relatively _____.

29. _____

30. After all damage is removed, make a(n) _____ cut.

30. _____

31. If you accidentally remove too much metal from the rotor, what should you do to correct the problem?

_____

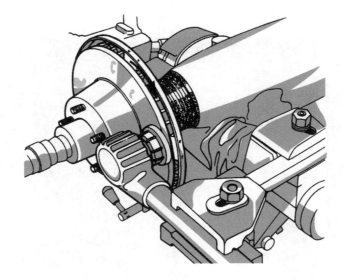

32. This figure shows a(n) _____ being used to remove hot spots on a rotor.

32. _____

33. Swirl grinding is used to make a(n) _____ finish on the rotor surface.

33. _____

34. After reassembling the brakes, road test and make at least _____ gentle stops to bed in the brakes.

34. _____

35. After brake service advise the vehicle driver to avoid _____ for the first 200 miles (320 km).

35. _____

36. A brake wear indicator is a small piece of sheet metal attached to the pad assembly. When the pad wears down enough, the indicator makes contact with the rotor, resulting in a(n) _____ whenever brakes are applied.

36. _____

Copyright Goodheart-Willcox Co., Inc.
May not be reproduced or posted to a publicly accessible website

Chapter 14

Drum Brake System Components and Operation

After studying this chapter, you will be able to:
- ❑ Identify major drum brake components.
- ❑ Explain the purpose of backing plates.
- ❑ Identify the construction and purpose of brake shoes.
- ❑ Identify and explain the purpose of brake springs.
- ❑ Identify types of brake drums.
- ❑ Explain self-energizing, leverage, and servo action.
- ❑ Identify servo and non-servo brakes and explain their operation.

1. What are the two purposes of the drum brake backing plate?

   _____

   _____

2. The brake anchors are stationary anchoring points for the brake _____ and _____.

   2. _____

   _____

3. The two parts of the brake shoe are the _____ and _____.

   3. _____

   _____

4. The support pads are part of the _____.
   (A) shoe table
   (B) shoe web
   (C) backing plate
   (D) anchor plate

   4. _____

5. The brake shoe may press directly on the wheel cylinder piston or may be connected through a link, often called a(n) _____ or _____.

   5. _____

   _____

Copyright Goodheart-Willcox Co., Inc.
May not be reproduced or posted to a publicly accessible website

6. Define the term *drum brake lining*.

_____

_____

7. All of the following statements about drum brake linings are true, EXCEPT:
   (A) older vehicles used large relatively thin brake linings on the front brakes.
   (B) current vehicles use small thick brake linings on the rear brakes.
   (C) each lining is riveted and bonded to ensure solid attachment.
   (D) every drum brake assembly has a primary and a secondary shoe.

7. _____

8. A(n) _____ contacts the drum evenly.

8. _____

9. _____ are cut in the linings of very large brake shoes.

9. _____

10. The two main types of brake shoe springs are the _____ spring and the _____ spring.

10. _____

   _____

11. Hold-down springs hold the shoes against the _____ when the brakes are not applied.
    (A) anchors
    (B) backing plate
    (C) wheel cylinder pistons
    (D) self-adjuster

11. _____

12. Brake shoe return springs are sometimes _____ to identify their proper location.
    (A) shaped differently
    (B) stamped with a number
    (C) stamped with a letter
    (D) color-coded

12. _____

13. What type of vehicle is *most likely* to have an eccentric cam drum brake adjuster?
    (A) Older car.
    (B) Newer pickup truck.
    (C) Newer SUV.
    (D) Any age minivan.

13. _____

Copyright Goodheart-Willcox Co., Inc.
May not be reproduced or posted to a publicly accessible website

Name _____

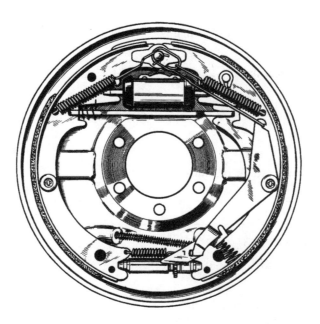

14. What type of brake adjuster is used on the drum brake assembly shown above?

14. _____

15. Star wheel adjusters are being discussed. Technician A says star wheel adjusters can be swapped between the right and left sides of the vehicle to equalize wear. Technician B says star wheel adjusters only operate if the brakes are applied when the vehicle is moving in reverse. Who is right?
    (A) A only.
    (B) B only.
    (C) Both A and B.
    (D) Neither A nor B.

15. _____

16. List the three main classes of automatic star wheel adjuster.

16. _____

    _____

    _____

17. When do the self-adjusters operate to reduce clearance?
    (A) When the brakes are applied at high speeds.
    (B) When the brakes are applied at low speeds.
    (C) When the brake pedal is released.
    (D) When the brakes are applied in reverse.

17. _____

18. All of the following statements about drum brake self-adjusters are true, EXCEPT:
    (A) most self-adjusters have an override mechanism to prevent linkage damage.
    (B) ratchet type adjusters are used on non-servo brakes.
    (C) adjusters used on servo brakes are located between the primary and secondary shoes.
    (D) ratchet-type adjusters have no provision for manual adjustment.

18. _____

19. In addition to the automatic adjuster, all drum brakes have a way to make a(n) _____ brake shoe adjustment.

19. _____

Copyright Goodheart-Willcox Co., Inc.
May not be reproduced or posted to a publicly accessible website

20. All modern brake drums have a(n) _____ surface that is machined smooth.

20. _____

21. On a rear-wheel drive vehicle, the rear drum assemblies are held to the axle flange by _____.
    (A) a cotter pin
    (B) the lug bolts and nuts
    (C) a part of the flange
    (D) None of the above.

21. _____

22. What is the purpose of the fins cast into the outside of some drums?

_____

_____

23. An aluminum drum must have a cast iron _____.

23. _____

24. When the rotation of the drum tries to pull the shoe into the drum, _____ occurs.

24. _____

25. Before the brake pedal pressure can be assisted by the self-energizing principle, the shoe must be brought into contact with the drum by _____.
    (A) the wheel cylinder piston
    (B) shoe leverage
    (C) servo action
    (D) star wheel adjuster

25. _____

26. Servo action occurs when power is transferred from the _____ shoe to the _____ shoe.

26. _____

    _____

27. Technician A says servo brakes only operate when moving forward. Technician B says brake shoes that are anchored at the bottom are not servo brakes. Who is right?
    (A) A only.
    (B) B only.
    (C) Both A and B.
    (D) Neither A nor B.

27. _____

28. When servo action drum brakes are used, the _____ shoe always has the longest lining.

28. _____

29. Non-servo brakes are *most likely* to be found on which of the following vehicles?
    (A) Large car.
    (B) Small car.
    (C) Large sport-utility vehicles.
    (D) Small truck.

29. _____

30. When a non-servo drum brake is applied while the vehicle is moving forward, which shoe is applied by hydraulic pressure *only?*

30. _____

Copyright Goodheart-Willcox Co., Inc.
May not be reproduced or posted to a publicly accessible website

Chapter 15

Drum Brake Service

After studying this chapter, you will be able to:
- ❏ Identify common drum brake problems.
- ❏ Diagnose drum brake problems.
- ❏ Remove and replace brake drums.
- ❏ Check brake shoe condition.
- ❏ Check brake springs for damage.
- ❏ Check condition of brake shoe adjuster mechanisms.
- ❏ Check drum diameter and compare with maximum wear limits.
- ❏ Remove and replace brake shoes.
- ❏ Refinish brake drums.
- ❏ Adjust drum brake clearance.

1. Technician A says glazed linings may cause squeaking drum brakes. Technician B says completely worn down linings may cause clicking noises. Who is right?
   (A) A only.
   (B) B only.
   (C) Both A and B.
   (D) Neither A nor B.

1. _____

2. Out-of-round drums can cause _____.

2. _____

3. Thin drums may cause the brakes to _____.

3. _____

4. Technician A says oil on the linings causes grabbing. Technician B says weak retracting springs can cause grabbing. Who is right?
   (A) A only.
   (B) B only.
   (C) Both A and B.
   (D) Neither A nor B.

4. _____

Copyright Goodheart-Willcox Co., Inc.
May not be reproduced or posted to a publicly accessible website

5. It may be necessary to back off the adjuster to remove the drums if they are badly _____.

5. _____

6. The adjuster access hole may contain a(n) _____ plug, which must be removed with a punch and hammer.

6. _____

7. The _____ must be disengaged before the star wheel can be turned.
   (A) hold-down springs
   (B) retracting springs
   (C) wheel cylinder hose
   (D) self-adjusting lever

7. _____

8. Why should you *not* hit the centering flange when removing a drum?

_____

_____

9. To remove an integral drum, the technician must first remove the cotter pin and nut holding the _____.

9. _____

10. All of the following conditions require brake shoe replacement, EXCEPT:
    (A) darkening.
    (B) glazing.
    (C) cracks.
    (D) scoring.

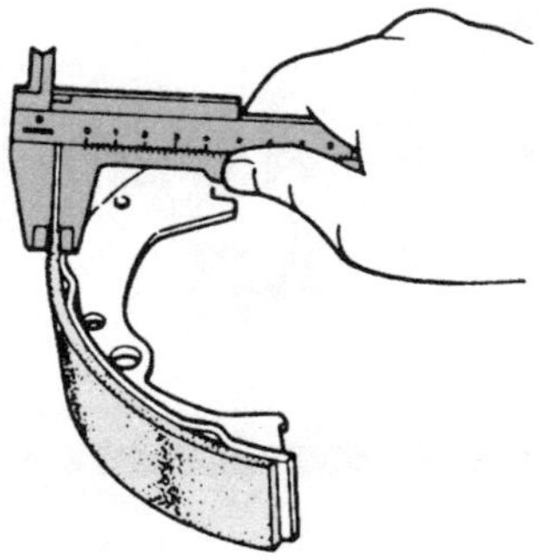

10. _____

11. Technician A says the above figure shows a technician checking a brake lining for thickness. Technician B says the above figure shows a technician checking a brake lining for glazing. Who is right?
    (A) A only.
    (B) B only.
    (C) Both A and B.
    (D) Neither A nor B.

11. _____

12. If the brake assembly has been severely overheated, it is common practice to replace the brake _____, even though no damage is evident.

12. _____

Copyright Goodheart-Willcox Co., Inc.
May not be reproduced or posted to a publicly accessible website

Name _____

13. If pulling back the dust cover of the wheel cylinder causes fluid to drip, the wheel cylinder should be _____.
   (A) overhauled
   (B) replaced
   (C) left alone
   (D) Both A and B.

13. _____

14. If the outer diameter of the machined surface of a drum is larger than the inner diameter, the drum is _____.

14. _____

15. A drum has different diameters when it is measured at every 45° around its internal surface. What does this mean?
   (A) The drum can be reused.
   (B) The drum is too thin.
   (C) The drum is out-of-round.
   (D) The drum is tapered.

15. _____

16. Most servo type brake shoes can be removed from the backing plate as a(n) _____ with the _____.

16. _____
   _____

17. Many _____ springs are not interchangeable between the front and rear shoes.
   (A) hold down
   (B) retracting
   (C) adjuster
   (D) Both A and B.

17. _____

18. Before rear brakes are removed from the vehicle, the parking brake _____ must be removed from the rear shoe.

18. _____

19. The backing plate should not be removed unless it is _____

19. _____

20. After cleaning the brake parts, do not dry them using _____.

20. _____

21. If a star wheel adjuster does not turn easily, what can be done to loosen it?

_____

22. If the paint has been burned off a brake spring, this is a symptom of:
   (A) brake overheating.
   (B) a warped drum.
   (C) a stuck wheel cylinder.
   (D) this is a normal condition of used brakes.

22. _____

23. What part of the self-adjuster should *never* be lubricated?

23. _____

24. When new brake shoes are installed, the primary shoe should face the _____ of the vehicle.

24. _____

25. Before turning a drum with an integral hub, the inner _____ must be removed.

25. _____

Copyright Goodheart-Willcox Co., Inc.
May not be reproduced or posted to a publicly accessible website

26. Technician A says you should make sure the lathe arbor is clean before mounting a drum. Technician B says since drums require adapters, arbor cleanliness is not a factor. Who is right?
    (A) A only.
    (B) B only.
    (C) Both A and B.
    (D) Neither A nor B.

26. _____

27. The drum brake lathe feed dial sets the _____ of the cut. The feed speed dial sets the _____ of the cut.

27. _____

    _____

28. All of the following statements about machining brake drums are true, EXCEPT:
    (A) cutting speed should be relatively fast for a rough cut.
    (B) cutting depth should be relatively deep for a finish cut.
    (C) cutting speed should be relatively slow for a finish cut.
    (D) the rough cut is always done first.

28. _____

29. Before the drum is reinstalled after turning, remove all _____.

29. _____

30. What operation does this figure show?

    _____

    _____

Copyright Goodheart-Willcox Co., Inc.
May not be reproduced or posted to a publicly accessible website

Chapter 16

Wheel Bearings and Oil Seals

After studying this chapter, you will be able to:
- ❑ Identify types of wheel hubs and axle flanges.
- ❑ Identify types of wheel bearings.
- ❑ Recall common locations and usage of each wheel bearing type.
- ❑ Explain how each type of wheel bearing is installed on spindles and bearing hubs.
- ❑ Explain how oil seals are constructed.
- ❑ Identify places where oil seals are installed.
- ❑ Recall brake-related locations where gaskets or O-rings are used.

1. Wheel hubs on front-wheel-drive vehicles are _____ from the axle.

1. _____

2. The largest part of a lug bolt is _____ so it will hold tightly in the hub or flange. The rear _____ keeps the lug bolt from coming through the hub or flange.

2. _____
_____

3. Technician A says friction bearings are used as wheel bearings on some vehicles. Technician B says antifriction bearings are used where space is limited, such as engines. Who is right?
(A) A only.
(B) B only.
(C) Both A and B.
(D) Neither A nor B.

3. _____

4. Bearings are designed to form a low _____ connection between the rotating wheel and stationary body.

4. _____

Copyright Goodheart-Willcox Co., Inc.
May not be reproduced or posted to a publicly accessible website

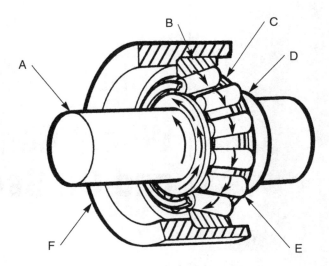

5. Identify the bearing parts shown above.

(A)_____   (D)_____

(B)_____   (E)_____

(C)_____   (F)_____

6. The advantage of using rolling elements in a bearing is
   the large reduction in _____.

6. _____

7. The bearing cage keeps the rolling elements _____.

7. _____

8. Technician A says vehicle weight causes radial loads on
   the bearings. Technician B says centrifugal force causes
   radial loads on the bearings. Who is right?
   (A) A only.
   (B) B only.
   (C) Both A and B.
   (D) Neither A nor B.

8. _____

9. The two types of loads placed on a bearing are _____
   loads caused by vehicle weight, and _____ loads caused
   when the vehicle turns.

9. _____

   _____

10. Preload can be adjusted on which of the following
    bearings?
    (A) Ball bearing.
    (B) Flat roller bearing.
    (C) Tapered roller bearing.
    (D) Needle bearing.

10. _____

11. Ball bearings are *most likely* to be used on which of the
    following vehicle designs?
    (A) Front axle of front-wheel drive vehicles.
    (B) Rear axle of rear-wheel drive vehicles.
    (C) Front axle of rear-wheel drive vehicles.
    (D) Rear axle of front-wheel drive vehicles.

11. _____

12. The _____ on ball bearing assemblies is factory set and
    cannot be adjusted.

12. _____

Copyright Goodheart-Willcox Co., Inc.
May not be reproduced or posted to a publicly accessible website

Name _____

13. All of the following statements about antifriction bearing
    and rolling element design are true, EXCEPT:
    (A) small rollers may shatter under shock loads.
    (B) front bearings are usually larger than rear bearings.
    (C) ball bearings cannot be adjusted.
    (D) only tapered bearings can handle axial loads in both
        directions.

13. _____

14. List two ways of holding a spindle nut in place.

    _____

    _____

15. A(n) _____ and _____ is used to stake the outer part of
    a nut into a slot on the spindle.

15. _____
    _____

16. Technician A says the grease in wheel bearings must be
    periodically changed. Technician B says gear oil is
    splashed on some rear axle bearings. Who is right?
    (A) A only.
    (B) B only.
    (C) Both A and B.
    (D) Neither A nor B.

16. _____

17. _____ is a semisolid lubricant.

17. _____

18. Modern grease usually contains all of the following,
    EXCEPT:
    (A) lithium.
    (B) long fibers.
    (C) polymers.
    (D) oils.

18. _____

19. Most cars and light trucks use gear oil with a(n)
    _____ rating.

19. _____

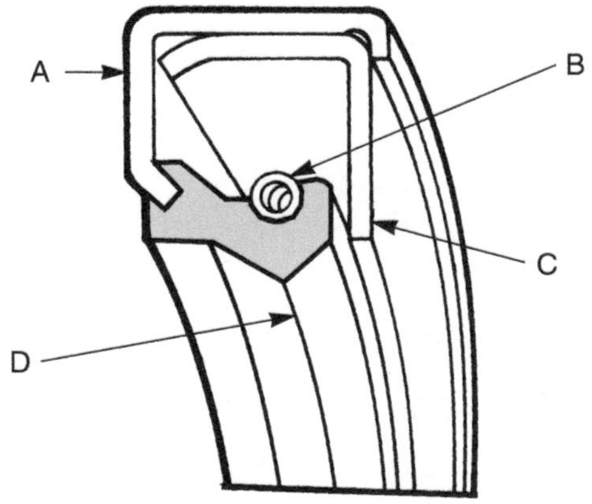

20. Identify the lip seal parts shown in the above figure.

    (A)_____   (C)_____

    (B)_____   (D)_____

Copyright Goodheart-Willcox Co., Inc.
May not be reproduced or posted to a publicly accessible website

21. What are the two purposes of the oil film that forms on a lip seal?

_____

_____

22. Most lip type oil seals are _____ into the hub or axle.   22. _____
    (A) bolted
    (B) staked
    (C) glued
    (D) pressed

23. Slight amounts of lubricant that get past the seal may be   23. _____
    absorbed by a(n) _____.

24. Gaskets prevent leaks between _____ parts.   24. _____

25. What is the advantage of an O-ring over a gasket?

_____

_____

Copyright Goodheart-Willcox Co., Inc.
May not be reproduced or posted to a publicly accessible website

Chapter 17

Wheel Bearing and Oil Seal Service

After studying this chapter, you will be able to:
- ❑ Identify common wheel bearing defects.
- ❑ Diagnose wheel bearing problems.
- ❑ Remove and clean tapered wheel bearings.
- ❑ Inspect tapered roller wheel bearings and identify defects.
- ❑ Remove and replace pressed in wheel bearing races.
- ❑ Lubricate, install, and adjust tapered roller wheel bearings.
- ❑ Remove and replace ball and flat roller wheel bearings.
- ❑ Identify leaking oil seals, gaskets, and O-rings.
- ❑ Remove and replace oil seals.
- ❑ Remove and replace gaskets and O-rings.
- ❑ Remove and replace wheel studs.

1. The usual cause of wheel bearing problems is worn out _____ or _____ entering the bearing.

2. Severe pitting or cratering of the bearing rollers or races is called _____.

3. Worn wheel bearings may make a roaring noise that increases and decreases with _____.

4. *True or False?* A cracked bearing race can be replaced without replacing the rollers.

5. Technician A says shaking a wheel can often isolate a worn bearing. Technician B says shaking the wheel may also locate a worn suspension part. Who is right?
   (A) A only.
   (B) B only.
   (C) Both A and B.
   (D) Neither A nor B.

1. _____

_____

2. _____

3. _____

4. _____

5. _____

Copyright Goodheart-Willcox Co., Inc.
May not be reproduced or posted to a publicly accessible website

6. *True or False?* It is *not* necessary to remove an integral brake drum to service tapered wheel bearings.

6. _____

7. All of the following statements about tapered bearing removal are true, EXCEPT:
   (A) use diagonal pliers to remove the cotter pin.
   (B) shake the hub to unseat the outer bearing.
   (C) lift the inner bearing from the hub after removing the seal.
   (D) save the inner seal for reuse.

7. _____

8. *True or False?* A brass drift may damage the bearing race.

8. _____

9. Technician A says bearings can be successfully hand lubricated. Technician B says a new seal should be used whenever the bearings are repacked. Who is right?
   (A) A only.
   (B) B only.
   (C) Both A and B.
   (D) Neither A nor B.

9. _____

10. The figure above illustrates which of the following bearing service steps?
    (A) Seal removal.
    (B) Seal installation.
    (C) Bearing race removal.
    (D) Bearing installation.

10. _____

11. _____ is the oldest and perhaps best method of lubricating wheel bearings.

11. _____

12. The seal manufacturer usually coats the outer housing of a lip seal with _____.

12. _____

13. Explain why you should tighten the wheel bearing adjusting nut to 100 ft-lbs. (135.5 N•m) before adjusting the bearings.

_____

_____

14. What part of a wheel bearing assembly should *always* be replaced as part of wheel bearing service?

14. _____

Copyright Goodheart-Willcox Co., Inc.
May not be reproduced or posted to a publicly accessible website

Name _____

15. Some front-wheel drive bearings are pressed into the hub, while others are held by a(n) _____.

15. _____

16. *True or False?* Some bearing nuts may have left-hand threads.

16. _____

17. To remove a hub and knuckle assembly, you must remove all of the following parts, EXCEPT:
    (A) lower ball joint.
    (B) tie rod end.
    (C) brake hose.
    (D) lower control arm.

17. _____

18. To remove a pressed-in bearing, you will need a(n) _____ press.

18. _____

19. Where should you apply pressure when pressing in a new bearing?

_____

20. To remove a C-lock, the _____ must be removed.

20. _____

21. On a C-lock solid axle, a(n) _____ is pressed into the rear axle housing.

21. _____

22. If the solid rear axle is held in place by a retainer plate, the bearing is lubricated by _____.

22. _____

23. If a seal is installed backward, it will:
    (A) squeak.
    (B) leak.
    (C) wear the shaft surface.
    (D) cause the drive shaft to lock up.

23. _____

24. Rear axle bearing collar removal is being discussed. Technician A says the collar must be ground completely through before removal. Technician B says the collar must be cracked with a hammer and chisel to remove it from the shaft. Who is right?
    (A) A only.
    (B) B only.
    (C) Both A and B.
    (D) Neither A nor B.

24. _____

25. A replacement seal is placed over the shaft at its normal riding position. It feels snug against the shaft. This means that:
    (A) it is the wrong seal.
    (B) it is the right seal.
    (C) the shaft must be sanded to remove deposits.
    (D) the shaft must be replaced.

25. _____

26. A gasket sealing surface on a part has some deep scratches. What should be done to prevent leaks?

_____

27. *True or False?* A gasket must face in the proper direction to seal properly.

27. _____

28. What three things should an O-ring groove be checked for?

_____

_____

Copyright Goodheart-Willcox Co., Inc.
May not be reproduced or posted to a publicly accessible website

29. The tool used to clean an O-ring groove should be made from _____ or _____.

29. _____

_____

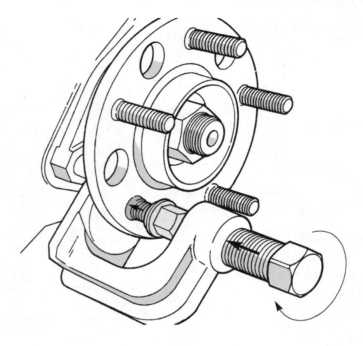

30. The figure above shows a special tool being used to _____ a wheel stud.

30. _____

Copyright Goodheart-Willcox Co., Inc.
May not be reproduced or posted to a publicly accessible website

Chapter 18

Parking Brakes

After studying this chapter, you will be able to:
- ❑ Explain the function of the parking brake.
- ❑ Identify the components and explain the operation of driver-applied parking brake levers.
- ❑ Describe the construction and explain the operation of automatic parking brake release mechanisms.
- ❑ Identify the components and operation of parking brake warning lights.
- ❑ Identify the components of parking brake linkage.
- ❑ Explain the operation of parking brake levers and linkage.
- ❑ Describe the construction and operation of drum brake parking brakes.
- ❑ Describe the construction and operation of disc brake parking brakes.

1. Which kind of driver-operated parking brake actuator is the *least* common?
   (A) Foot-operated pedal.
   (B) Hand lever between front seats.
   (C) Hand lever under dashboard.
   (D) Hand lever beside the driver's seat.

1. _____

2. In a foot-operated parking brake, the lever is usually called the _____.

2. _____

3. Foot-operated and floor-mounted parking brake levers are being discussed. Technician A says both types have similar operating principles. Technician B says the parking pawl on either type must be engaged with the stationary teeth before the brake will release. Who is right?
   (A) A only.
   (B) B only.
   (C) Both A and B.
   (D) Neither A nor B.

3. _____

Copyright Goodheart-Willcox Co., Inc.
May not be reproduced or posted to a publicly accessible website

4. A(n) _____ requires several applications of the pedal arm to set the brake.

4. _____

5. Some foot-operated parking brakes are automatically released by _____.

5. _____

6. *True or False?* Most automatic release parking brakes have an emergency manual release lever.

6. _____

7. Turning the _____ disengages a hand-operated under-dashboard parking brake lever.

7. _____

8. A floor-mounted hand lever is held in the applied position when a(n) _____ contacts the _____ on a stationary support bracket.

8. _____
_____

9. A(n) _____ is used to tell the driver the parking brake is on.

9. _____

10. Parking brake cables are made from stranded _____.

10. _____

11. _____ may be used to carry the cable around sharp corners.

11. _____

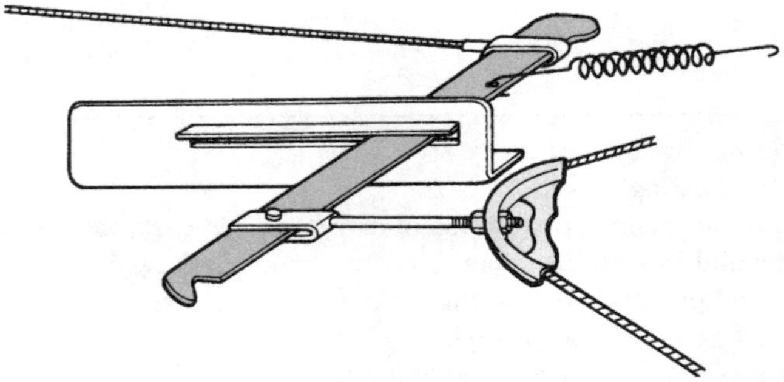

12. This illustration shows all of the following parking brake components, EXCEPT:
    (A) release mechanism.
    (B) force multiplier.
    (C) parking brake adjuster.
    (D) force equalizer.

12. _____

13. Brake leverage is increased by a(n) _____. Brake leverage is balanced by a(n) _____.

13. _____
_____

14. List two types of parking brake linkage adjustment devices.

14. _____
_____

15. The brake friction members that are operated by the hydraulic system are called the _____ brakes.

15. _____

16. List the three types of parking brakes.

16. _____
_____
_____

Copyright Goodheart-Willcox Co., Inc.
May not be reproduced or posted to a publicly accessible website

Name _____

17. Technician A says the parking brake lever applies both brake shoes of a servo action drum brake. Technician B says the parking brake lever applies both brake shoes of a non-servo action drum brake. Who is right?
(A) A only.
(B) B only.
(C) Both A and B.
(D) Neither A nor B.

17. _____

18. The _____ in a non-servo parking brake arrangement performs the same function as the lever strut in a servo parking brake arrangement.

18. _____

19. A self-contained drum parking brake is *most likely* to be used on which of the following brake systems?
(A) Front drum.
(B) Rear drum.
(C) Front disc.
(D) Rear disc.

19. _____

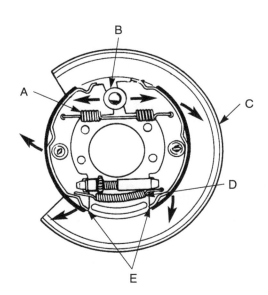

20. List the components of the self-contained brake assembly shown above.

(A) _____   (D) _____

(B) _____   (E) _____

(C) _____

21. The _____ is the most common type of caliper parking brake actuator.

21. _____

Copyright Goodheart-Willcox Co., Inc.
May not be reproduced or posted to a publicly accessible website

22. Match the type of integral disc parking brake with its components.
    (A) Screw type
    (B) Ball-and-ramp type
    (C) Cam type
    (D) All of the above

23. In a screw disc parking brake, what pulls the actuator lever back to its released position?

24. Which of the following integral disc parking brakes is self-adjusting?
    (A) Screw type.
    (B) Ball-and-ramp type.
    (C) Cam type.
    (D) All of the above.

25. In a cam disc parking brake, what is the cam sometimes called?

22. __A__ Nut and cone assembly
     __B__ Thrust screw
     __A__ Actuator screw
     __C__ Actuator rod
     __C__ Eccentric
     __B__ Operating shaft
     __B__ Three steel balls

23. _____

24. _____

25. _____

Copyright Goodheart-Willcox Co., Inc.
May not be reproduced or posted to a publicly accessible website

Chapter 19

Parking Brake Service

After studying this chapter, you will be able to:
- ☐ Identify common parking brake problems.
- ☐ Diagnose parking brake problems.
- ☐ Adjust parking brakes.
- ☐ Service parking brake cables and related parts.
- ☐ Service automatic vacuum brake release mechanisms.
- ☐ Service warning lights.
- ☐ Adjust drum parking brake wheel assemblies.
- ☐ Adjust disc parking brake wheel assemblies.

1. What is the most common cause of poor parking brake holding power?

    _____

    _____

2. If the parking brake does not work, the driver may blame the _____ or the _____.

    2. _____

    _____

3. Describe the parking brake click test.

    _____

    _____

    _____

4. The click test is not accurate on vehicles with _____ levers.

    4. _____

5. A vacuum release parking brake should release when the vehicle is shifted into _____.

    5. _____

6. Some forward movement with resistance is considered normal in most vehicles with _____.

    6. _____

Copyright Goodheart-Willcox Co., Inc.
May not be reproduced or posted to a publicly accessible website

7. Where should you start checking for parking brake problems?

   _____

8. What should you look for when inspecting hand-operated parking levers?

   _____

   _____

9. The parking brake warning light does not illuminate. Technician A says the bulb should always be checked first. Technician B says the parking brake switch can be checked with an ohmmeter or test light. Who is right?
   (A) A only.
   (B) B only.
   (C) Both A and B.
   (D) Neither A nor B.

9. _____

10. Most parking brake cable adjusters are located at the:
    (A) driver-operated lever.
    (B) equalizer.
    (C) rear brake assembly.
    (D) multiplier.

10. _____

11. *True or False?* Loose brake cable strands can be cut off and the cable reused.

11. _____

12. Technician A says if the brake lever can be pulled out to its limit, the cable is properly adjusted. Technician B says always adjust the service brakes before adjusting the parking brake. Who is right?
    (A) A only.
    (B) B only.
    (C) Both A and B.
    (D) Neither A nor B.

12. _____

13. If the _____ are worn out, do not attempt to adjust the parking brake.

13. _____

14. _____ should be checked whenever the disc brake caliper is removed.

14. _____

15. *True or False?* If light tapping does not free up a caliper piston, the caliper should be overhauled.

15. _____

Copyright Goodheart-Willcox Co., Inc.
May not be reproduced or posted to a publicly accessible website

Name _____

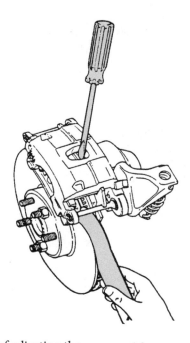

16. The illustration above shows a method of adjusting the
    rear brake _____.
    (A) cables
    (B) equalizer
    (C) pads
    (D) caliper piston

16. _____

17. You are removing a floor-mounted hand parking brake
    lever. Which of the following steps should be taken *first*?
    (A) Pull up the carpet.
    (B) Remove the electrical connector.
    (C) Remove the cable end.
    (D) Remove the lever-to-floor fasteners.

17. _____

18. Foot brakes are replaced as a(n) _____.

18. _____

19. Before removing any brake cables or linkage, make sure
    that the vehicle cannot _____.

19. _____

20. Most warning light switches can be _____.

20. _____

21. Technician A says parking brake cables may become
    corroded and stick. Technician B says parking brake
    cables and levers usually last the life of the vehicle. Who
    is right?
    (A) A only.
    (B) B only.
    (C) Both A and B.
    (D) Neither A nor B.

21. _____

22. To remove an intermediate cable, you may need to
    remove the _____ and/or _____.

22. _____

_____

23. If a(n) _____ -type retainer is used to hold the cable
    sheath to the backing plate, it can usually be compressed
    with a hose clamp.

23. _____

Copyright Goodheart-Willcox Co., Inc.
May not be reproduced or posted to a publicly accessible website

24. All of the following are used to hold a rear brake cable to the drum brake backing plate, EXCEPT:
    (A) retainer plate.
    (B) finger assembly.
    (C) snap ring.
    (D) clip.

24. _____

25. Before attempting to remove the clip or finger assembly holding the rear brake cable to the backing plate of a drum brake, always start by first removing the _____.
    (A) primary shoe
    (B) secondary shoe
    (C) parking brake lever
    (D) brake dust

25. _____

Copyright Goodheart-Willcox Co., Inc.
May not be reproduced or posted to a publicly accessible website

Chapter 20

Brake System Electrical and Electronic Components

After studying this chapter, you will be able to:
- ❏ Explain theories of electricity.
- ❏ Identify basic electrical measurements.
- ❏ Identify basic vehicle electrical circuits.
- ❏ Identify and explain the purpose of vehicle wiring and connectors.
- ❏ Explain how to diagnose brake warning light problems.
- ❏ Explain the construction and operation of the automotive computer.
- ❏ Identify the major parts of vehicle computers.
- ❏ Explain the operation of control loops.

1. *True or False?* All modern vehicles use 12-volt electrical systems.

1. _____

2. Technician A says current is measured in volts. Technician B says resistance is measured in ohms. Who is right?
   (A) A only.
   (B) B only.
   (C) Both A and B.
   (D) Neither A nor B.

2. _____

3. _____ flows in one direction.

3. _____

4. If current flow through a 12-volt circuit is six amps, the resistance in the circuit must be _____.

4. _____

5. If resistance in a 12-volt circuit is three ohms, the amperage in the circuit must be _____.

5. _____

6. A(n) _____ allows current to flow.

6. _____

Copyright Goodheart-Willcox Co., Inc.
May not be reproduced or posted to a publicly accessible website

7. What type of signal is shown in the following illustration?

7.

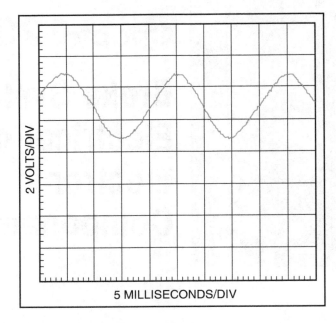

8. Technician A says when same amount of current flows through every part of a circuit, the circuit is a series circuit. Technician B says brake light circuits are series circuits. Who is right?
(A) A only.
(B) B only.
(C) Both A and B.
(D) Neither A nor B.

8.

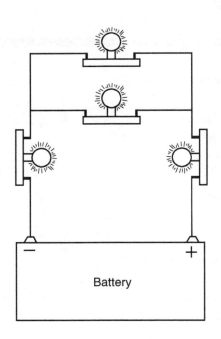

9. The above illustration shows a(n) _____ circuit.

9. _____

10. A(n) _____ is caused when the wire insulation fails or is removed and the wires contact each other.

10. _____

Copyright Goodheart-Willcox Co., Inc.
May not be reproduced or posted to a publicly accessible website

Name _____

11. All of the following statements about circuit defects are true, EXCEPT:
   (A) no current can flow in an open circuit.
   (B) a grounded circuit is similar to a short circuit.
   (C) short circuits are usually caused by insulation failure.
   (D) a high-resistance circuit allows excessive current to flow.

11. _____

12. All of the following are possible causes of an open circuit, EXCEPT:
   (A) disconnected wires.
   (B) low-resistance electrical connection.
   (C) loose connection.
   (D) defective electrical component.

12. _____

13. What two metals are commonly used in automotive wiring?

13. _____

   _____

14. Most wires are assembled into wire _____.

14. _____

15. Why are wires color-coded?

_____

16. _____ is the rating system for wire diameter.

16. _____

17. Shielded wires are used to protect low-voltage circuits from _____.

17. _____

18. Modern _____ are often thoroughly sealed.

18. _____

19. List the three most common types of circuit protection devices.

19. _____

   _____

   _____

20. A red Maxifuse has what amperage rating?

20. _____

21. A rear bulb on an older vehicle may have two filaments. What light function do these filaments perform?

_____

22. No brake lights come on when the brake pedal is pressed. Which of the following is the *least likely* cause?
   (A) Brake light fuse blown.
   (B) Brake switch misadjusted.
   (C) All bulb filaments burned out.
   (D) Brake switch wiring defect.

22. _____

23. If a warning light is on at all times, which of the following is the *most likely* cause?
   (A) The circuit is always open.
   (B) The circuit has high resistance.
   (C) The circuit is always closed.
   (D) The circuit switch is open.

23. _____

Copyright Goodheart-Willcox Co., Inc.
May not be reproduced or posted to a publicly accessible website

24. All of the following statements about electromagnetism
    are true, EXCEPT:
    (A) all magnetic fields have polarity.
    (B) induction is the use of current to produce magnetism.
    (C) if a wire moves through a magnetic field, current
         starts to flow in the wire.
    (D) electromagnets are the basic components of solenoids.

24. _____

25. A motor turns electricity into _____.

25. _____

26. To stop ABS motor rotation, _____ are used.

26. _____

27. Radio frequency and electromagnetic are two types of
    electrical _____.

27. _____

28. Diodes and transistors are examples of _____.

28. _____

29. All of the following statements about computer sections
    are true, EXCEPT:
    (A) the CPU performs calculations.
    (B) removing the battery cable can erase RAM memory.
    (C) removing the computer system fuse can erase
         ROM memory.
    (D) trouble codes are a computer output.

29. _____

30. Applied to computer systems, an endless circle of cause
    and effect is called a(n) _____.

30. _____

Copyright Goodheart-Willcox Co., Inc.
May not be reproduced or posted to a publicly accessible website

Chapter 21

Anti-Lock Brake, Traction Control, and Electronic Stability Control System Components and Operation

After studying this chapter, you will be able to:
- ❏ Explain why anti-lock brake systems were developed.
- ❏ Explain anti-lock brake system operation.
- ❏ Identify and explain the purpose of anti-lock brake system components.
- ❏ Explain traction control system operation.
- ❏ Identify and explain the purpose of traction control system components.
- ❏ Explain how the traction control system can affect engine and drive train operation.
- ❏ Explain electronic stability control system operation.
- ❏ Identify and explain the purpose of a yaw rate sensor.
- ❏ Identify common components of anti-lock brake, traction control, and electronic stability control systems.

1. At 100% negative slip, the brakes stop the _____ but not the _____.

1. _____
_____

2. At 100% positive or negative slip, the tire has no _____.

2. _____

3. During very hard braking on dry pavement, the wheel may slide on _____. This may cause a(n) _____ on the bottom of the tire.

3. _____
_____

4. The ABS system is a method of rapidly _____ the brake during hard braking.

4. _____

5. If a tire can continue to rotate during a panic stop, tire wear will be _____.

5. _____

6. The _____ will operate if the ABS system fails.

6. _____

Copyright Goodheart-Willcox Co., Inc.
May not be reproduced or posted to a publicly accessible website

7. Technician A says limited-slip differentials are the best kind of traction control. Technician B says a TCS system applies the brakes on wheels with the most traction. Who is right?
   (A) A only.
   (B) B only.
   (C) Both A and B.
   (D) Neither A nor B.

7. _____

8. *True or False?* Many drivers do not use ABS properly.

8. _____

9. *True or False?* Brake pedal pulsation during hard braking is a sign of normal ABS operation.

9. _____

10. RWAL stands for _____.

10. _____

11. Riding the brakes while driving a vehicle can cause all of the following conditions, EXCEPT:
    (A) setting a diagnostic code and disabling the ABS system. ✓
    (B) forcing the control module to disable the TCS system. ✓
    (C) preventing panic stops since the slight brake pad-to-rotor clearance is eliminated when driving.
    (D) overheating and causing premature wear of the ✓ base brakes.

11. _____

12. *True or False?* Electronic stability control operates in the same manner as traction control and is the name used for traction control systems equipped in vehicles manufactured before the 2000 model year.

12. _____

13. A typical ABS system could have as many as _____ channels.

13. _____

14. A tone wheel speed sensor acts like a small electrical _____.

14. _____

15. A G-force sensor measures rate of vehicle deceleration by sensing vehicle _____ during braking. A lateral acceleration sensor measures _____ speed.

15. _____
    _____

16. Two switches are attached to the brake pedal to provide input to the ABS system. They are the _____ switch and the _____ switch.

16. _____
    _____

17. ABS control modules can be installed in all the following places, EXCEPT:
    (A) as part of the instrument cluster. ✗
    (B) in the trunk. ✓
    (C) under the hood. ✓
    (D) at or near the master cylinder. ✓

17. _____

18. Wheel speed sensors in a(n) _____ system produce their own output signals by the use of magnets.

18. _____

19. Describe the operation of a magneto resistive element (MRE) wheel speed sensor.

_____

_____

_____

Copyright Goodheart-Willcox Co., Inc.
May not be reproduced or posted to a publicly accessible website

Name _____

20. All of the following statements about the ABS electrical
power supply are true, EXCEPT:
   (A) an unfused wire from the battery maintains the RAM.
   (B) one circuit turns on the ABS dashboard light when
       the ignition is turned to the run position.
   (C) some ABS/TCS systems have four separate
       electrical inputs.
   (D) most ABS systems will be disabled if input power
       drops below 9.5 volts.

20. _____

21. Once the vehicle reaches 3–9 mph (4–12 kph) after start-
up, many ABS systems perform a(n) _____ that consists
of cycling the valves in the hydraulic actuator for a
period of 1–2 seconds.

21. _____

22. In addition to hydraulic actuators, output devices consist
of _____ installed on the vehicle _____.

22. _____

_____

23. Hydraulic actuators are often operated through what type of electrical device?

_____

24. What type of electrical device operates the most common hydraulic actuators?

_____

25. Pressure for the hydraulic actuators is provided by
a(n) _____.

25. _____

26. The ABS system accumulator stores:
   (A) trouble codes.
   (B) pressurized brake fluid.
   (C) self-test data.
   (D) vehicle electrical system data.

26. _____

27. The piston-operated hydraulic actuator does not have a
separate hydraulic _____.

27. _____

28. Some ABS/TCS systems have a lamp _____ module that
is separate from the main control module.

28. _____

29. Trouble codes that are used in all makes of vehicles are
called _____ codes.

29. _____

30. Match the condition with the ABS system response.
   (A) Bleed or reduce pressure to the wheel.
   (B) Increase pressure to the wheel.
   (C) seal the passage between the master
       cylinder and wheel

30. __A__ First action when one wheel begins to skid.
    __B__ Action if the wheel continues to skid.
    __C__ Action if the wheel rotation increases.

Copyright Goodheart-Willcox Co., Inc.
May not be reproduced or posted to a publicly accessible website

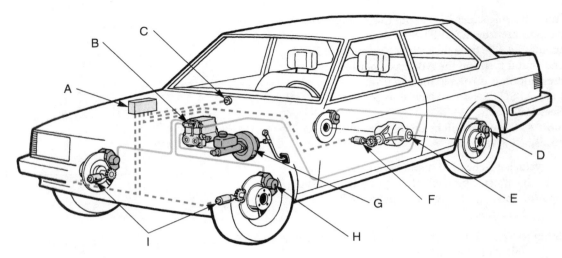

31. Identify the anti-lock brake system components in the above figure.

(A)_____   (F)_____

(B)_____   (G)_____

(C)_____   (H)_____

(D)_____   (I)_____

(E)_____

32. When a vehicle drive wheel begins to slip during acceler-   32. _____
    ation, any needed TCS pressure will be provided by the   _____
    _____ or the _____.

33. The TCS system may reduce engine output by all of the   33. _____
    following methods, EXCEPT:
    (A) upshifting the transmission. ✓
    (B) disabling cylinders. ✓
    (C) opening the EGR valve. ✓
    (D) advancing ignition timing.

34. All of the following statements about yaw and yaw rate   34. _____
    sensors are true, EXCEPT:
    ✓(A) yaw rate sensor inputs help operate the anti-lock
         and stability control systems.
    ✓(B) they are manufactured as either piezoelectric or
         micromechanical types.
    ✓(C) yaw is the rotation of the vehicle around an imagi-
         nary line running vertically through the center of
         the vehicle.
    (D) yaw rate is calculated by inputs from the brake
        pedal travel switch and brake fluid level sensor.

35. Hydraulic control during electronic stability control   35. _____
    operation involves the control system applying which
    brake if a vehicle is turning too quickly to the left?
    (A) Brakes at all four wheels.
    (B) Both rear brakes.
    (C) The right front brake and maybe a rear brake.
    (D) The vehicle emergency brake.

Copyright Goodheart-Willcox Co., Inc.
May not be reproduced or posted to a publicly accessible website

Name _____

36. Technician A says the following figure shows a
pump-operated hydraulic actuator in an anti-lock brake
system. Technician B says the system shown in the
following figure has no hydraulic pump. Who is right?
(A) A only.
(B) B only.
(C) Both A and B.
(D) Neither A nor B.

36. _____

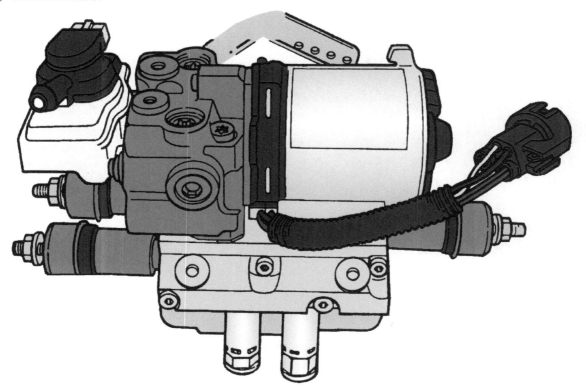

Copyright Goodheart-Willcox Co., Inc.
May not be reproduced or posted to a publicly accessible website

Copyright Goodheart-Willcox Co., Inc.
May not be reproduced or posted to a publicly accessible website

Name _____

Date _____ Class _____

Chapter 22

Anti-Lock Brake, Traction Control, and Electronic Stability Control System Service

After studying this chapter, you will be able to:
- ❑ Perform anti-lock brake, traction control, and electronic stability control system maintenance.
- ❑ Use scan tools to retrieve trouble codes from an anti-lock brake, traction control, or electronic stability control system.
- ❑ Use scan tools to diagnose problems in an anti-lock brake, traction control, or electronic stability control system.
- ❑ Check electrical and electronic components of ABS/TCS/ESC systems.
- ❑ Make pressure checks of ABS/TCS/ESC hydraulic components.
- ❑ Diagnose ABS/TCS/ESC system problems.
- ❑ Isolate defective ABS/TCS/ESC system components.
- ❑ Adjust ABS/TCS/ESC wheel sensors and brake pedal-travel switches.
- ❑ Replace defective ABS/TCS/ESC system components.

1. When the red brake light is on, which system should the technician test *first*?
   (A) ABS.
   (B) TCS.
   (C) Base brakes.
   (D) Engine controls.

1. _____

2. You must _____ a defective ABS/TCS system, since replacement parts are very _____.

2. _____
_____

3. *True or False?* Technicians must make major procedural changes when performing routine brake service (pad replacement or rotor work) on an ABS/TCS/ESC-equipped vehicle.

3. _____

Copyright Goodheart-Willcox Co., Inc.
May not be reproduced or posted to a publicly accessible website

4. Always begin diagnosing a defective ABS/TCS system by _____.
   (A) performing a road test
   (B) retrieving trouble codes
   (C) checking fluid level
   (D) talking to the driver

4. _____

5. When the vehicle reaches a speed of 3 to 9 mph (4.8 to 14.4 kph) you may hear a(n) _____ or _____.

5. _____
   _____

6. What tire noise is considered normal during an ABS assisted stop?

_____

7. Sometimes a driver may think normal operation of the TCS system is a lack of engine power. Why?

_____
_____

8. One of the few ways that an ABS defect can affect normal braking operation is pulling caused by a defective _____.

8. _____

9. A defective _____ may cause a falling brake pedal on some ABS systems.

9. _____

10. Why is it important to use the correct service information when working on ABS, TCS, or ESC systems?

_____
_____

11. Which of the following is an actual ABS defect and not an outside defect that could cause an ABS malfunction?
    (A) Mismatched tires. ✔
    (B) Disconnected wheel speed sensor.
    (C) Charging system defect. ✔
    (D) Defective power brake booster. ✔

11. _____

12. A shorted alternator diode could cause _____.

12. _____

13. All of the following statements regarding scan tool retrieval of ABS, TCS, or ESC trouble codes is true, EXCEPT:
    (A) modern systems use a standardized trouble code system. ✔
    (B) retrieved codes are compared to the appropriate trouble code chart to determine potential problems. ✔
    (C) trouble codes pinpoint the exact location of ABS/TCS/ESC electrical problems.
    (D) the computer stores data about ABS/TCS/ESC ✔ problems.

13. _____

14. Scan tools may have a(n) _____ mode that enables the control module to display the system readings present at the time the malfunction occurred.
    (A) pending code
    (B) snapshot or freeze frame
    (C) interference
    (D) false data signal

14. _____

15. *True or False?* Disconnecting the vehicle's battery or ECM is what many vehicle manufacturers recommended to permanently erase diagnostic trouble codes.

15. _____

Copyright Goodheart-Willcox Co., Inc.
May not be reproduced or posted to a publicly accessible website

Name _____

16. _____ will reset as soon as the ignition switch is turned on.

16. _____

17. Technician A says hard codes can be caused by a bad sensor connection. Technician B says only defective sensors set intermittent codes. Who is right?
    (A) A only.
    (B) B only.
    (C) Both A and B.
    (D) Neither A nor B.

17. _____

18. *True or False?* Electrical trouble codes are always evidence of an ABS defect.

18. _____

19. Technician A says a hard code indicates an occasional problem. Technician B says intermittent codes are harder to diagnose than hard codes. Who is right?
    (A) A only.
    (B) B only.
    (C) Both A and B.
    (D) Neither A nor B.

19. _____

20. Before checking wheel speed sensor resistance, visually check the sensor and wheel ring for _____.

20. _____

21. If the tone wheel has the wrong number of _____ it could send a false signal.

21. _____

Sensor Monitor

LF Wheel Speed: 22
RF Wheel Speed: 22
LR Wheel Speed: 22
RR Wheel Speed: 0
Brake Switch: Released
Pressure Switch: Open

---

22. The ABS light on a vehicle comes on whenever the vehicle is moving. A scan tool reading from the vehicle is shown above. According to these readings, which of the following components is causing the ABS light to come on?
    (A) Defective brake light switch.
    (B) Defective left front wheel speed sensor.
    (C) Defective pressure switch.
    (D) Defective right rear wheel speed sensor.

22. _____

23. Some G-force sensors have continuity when _____ while others have continuity when _____.

23. _____

    _____

24. Electronic circuitry inside of a module can be destroyed by improper _____ tests.

24. _____

25. Before installing a new module, check all related electrical devices such as _____ and _____.

25. _____

    _____

Copyright Goodheart-Willcox Co., Inc.
May not be reproduced or posted to a publicly accessible website

26. As a general rule, a steering angle sensor produces _____ signals when the steering wheel is turned to the right and _____ signals when the wheel is turned left.
    (A) negative voltage, positive voltage
    (B) square wave, sine wave
    (C) positive voltage, negative voltage
    (D) sine wave, square wave

26. _____

27. During testing, ohmmeter resistance measurements vary by the same amount regardless of the degree of yaw sensor rotation. Technician A says that the sensor is defective and should be replaced. Technician B says that the sensor needs to be reprogrammed. Who is right?
    (A) A only.
    (B) B only.
    (C) Both A and B.
    (D) Neither A nor B.

27. _____

28. If operating correctly, wheel speed sensors with a tone ring or encoder ring should produce a pattern of sine waves whose frequency and _____ increase as wheel speed increases.

28. _____

29. What should you check if the pump runs continuously?

_____

30. The TCS light should be on for a few seconds after the vehicle is _____.

30. _____

31. If engine power is reduced at all times, you should start by checking the _____ for codes.

31. _____

32. What position should the ignition switch be in during the entire time the ABS or TCS system is being serviced?

32. _____

33. After replacing a speed sensor, always check the _____ if it is adjustable.

33. _____

34. Hammering or heating can be used to remove a used speed sensor tone wheel. However, the new tone wheel should be carefully _____ into position.

34. _____

35. G-force sensors and yaw sensors are usually located in the _____ compartment.

35. _____

36. Brake light and pedal position switches are almost always located on the _____.

36. _____

37. When replacing an ABS control module, always follow the manufacturers' _____ discharge instructions.

37. _____

38. Before replacing any ABS or TCS hydraulic component, what should the technician *always* do?

_____

39. When overhauling any ABS/TCS hydraulic unit, use *all* of the _____.

39. _____

40. Most ABS accumulators are _____ into the master cylinder or valve body.

40. _____

Copyright Goodheart-Willcox Co., Inc.
May not be reproduced or posted to a publicly accessible website

Name _____

41. A(n) _____ may be needed to loosen some
    pressure switches.

41. _____

42. *True or False?* When replacing a magneto resistive element
    (MRE) encoder ring, install the wheel bearing assembly so
    that the encoder ring is facing the MRE sensor.

42. _____

43. Most ABS/TCS/ESC systems can be bled manually, while
    others must be bled using a(n) _____.

43. _____

44. If air becomes trapped in the ABS/TCS/ESC hydraulic
    actuator, it may not be noticed until the first time the:
    (A) engine is started.
    (B) service brakes are applied.
    (C) parking brake is applied.
    (D) ABS/TCS/ESC is used.

44. _____

45. If water, dirt, or metal contaminates a hydraulic actuator,
    the actuator should be:
    (A) bled.
    (B) flushed.
    (C) manually cleaned.
    (D) replaced.

45. _____

Copyright Goodheart-Willcox Co., Inc.
May not be reproduced or posted to a publicly accessible website

Copyright Goodheart-Willcox Co., Inc.
May not be reproduced or posted to a publicly accessible website

Chapter 23

Troubleshooting Brake Systems

After studying this chapter, you will be able to:
- ❑ Complete a work order based on the necessary repairs and service required to fix a vehicle.
- ❑ Use logical procedures when applying the seven-step troubleshooting process to diagnose brake problems.
- ❑ Question drivers concerning suspected brake problems.
- ❑ Safely road test vehicles to determine actual brake system problems.
- ❑ Separate brake system problems from other vehicle problems.
- ❑ Use correct diagnosis charts and test procedures.
- ❑ Inspect brake components for wear and damage related to a driver's complaint.
- ❑ Determine what repairs must be made to correct brake problems and draft a repair plan to complete them.
- ❑ Recheck brake operation after repairs.
- ❑ Perform a diagnosis follow-up to determine if the discovered problem was accurately located and corrected.
- ❑ Summarize noise, vibration, and harshness (NVH) diagnostics and the techniques used to eliminate NVH complaints.

1. Describe strategy-based diagnostics.

   _____

   _____

   _____

2. List in order, the seven-step diagnostic process outlined in this chapter.

   _____

   _____

   _____

   _____

   _____

   _____

   _____

Copyright Goodheart-Willcox Co., Inc.
May not be reproduced or posted to a publicly accessible website

3. When should you *not* perform a brake road test?

_____

_____

4. Always try to road test the vehicle with the _____.   4. _____

5. During the road test do not adjust anything in the   5. _____
   interior of the vehicle, except the _____ if necessary.

6. When is it okay to make panic stops during a road test?

_____

_____

7. Name at least three things you should look for as part of a visual inspection of the brake system.

_____

_____

_____

8. Wheel brake inspection is being discussed. Technician A   8. _____
   says it is often necessary to remove all wheels to determine
   the exact cause of a brake problem. Technician B says the
   rotor and drum thickness do not have to be checked
   during an inspection of the brake linings. Who is right?
   (A) A only.
   (B) B only.
   (C) Both A and B.
   (D) Neither A nor B.

9. When trying to diagnose an intermittent brake problem, what should the technician try to recreate?

_____

_____

10. In Step 5 the technician should do all of the following,   10. _____
    EXCEPT:
    (A) decide whether a part should be rebuilt or replaced. ✔
    (B) perform additional tests. ✔
    (C) recheck the condition of the suspected part. ✔
    (D) replace the suspected part.

11. In Step 5 of the seven-step troubleshooting process the   11. _____
    suspected problem is _____ and _____.
                                                                _____

12. To reduce the possibility of future problems, the technician should service what other brake system parts?

_____

_____

13. The price of a new part may be less than the _____ to   13. _____
    rebuild the old part.

14. Before beginning any repairs, be sure the _____ under-   14. _____
    stands what needs to be done, and the _____ involved.
                                                                _____

Copyright Goodheart-Willcox Co., Inc.
May not be reproduced or posted to a publicly accessible website

Name _____

15. When diagnosing a problem, always check the _____ things first.

15. _____

16. Every repair order should contain what three things (list in order)?

16. _____

_____

_____

_____

17. Only a(n) _____ person can think logically.
   (A) experienced
   (B) calm
   (C) old
   (D) educated

17. _____

18. Noise, vibration, and harshness (NVH) problems are usually associated with what two automotive systems?

18. _____

_____

19. Most vibration comes from automotive parts that _____.
   (A) rotate
   (B) contact the body
   (C) move up and down
   (D) are poorly lubricated

19. _____

20. Order of vibration refers to how many times a vibration occurs during one _____ of the affected part.

20. _____

21. The source of all _____ complaints is a vibration.

21. _____

22. Harshness is caused by excessive _____ between two parts.

22. _____

23. All of the following statements about noise, vibration, and harshness (NVH) are true, EXCEPT:
   (A) the source of vibration is the transmitter.
   (B) the path of vibration is called the collector.
   (C) balancing can cancel out vibration.
   (D) dampening is used when a vibration cannot be eliminated.

23. _____

24. The ideal way to fix an NVH problem is to correct the _____ cause of the problem.

24. _____

25. The above illustration shows a drum being checked to find out if it is a source of _____.

25. _____

Copyright Goodheart-Willcox Co., Inc.
May not be reproduced or posted to a publicly accessible website

Copyright Goodheart-Willcox Co., Inc.
May not be reproduced or posted to a publicly accessible website

Chapter 24

ASE Certification

After studying this chapter, you will be able to:
- ❑ Explain why technician certification is necessary.
- ❑ Explain the process of registering for ASE tests.
- ❑ Explain how to take the ASE tests.
- ❑ Identify typical ASE test questions.
- ❑ Identify the content of the Brakes Test.
- ❑ Explain what is done with ASE test results.

1. Automotive repair standards have been difficult to set because of the large number of _____.

1. _____

2. When speaking of ASE certification, what does the word *certified* mean?

_____

_____

3. A certified Master Technician has passed _____ tests in automotive or heavy truck areas.

3. _____

4. Technician A says ASE does not conduct hands-on tests. Technician B says ASE written tests are given every month. Who is right?
   (A) A only.
   (B) B only.
   (C) Both A and B.
   (D) Neither A nor B.

4. _____

5. ASE tests are given _____ times each year.

5. _____

6. The North American Council of Automotive Teachers (NACAT) supports all of the following missions, EXCEPT:
   (A) update and improve automotive service education.
   (B) manage and host the hands-on lab portion of each ASE certification test.
   (C) promote the automotive service education community.
   (D) develop and maintain a strong professional organization of automotive technology teachers and trainers.

6. _____

Copyright Goodheart-Willcox Co., Inc.
May not be reproduced or posted to a publicly accessible website

7. Without _____ years of work experience, a technician will not be certified, even if he or she passes an ASE test.

7. _____

8. To apply for an ASE certification test, you have to _____.
   (A) access the ASE website and follow the registration instructions
   (B) speak to an ASE-certified Master Technician at a local automotive shop
   (C) be currently enrolled in an ASE-accredited automotive training program
   (D) All of the above.

8. _____

9. *True or False?* Technicians are allowed to take a maximum of two ASE certification tests a year if they have under five years of applicable automotive service experience.

9. _____

10. Technician A says that ASE certification tests can be paid for online at the ASE website. Technician B says that passing a single recertification test every three years will maintain all your current ASE certifications. Who is right?
    (A) A only.
    (B) B only.
    (C) Both A and B.
    (D) Neither A nor B.

10. _____

11. Once the test payment is made, you will be able to print out a(n) _____.

11. _____

12. ASE test questions are all formatted as _____ questions.

12. _____

13. During the test, carefully read _____ of the test question before deciding on your answer.

13. _____

14. Each ASE certification test contains between _____ and _____ test questions.

14. _____
    _____

15. What is the type of question that you are reading now?
    (A) One-part.
    (B) Two-part.
    (C) Negative.
    (D) Incomplete.

15. _____

16. How many times can a technician take a certification test?

16. _____

17. Who is entitled to give your employer a copy of your ASE test results?

_____

18. ASE two-part questions always refer to statements made by _____.

18. _____

19. A negative question uses the word _____.

19. _____

20. Computer-based tests are scored _____ and the technician will know whether he passed or failed any tests before he or she _____ the test center.

20. _____
    _____

Copyright Goodheart-Willcox Co., Inc.
May not be reproduced or posted to a publicly accessible website

Chapter 25

Career Preparation

After studying this chapter, you will be able to:
- ❑ Identify three classifications of automotive technicians.
- ❑ Identify the major sources of employment in the automotive industry.
- ❑ Reorganize advancement possibilities for automotive technicians.
- ❑ Explain job search strategies and how to fill out a job application.
- ❑ Explain how to conduct yourself during a job interview.
- ❑ Recall ethical workplace practices for working in an automotive repair shop.
- ❑ Describe why developing professional workplace habits and procedures is important.

1. The _____ performs the easiest types of service and maintenance.

1. _____

2. What is the main job of the apprentice technician?

_____

_____

3. An apprentice may work and study to become a(n) _____.

3. _____

4. Before beginning service, install _____ to protect the vehicle's front bumper and panels.

4. _____

5. Technician A says that an itemized repair bill with a clear explanation of service should always be provided to the customer. Technician B says that adding "mysterious" fees to the final bill of a disrespectful customer is an ethical shop policy. Who is right?
   (A) A only.
   (B) B only.
   (C) Both A and B.
   (D) Neither A nor B.

5. _____

6. A technician on salary is paid by the _____.
   A technician on commission is paid by the _____.

6. _____

   _____

7. Match the type of shop with the work performed.
   (A) Various repairs on newer vehicles.
   (B) Few types of repairs.
   (C) Concentrating on one type of repair.
   (C) Large variety of work.
   (D) Trim and upholstery repair.
   (F) Inspect vehicles coming in for resale.
   (G) Work on government vehicles.

7. _____ New vehicle dealer

   _____ Used vehicle superstore

   _____ Chain store automotive shop

   _____ Specialty shop

   _____ Independent shop

   _____ Government agency

8. The technician at a new vehicle dealership must supply
   his or her own:
   (A) cleaning equipment.
   (B) hand tools.
   (C) special testers.
   (D) press.

8. _____

9. Which of the following is *not* an example of an
   independent specialty repair shop?
   (A) An alignment shop.
   (B) A transmission repair shop.
   (C) An air conditioning repair shop.
   (D) Department store.

9. _____

10. Shop foremen often have to deal with _____ and _____
    as well as vehicles.

10. _____

    _____

11. Which of the following businesses would be *most likely* to
    have separate service sales persons or service advisors?
    (A) Government garages.
    (B) Chain or department store auto centers.
    (C) Independent shops.
    (D) Specialty shops.

11. _____

12. *True or False?* Parts stores must keep large numbers of
    parts in stock.

12. _____

13. *True or False?* There are few job openings in the
    automotive service field.

13. _____

14. All of the following are places where the beginning auto-
    motive technician should look for a job, EXCEPT:
    (A) national automotive magazines.
    (B) newspaper classified advertisements.
    (C) state employment agencies.
    (D) auto center personnel departments.

14. _____

15. *True or False?* Arrive slightly early for a job interview.

15. _____

Copyright Goodheart-Willcox Co., Inc.
May not be reproduced or posted to a publicly accessible website

C0-BVV-422

3014 00137 4216

RESEARCH ON AFRICAN-AMERICAN
FAMILIES: A HOLISTIC PERSPECTIVE

DATE DUE

JUN 2 4 1991	
NOV 1 1 1991	
MAR 0 7 2008	

Un

UPI 261-2505   PRINTED IN U.S.A.

1989

Framingham State College
Framingham, Massachusetts

© 1989 by William Monroe Trotter Institute
ISBN 1-878358-02-2

E
185.86
A75
1990
V.2

TABLE OF CONTENTS

PREFACE

In the Spring of 1987 the William Monroe Trotter Institute at the University of Massachusetts at Boston initiated a project entitled, "The Assessment of the Status of African-Americans." Thirty-five scholars were organized into study groups, one for each of six topics: education; employment, income, and occupations; political participation and the administration of justice; social and cultural change; health status and medical care; and the family. The study groups were established to analyze the status of African-Americans in each of the topical areas in anticipation of the results and analyses of the National Research Council's Study Committee on the Status of Black Americans. We wanted to have the widest possible discussion of the present condition of blacks and the social policy implications of that condition.

The multidisciplinary group of scholars comprising the study groups included persons from all sections of the country and from varied settings–private and public universities, historically black universities, and private agencies. A list of these scholars by study group is given in the Appendix. Each of the study groups met and drafted an agenda for examining significant issues under their respective topics. Members chose issues from this agenda within their areas of expertise and identified other scholars who had written extensively on other issues on the agenda. These other scholars made a variety of contributions, including original papers, reprints, notes and materials, and/or substantial commentaries on draft documents.

Despite the pressures of limited time and limited financial support for this work, five volumes were produced:

Volume I: Summary
Volume II: Research on the African-American Family: A Holistic Perspective
Volume III: Education of African-Americans
Volume IV: Social, Political, and Economic Issues in Black America
Volume V: Health and Medical Care of African-Americans

Each of the study groups developed its own conclusion and policy recommendations.

In addition to study group members and other contributors, we are indebted to a number of individuals for the production of this study. We owe thanks to Phillip Hallen and the Maurice Falk Foundation for underwriting the costs of producing these volumes. Special thanks are also offered to the following persons: our editors–Duncan Nelson, Manuscript Editor; Linda Kluz and Suzanne Baker, Production Editors; the office staff–Eva Hendricks, Tina Wilson, Patricia Wellington, and Gemima Remy; and Assistant Director Frances Stubbs.

Wornie L. Reed

I. INTRODUCTION

The strong social and economic gains of black families during the 1960s were severely eroded during the 1970s and 1980s (Swinton, 1988). While unemployment rates among black adults and youth fell markedly between 1964 and 1969, poverty rates among two-parent and one-parent black families also declined to record lows. Moreover, the narrowing of the income gap between black and white families resulted in unprecedented increases in the number of working-class and middle-class black families during the 1960s. However, between 1969 and 1983, the jobless rate among all blacks soared from 6% to 20%–the highest level ever recorded for blacks by the U.S. Department of Labor. Although the official jobless rate for blacks fell to 14% by 1987, unofficially a depression-level one out of four black workers is still unemployed (National Urban League, 1978b).

Black families were affected by soaring unemployment during the 1970s and 1980s–regardless of family structure. Four back-to-back recessions between 1970 and 1985 led to a tripling in the jobless rates among husbands and wives in two-parent families as well as among women heading single families (Hill, 1986). Like their parents, black youth also registered unprecedented increases in joblessness. Between 1969 and 1983, the jobless rate of black teenagers, 16 to 19 years old, doubled from one-fourth to one-half. Although the official jobless rate for black teenagers fell to two out of five by 1987, unofficially three out of five black youth are still unemployed (National Urban League, 1978b).

Not surprisingly, rising unemployment led to a resurgence in poverty among black families. As the number of poor black families declined from 1.9 million to 1.4 million between 1959 and 1969, their poverty rate plummeted from 48% to 28%. Although the proportion of black families in poverty remained at 28% in 1986, the number of poor black families had risen to 2 million. Increasing economic instability among black families has contributed to many social problems, such as single-parent families, adolescent pregnancies, school dropouts, welfare recipiency, ill health, drug abuse, alcohol abuse, delinquency, crime, homelessness, child neglect, and family violence (National Urban League, 1986, 1987a, 1988).

Although sizable numbers of black families experienced increased economic and social deprivation over the past decade and a half, the majority of working-class and middle-class black families made some important gains. The total number of employed black family heads rose from 3.4 million to 3.9 million between 1969 and 1985 and the number of black female family heads with jobs more than doubled from 637,000 to 1.4 million. Moreover, the proportion of family heads in higher-paying jobs rose sharply among female heads of families as well as among husbands and wives in two-parent families. However, these economic gains were precarious for many black families who were still one paycheck away from poverty (Landry, 1987; Swinton, 1988).

The increasing gravity of the situation among black families has become a widely-discussed issue. Hundreds of black organizations at national and local level have given top priority to initiatives designed to strengthen the social and economic functioning of black families (National Urban League, 1983; Joint Center for Political Studies, 1987).

A. CONVENTIONAL TREATMENT OF BLACK FAMILIES

Unfortunately, the quality of the national dialogue reveals that the American public's comprehension of the circumstances of black families has not progressed much farther than it was 20 years ago. Many policymakers are genuinely puzzled as to why the social and economic instability of black families increased so sharply during the 1970s and 1980s–when government spending on programs for the poor and disadvantaged minorities was at record levels. Such widespread lack of understanding is due mainly to the fact that the news media, along with many social scientists (Moynihan, 1967; Banfield, 1968; Gilder, 1981; Murray, 1984) and policymakers employ the "conventional" perspective to examine black families, a framework with the following fundamental deficiencies:

- It reflects a superficial treatment of black families. Black families are not considered to be an important unit of focus and thus are omitted entirely or treated peripherally. This perspective assumes that black families are automatically treated in all analyses that focus on blacks as individuals.

- It accepts uncritically the assumptions of the "deficit model," which attributes most of the problems of black families to internal deficiencies or pathologies.

- It fails to incorporate numerous new research findings and programmatic insights produced over the past two decades concerning black families–many of which contradict basic tenets of the deficit model.

- It fails to focus on positive policies, programs, services, self-help efforts, and coping strategies that are successful in strengthening the functioning of black families.

In the appendix to his work, *Black Families in White America*, Billingsley (1968) provides an in-depth critique of the conventional treatment of black families in American social science. Whether it was in the field of family studies, ethnic assimilation, race relations, or social welfare, black families were examined in a superficial, pathological, and theoretical manner. Recent content analyses of social science treatment of black families by Johnson (1981), Peters and Massey (1983), Rubin (1978) and other scholars (Allen, et al., 1986), have reinforced Billingsley's findings. We shall now examine some of the major shortcomings of the conventional approach

2

that impedes understanding of the causes and nature of the current crisis among black families.

1.   Superficial

Johnson's (1981) content analysis of 10 key journals in sociology and social work revealed that articles on black families comprised only 3% of 3,547 empirical studies of American families published between 1965 and 1975. Despite social work's emphasis on family issues, only one article on black families was published in its two major journals, *Social Casework* and *Social Work,* over a 13-year span (1965 to 1978). Consequently, studies of black families tend to be concentrated in special issues on minority families. For example, the special issue on black families in the *Journal of Marriage and the Family* (November 1978) accounted for two-fifths of all articles on black families appearing in the 10 key journals between 1965 and 1978.

An analysis of the special issue of *Family Relations* (October, 1980) on "Family Stress, Coping and Adaptation" by Peters and Massey (1983) reveals comparable inadequancies. Although 12 of the articles in one section, "Change and Stress over the Life Span," covered topics which were relevant to the experiences of blacks and other minorities, Peters and Massey (1983) found that:

> . . . even in areas where black representation is higher than the average for American families–such as unemployment and divorce/separation–the three relevant articles did not indicate that blacks were included in their sample. . . . Additionally, in this same issue, the five articles under the section, "Social Support and Intervention" did not include black families in their discussion. (p. 198)

A more recent example of the superficial treatment of black families is reflected in the National Research Council's (NRC) *Study on the Status of Black Americans.* The proposal for this three-year (1984-87) study makes it clear that its primary objective is to assess changes in the status of black individuals from 1940 to the present. Consequently, five study panels were established to focus on the following topics:
(1) education; (2) employment, income, and occupation; (3) health status and demography; (4) political participation and administration of justice; and (5) social and cultural change and continuity.

Although papers on black families have been commissioned by several panels, black families was not a central foci of the NRC project. Assessments of the status of black individuals without using families as the major unit of analysis are often misleading, since black economic mobility is largely determined by the pooling of resources among family members. Thus, the NRC project confirms Billingsley's observation, ". . . [American] scholars do not yet seem to be interested in the Negro family as an institution for its own sake, and for what an understanding of it can tell us about our society" (1968, p 207).

2.   Pathological: The Deficit Model

The deficit model is an ideological perspective that attributes the social ills afflicting minority and low-income groups to internal rather than external factors. It is popularly known as the "blaming the victim" syndrome (Staples, 1971a, 1971b; Engram, 1982). As Valentine observed in *Culture and Poverty*, (1968) this mode of thought has a very long tradition:

> [these are] . . . doctrines that point to presumed defects in the mentality or behavior of disadvantaged classes, then go on to explain their social position and deprivation as resulting from their internal deficiencies. There is of course a long philosophical evolution behind the emergence of these doctrines. (p. 18)

The contemporary work that best characterizes the deficit perspective is Daniel P. Moynihan's 1965 report, *The Negro Family: A Case for National Action* (Rainwater & Yancey, 1967), which depicted low-income black families as "a tangle of pathology" because of disproportionately high rates of one-parent families, poverty, unemployment, welfare recipiency, and crime. Although some external forces (such as racism and recessions) were acknowledged to have contributed to these "pathologies," the Moynihan Report deemphasized their significance and concluded that the internal "matriarchal" structure of black families was "at the center of the tangle of pathology and was mainly responsible for the problems in the black community" (Staples, 1971a).

Rubin found the "matriarchal" theme to be pervasive in his review of works on black families (1978). More specifically, he revealed that sweeping generalizations were often made about dysfunctional male-female relations, self-concepts of males reared in female-headed families, attitudes about sexuality, etc., all based on very small samples of unrepresentative disadvantaged black individuals or families. In her review of the treatment of black families in family sociology textbooks, Peters (1974) also noted an overemphasis on pathology, deviance, and irresponsible sexuality.

Over the past two decades, the deficit model has been the predominant perspective projected by the news media in their coverage of black families. In late 1983 the *New York Times* presented a series of articles on "The Black Family," which focused almost solely on poor one-parent families on welfare–a group that comprises only about 15% of all black families. In 1984 the *Baltimore Sun* also ran a series of articles on "The Black Family" that was so stereotyped that the black community launched a boycott of that newspaper. And in January 1986, Bill Moyers produced a CBS-TV documentary on black families that characterized single-parent families as "vanishing" nonfamilies (Billingsley, 1987). A recent analysis of the media conducted by the University of Michigan (Jackson, 1982) reveals that black families continue to be portrayed stereotypically in both the television and print media.

4

3. Ad Hoc: A-Theoretical

A major impediment to understanding the functioning of black families has been the failure of most analysts to use a theoretical or conceptual framework that viewed the totality of black family life. Consequently, conventional accounts of black families are: (a) fragmented, i.e., they exclude the bulk of black families by focusing on only one subgroup; (b) *ad hoc*, i.e., they apply arbitrary explanations that are not derived from systematic theoretical formulations which have been empirically substantiated; (c) negative, i.e., focus exclusively on the "weaknesses" of black families; and (d) internally oriented, i.e., exclude any systematic consideration of the role of forces in the wider society on black family life. Billingsley (1968, 1970), Staples (1971a, 1971b), Allen (1978), and Engram (1982) provide informative critiques of the a-theoretical and unsystematic treatment of traditional studies of black families.

Billingsley (1968) underscored this defect in his critique of "scientific" studies of black families:

> But most important, insofar as they have focused on the Negro experience or race relations in America, they have been *ad hoc* studies without a limiting range of guiding and overarching theories. This last characteristic is the most serious and crippling. For while it is true that the methodological tools most in vogue for social science during recent years do not lend themselves to the study of family life, it is a more searching indictment that these disciplines have had so few theories to guide their studies of the Negro situation. Had they had such overarching and comprehensive theories of group life, it might have been clearer to them that some glaring omissions were being made in their researches regarding Negro family life. (p. 213)

Despite these severe shortcomings, the "deficit" perspective continues to be the common view of black families promulgated to the American public by the news media, policymakers, and by many social scientists (Gilder, 1981; Murray, 1984; Lemann, 1986). Since the conventional "pathological" perspective focuses on black families in a superficial, unbalanced, and *ad hoc* manner, it impedes the development of viable policies for strengthening them. For example, it is widely assumed that the problem of poverty in the black community can be resolved by simply reforming the welfare system. Yet such an assumption fails to realize that half of poor blacks are not on welfare and thus, would remain in poverty after such "reform" (Ellwood & Summers, 1986). Similarly, it is widely believed that poverty can be eliminated by simply providing jobs. However, such a policy fails to confront the fact that two million people in the United States currently work year-round, full-time, but still remain in poverty (Levitan, 1985). The deficit framework also contributes to such misguided policies as *reducing* work incentives for welfare families by removing the working poor from the rolls (Center on Budget and Policy Priorities, 1984a, 1984b; Children's Defense Fund, 1984, 1986).

B. A HOLISTIC PERSPECTIVE

The social and economic functioning of black families can be enhanced significantly through research strategies and policy initiatives that are based on a "holistic" framework in which families are the central unit of analysis. Since families continue to be the preeminent mechanism for socialization and for pooling resources for upward mobility among blacks and whites (Bronfenner, 1979; Moroney, 1980; Duncan, 1984; Levy, 1987), it is essential that they should not be viewed as peripheral. Almost a century ago at the meeting of the American Academy of Political and Social Science, W. E. B. DuBois (1898) set forth a holistic framework for studying black people:

. . . we should seek to know and measure carefully all the forces and conditions that go to make up these different problems, to trace the historical development of these conditions and discover as far as possible the probable trend of further development. Without doubt this would be difficult work, and it can with much truth be objected that we cannot ascertain, by the methods of sociological research known to us, all such facts thoroughly and accurately. To this objection it is only necessary to answer that however difficult it may be to know all about the Negro, it is certain that we can know vastly more than we do and that we can have our knowledge in more systematic and intelligible form. As things are, our opinions upon the Negro are more matters of faith than of knowledge. . .

. . . the [past] work done has been lamentably unsystematic and fragmentary. Scientific work must be subdivided, but conclusions which affect the whole subject must be based on a study of the whole. One cannot study the Negro in freedom and come to general conclusions about his destiny without knowing his history in slavery. A vast set of problems having a common centre must , too, be studied according to some general plan, if the work of different students is to be compared or to go toward building a unified body of knowledge. (pp. 10, 12)

DuBois contended that a proper understanding of blacks in America could not be achieved without systematically assessing the influence of historical, cultural, social, economic and political forces. Such a holistic and systematic treatment of black families is evident in his two pioneering studies–*The Philadelphia Negro* (1899) and *The Negro Family* (1908). This perspective was also reflected in the breadth and depth of the issues covered in the annual monographs on black Americans published as the *Atlanta University Studies* between 1898 and 1914. Unfortunately, DuBois' recommendations to incorporate a holistic framework in the analyses of black individuals and families have not been heeded by mainstream social scientists.

6

Although Frazier has been considered an adherent of the deficit model, the major thrust of his prolific studies of black families never succumbed to the conventional approach of treating *symptoms* (e.g., female-headed family structures) as causes of the ills (i.e., poverty, unemployment, out-of-wedlock births, etc.) afflicting black families. In fact, Frazier customarily employed an ecological framework in his studies. Contrary to the deficit perspective, Frazier's ecological studies of Chicago and Harlem (1939; 1949) revealed that black families were diverse rather than monolithic. Moreover, his analyses consistently attributed the *primary* sources of family instability to *external* forces (e. g., racism, urbanization, technological changes, recessions, etc.) and not to *internal* characteristics of black families.

This report will: (1) examine recent social and economic trends among black families; (2) describe how the holistic framework enhances understanding of the causes and cures of the current crisis among black families; (3) assess the impact of external and internal factors on black families; (4) highlight new research and programmatic insights that facilitate the development of more effective strategies for strengthening black families; and (5) offer recommendations to public and private policymakers and to service providers and self-help institutions in the black community in order to enhance the viability of black families.

7

II. RECENT SOCIAL AND ECONOMIC TRENDS

A. ECONOMIC TRENDS

1. Employment Patterns

Joblessness has soared among the heads of both black and white families. The number of unemployed black family heads jumped from 122,000 to 504,000 between 1969 and 1985, while their jobless rate tripled from 3.5% to 11.1%. Over the same period, the number of unemployed white family heads tripled (from 631,000 to 1,944,000), raising their jobless rate from 1.7% to 4.7%. Since unemployment among whites rose less sharply than among blacks, the jobless gap between black and white family heads widened from 2.1 to a record level 2.4.

Heads of both two-parent and one-parent families were strongly affected by unemployment. The number of unemployed black husbands rose from 84,000 to 188,000 between 1969 and 1985, while their jobless rate rose from 2.9% to 7.1%. In 1969, only 38,000 (5.6%) of black women heading families were unemployed. By 1985, seven times as many female heads of black families were unemployed (273,000), while their jobless rate tripled to 16.4%. Among white families, the jobless rate went from 1.5% to 4.2% among husbands and from 3.6% to 7.9% among female heads between 1969 and 1985.

Although joblessness rose sharply among black families, the number of black family heads with jobs increased. The total number of employed black family heads went from 2.4 million to 3.9 million between 1969 and 1985. Interestingly, while the number of black female family heads with jobs rose from 637,000 to 1,390,000, the number of black male family heads with jobs declined from 2,766,000 to 2,353,000.

These opposing patterns were partly due to the fact that the total number of black families headed by women rose much faster than the total number of two-parent black families. These patterns also reflect the surge of women in the labor force during the 1970s and 1980s among blacks and whites. While the number of employed white husbands fell from 35.3 million to 33.6 million between 1969 and 1985, the number of white female family heads with jobs jumped from 2.0 million to 4.0 million.

2. Occupational Patterns

The increase in employment of black family heads was reflected in upward mobility in both one-parent and two-parent families. In 1970, 19% of all black family heads were in higher-paying jobs: managers (2%), professionals and technicians (8%), and crafts (9%). By 1985, 28% of black family heads were in those higher-status categories: managers (8%), professionals (8%), and crafts (12%). Among black female family heads, the proportion in higher-paying jobs rose from 14% to 16% between 1969 and 1985, while the proportion of husbands in two-parent black families holding higher-paying jobs jumped from 24% to 33%. The proportion of black family heads in moderate-paying clerical jobs (14% to 16%) and sales jobs (2% to 4%) also rose between 1969 and 1985. But these gains were much larger among female family heads (from 24% to 32%) than among husbands (from 10% to 15%).

However, despite this upward mobility, the overwhelming majority of black family heads are still in lower-paying jobs. Although the proportion of black family heads in lower-paying jobs (i.e., operatives, laborers, service and farm workers) fell from 64% to 55% between 1969 and 1985, there are still about twice as many black family heads in lower-paying jobs than white family heads (29%). Moreover, 53% of black husbands are currently in lower-paying jobs, compared to only 29% of white husbands. Similarly, one out of two black female family heads (52%) are in lower-paying jobs, compared to three out of ten white female family heads (31%).

Many recent studies that show a sharp increase in the proportion of black families in the "middle class" have committed the common fallacy of equating white collar jobs with "middle class" and blue-collar jobs with "working class" or "underclass." The major error in equating white collar jobs with the middle class is that only a small minority of black white collar workers have middle-income earnings. Moreover, sizable numbers of black operative and service workers have higher earnings than many black sales and clerical workers. Consequently, movement of blacks from such blue-collar to white-collar jobs is downward rather than upward mobility (Hill, 1978a; Pinkney, 1984; Collins, 1986).

3. Racial Income Gap

The widening unemployment gap between black and white families during the 1979s and 1980s led to a widening of the income gap between the two groups. Black families had a median income ($6,063) that was 61% of white family median income ($9,958). By 1986, the ratio of of black family income ($17,604) to white family income ($30,809) fell to 57%–one of its lowest levels since the 1960s. This widening income gap occurred in all regions. The black-to-white family income ratio fell from 67% to 63% in the Northeast, from 76% to 57% in the Midwest, from 75% to 71% in the West, and from 57% to 56% in the South between 1969 and 1986 (U. S. Bureau of the Census, 1987).

This decline in the black-to-white income ratio is partly due to the sharp rise in multiple earners among white families and the sharp decline in multiple earners among black families. Historically, black families had a higher proportion of two-earners than white families. During the 1970s and 1980s, however, there was a reversal of this pattern (Hill, 1981). While the proportion of black families with two or more earners fell steeply from 56% to 47% between 1969 and 1986, the proportion of white families with two or more earners rose from 54% to 58%. The drop in the black-to-white income ratio is also due to the disproportionate rise of female-headed black families. Consequently, it is necessary to assess whether the income gap widened among both two-parent and one-parent families. Although the income ratio widened

9

slightly from 61% to 59% among female-headed families between 1969 and 1986, the gap narrowed from 72% to 80% among married couples. The narrowing of this income gap also results from the higher proportion of working wives among black (64%) than white (53%) couples (Hill, 1987a; Landry, 1987).

Closer examination reveals that not all two-parent black families experienced income gains relative to two-parent white families. In fact, while the income gap narrowed from 77% to 82% among two-parent families with working wives, the gap widened from 62% to 60% among two-parent families with nonworking wives between 1969 and 1985, and then narrowed to 63% in 1986. Contrary to popular belief, it is the presence of more working wives–not the two-parent structure per se–that is mainly responsible for the economic gains that black couples have made relative to white couples over the past decade and a half.

4.   Real Income Trends

A proper assessment of the income gains of black families relative to white families during the 1970s and 1980s must take into account the disproportionate effects of double-digit inflation. While the real income of all white families increased by 5% between 1969 and 1986, the real income of all black families fell behind inflation by 2%. However, larger increases in purchasing power occurred among black (+22%) than white (+8%) two-parent families. This was mainly due to the higher proportion of working wives among blacks (65%) than whites (54%). While the real income of white couples with working wives increased by 10% between 1969 and 1986, the real income of black couples with working wives increased by 17%.

On the other hand, the income of couples without working wives–among blacks and whites–failed to keep ahead of inflation. The real income of white couples without working wives declined by 3% between 1969 and 1986, and the real income of black couples without working wives fell just under with inflation (-0.1%). The real income of families headed by white women declined by 4% and the real income of families headed by black women fell behind inflation by 7%.

Adjusting for inflation (in constant 1986 dollars) also permits us to examine the extent to which the income gap has widened between middle-income and poor black families since the end of the 1960s. The proportion of black families with incomes under $10,000 increased from 27% to 31% between 1970 and 1986 and the proportion of middle-income ($25,000-$49,999) black families declined from 28% to 27%. At the same time the proportion of upper-income ($50,000 and over) black families increased from 5% to 9%. Moreover, the proportion of near-poor ($10,000-$24,999) black families dropped sharply from 41% to 34%. Thus, the income gap has narrowed between middle-income and poor blacks, but widened between upper-income and poor blacks (Hill, 1986, 1987a).

There are similar patterns among white families. Although the proportion of low-income white families remained at 10% between 1970 and 1986, the proportion of middle-income white families fell sharply from 45% to 39%. Yet over the same period the proportion of upper-income white families jumped from 15% to 22%. Thus the economic cleavage appears to be widening most between upper-income and low-income among blacks and whites.

5.   Poverty Trends

The number of families with incomes below the official poverty levels rose markedly among blacks and whites. While the number of poor black families increased by 43% (from 1.4 to 2 million) between 1969 and 1986, the number of poor white families rose by 33% (from 3.6 to 4.8 million). Similarly, the number of poor black female-headed families doubled (from 737,000 to 1,488,000), while a comparable increase occurred among poor white female-headed families (from 1.1 to 2 million). But while the number of poor two-parent black families decreased from 629,000 to 500,000 between 1969 and 1986, the number of poor two-parent white families rose from 2.5 to 2.8 million (U.S. Bureau of the Census, 1987).

Moreover, while the poverty rate among all black families remained at 28% between 1969 and 1986, the poverty rate among all white families edged up from 8% to 9%. Among female-headed families, while the proportion of poor black families declined from 53% to 50%, the proportion of poor white families went from 26% to 28%. Similarly, among two-parent families, the proportion of poor black families dropped from 18% to 12%, while the proportion of poor white families held at 6%.

Poverty increased most sharply among children in black families. While the proportion of poor black children edged up from 42% to 43% between 1969 and 1986, the total number of black children in poor families jumped from 3.7 million to 4.0 million. The economic deprivation is particularly acute in single-parent families, where 80% of poor black children are concentrated. Between 1969 and 1986, the number of poor black children in female-headed families soared from 2.1 million to 3.3 million. Two out of three (67%) black children in families headed by women were poor in 1986–roughly the same proportion as in 1969 (68%). It should be emphasized, however, that the reason the proportion of poor black children in single-parent families remained the same over that 17-year span was that the number of nonpoor female-headed black families rose just as fast as the number of poor female-headed black families.

A major determinant of the rise in poverty among female-headed black families was the sharp rise in unemployment. Despite their higher educational and occupational levels, black women heading families are three times more likely to be unemployed today (16.4%) than they were a decade and a half ago (5.6%). Families headed by black women are disproportionately poor–not because they do not have husbands, but because they do not have jobs. Only one-fourth of employed women heading black families are poor, compared to three-fourths when unemployed (Hill, 1981).

11

6.   Welfare Trends

Interestingly, although poverty among black families rose from 29% to 31% between 1971 and 1984, welfare recipiency declined. The proportion of black families receiving public assistance fell from 25% to 20% between 1971 and 1984, while the proportion of white families on welfare remained at 4%. Similarly, while the proportion of two-parent black families on welfare fell from 12% to 6%, the proportion of female-headed black families on welfare plummeted from 54% to 39%. Thus, the proportions of black families on public assistance today are lower than they were at the onset of the 1970s. And most of this decline in welfare recipiency among blacks occurred *prior* to the sharp budget cuts by the Reagan administration during the 1980s.

Moreover, the proportion of poor black families on welfare remained at about one-half: in 1971 53%, in 1979 52%, and 1984 52%. In other words, about half of all poor black families received no public assistance during the past decade and a half. Similarly, the proportion of poor black female-headed families on welfare dropped from 70% in 1971 to 65% in 1979 and to 63% in 1984. Furthermore, contrary to the belief that black families are "overdependent" on welfare, public assistance accounts for only 4% of the total annual income of all black families, and for only 15% of the total annual income of families headed by black women.

7.   Noncash Benefits

Despite these facts and figures there is a popular assumption that blacks are the major recipients of both cash and noncash assistance for the poor. Not only do blacks comprise only two-fifths of the recipients of all forms of cash public assistance, they comprise between 30% and 40% of the recipients of major government in-kind programs for the poor–in line with their overall proportion of all poor families in the United States (30%). Blacks comprise 30% of medicaid recipients, 35% of food stamp recipients, 36% of school lunch recipients, and 39% of subsidized rent and public housing recipients.

Moreover, two-fifths or more of poor black families do not receive noncash benefits for the poor, with exception of the school lunch program. Two-fifths of poor blacks do not receive Medicaid (41%) or food stamps (43%), while two-thirds do not receive either subsidized rent or public housing (67%). A lower but still substantial percentage do not receive school lunches (28%). Furthermore, the extent of participation in multiple income support programs for the poor is quite low. For example, three-fifths (58%) of poor black households receive benefits from two or fewer of the seven major cash and noncash programs: welfare, SSI, Medicaid, public housing, subsidized rent, food stamps, and school lunches (Hill, 1981, 1983a).

8. Child Support

Black women are much less likely than white women to be awarded child support payments, and they also receive much smaller amounts when payments are awarded. According to a special 1983 survey of child support by the Census Bureau, two out of three (67%) single white mothers are awarded child support payments, compared to only one out of three (34%) single black mothers. Two-thirds (69%) of black mothers who were due support payments in 1983 received them, compared to three-fourths (77%) of white mothers. While white mothers received annual support payments of $2,475, black mothers received annual payments of $1,465. The lower payments to black mothers are partly due to the lower income of black fathers relative to white fathers (Everett, 1985).

B. SOCIAL TRENDS

1. Single-Parent Families

While the proportion of families headed by white women rose from 11% to 13% between 1970 and 1985, the proportion of families headed by black women jumped from 28% to 44%. However, the number of female-headed families with children increased at about the same rate among blacks (+13%) and whites (+16%). While the sharpest increases in one-parent white families occurred among separated and divorced women, the largest increases in one-parent black families occurred among never married women. For example, while separated and divorced women account for nine out of ten (86%) white female-headed families formed between 1970 and 1985, never married women account for two out of three (67%) of the black female-headed families formed during that 15-year span.

The number of single-parent families increased five times faster (+496%) among college-educated black women between 1970 and 1985 than among black women who failed to complete high school (+10%). Consequently, school dropouts comprised only 6% of the new black female-headed families formed over that 15-year span, while college-educated women comprised 35%. Thus, female-headed families increased much faster among the "middle class" than among the "underclass" among blacks–and whites–during the 1970s and 1980s (Hill, 1981, 1986).

The educational progress of black women heading families is most dramatic among mothers under 45 years old. The proportion of young black mothers who had not completed high school plummeted from 63% to 32% between 1971 and 1985, and the proportion who had gone to college tripled from 8% to 23%. Thus two-thirds (69%) of young black female heads of families had at least completed high school in 1985, compared to only one-third (37%) in 1970. Thus, the overwhelming majority of young black women heading families today have the educational credentials to hold jobs that will support them (Newman, et al., 1978; Farley, 1984; Farley & Allen, 1987).

13

2. Out-of-Wedlock Births

A sharp increase in out-of-wedlock births contributed to the rise in single-parent black families. There was a surge in out-of-wedlock births among both blacks and whites during the 1970s, partially a consequence of unprecedented numbers of young women coming to child-bearing age following the post-war "baby boom" (Farley, 1984; Moore, Simms, & Betsey, 1986; Allen & Farley, 1986) Interestingly, out-of-wedlock fertility rates have been declining among black women and rising among white women. As the birth rate for unmarried black women decreased 20% (from 95.5 to 76.8 per 1,000 unmarried women 15 to 44 years old) between 1969 and 1984, the out-of-birth rate for unmarried white women increased by 46% from (13.8 to 20.1 per 1,000 unmarried women 15 to 44 years old). Thus, while black women were seven times more likely than white women to have out-of-wedlock births in 1969, they were only four times more likely to do so in 1984. The proportion of all births that were out-of-wedlock went from 6% to 13% among whites between 1970 and 1984 and from 38% to 59% among blacks.

Although out-of-wedlock births have been declining recently among black and white teenagers, adolescent pregnancies will continue to have severe adverse consequences for black and white families in the coming decades. Out-of-wedlock birth rates fell among black teens (from 96.9 to 89.2 per 1,000 unmarried women 15 to 19 years old) between 1970 and 1980, and rose among white teens (from 10.9 to 16.2 per 1,000 unmarried women 15 to 19 years old). In 1984, birth rates for black and white teenagers fell to their lowest levels since 1940. Thus, with the aging of the baby boom cohort, "older" women, especially those 20 to 29 years old, are responsible for increasing proportions of out-of-wedlock births (Moore, Simms, & Betsey, 1986).

Nevertheless, it is estimated that teenagers will account for about one million pregnancies–400,000 abortions and 500,000 births–each year throughout this decade. Since over half of these adolescent out-of-wedlock births are likely to be among black teenagers, the social and economic viability of black families will be disproportionately affected. Since black teenage mothers are often in poor health because of inadequate health care and nutrition, their babies are at disproportionate risk of dying in infancy or having a critically low birth weight. And teenage mothers are at disproportionate risk of becoming welfare recipients because they lack the educational requirements to obtain employment at livable wages (McAdoo & Parham, 1985; Edelman, 1987).

However, although it is widely believed that teenage pregnancies were mainly responsible for the sharp growth in female-headed families among blacks during the 1970s and 1980s, this was not the case. The overwhelming majority (85%) of black unwed teenage mothers do not set up independent households, but continue to live in the homes of their parents or with other adult relatives after the birth of their babies. Thus, teenagers account for less than 5% of all black families headed by women. While about half of all AFDC recipients had their first child as teenagers, only one out of three teenage mothers are on welfare.

3. Child Care Patterns

The need for child care increased sharply over the past decade and a half because of the surge in employment of mothers in one-parent and two-parent black and white families (Children's Defense Fund, 1987). For wives with children under 18 years old, participation in the labor force between 1970 and 1984 rose from 56% to 70% among black women and from 38% to 58% among white women. Similarly, among mothers heading their own families, rates in the labor force rose from 53% to 62% among black women and from 63% to 72% among white women. Interestingly, while black wives are more likely to be in the labor force than white wives, white women heading families are more likely to be in the labor force than black women heading families.

Mothers of preschool children also entered the labor force in record numbers. Among wives with children under 6 years old, labor force participation rates between 1970 and 1984 rose from 50% to 72% among black women and from 29% to 51% among white women. Among single mothers with children under 6 years old, labor force rates increased from 44% to 51% among black women and from 49% to 58% among white women. However, despite the rise in their labor force participation rates, mothers of preschoolers are less likely to be in the labor force than mothers of school-age children. And single mothers are less likely to be in the labor force than wives in two-parent families—regardless of the age of their children.

According to a special 1982 survey of child care conducted by the U.S. Census Bureau (1983a), two-fifths of black (42%) and white (40%) working mothers had their youngest child under 5 years old cared for in the homes of relatives or nonrelatives, 18% of black and 16% of white working mothers had their children cared for at home by relatives or nonrelatives, and 12% of black and 9% of white working mothers placed their preschool children in formal day care centers. And black working mothers were almost twice as likely as white working mothers (45% to 27%) to use relatives for child care—whether inside or outside their homes.

Child care arrangements often differ according to the work status of the mothers. Black mothers who work part-time (53%) are more likely than those who work full-time (43%) to have their children cared for by relatives, while black mothers who work full-time (13%) are more likely than those who work part-time (8%) to use formal day care centers.

Due to the unavailability of day care for thousands of working parents, it has been estimated that between 6 and 7 million school-age children are "latchkey," returning from school to an unsupervised home. To obtain more precise figures, in December 1984 the U.S. Census Bureau conducted a special nationwide survey. This survey defined an "unsupervised" child as a 5- to 13-year-old who returned to a home where no adult or older sibling was present. Only 7.2% (or 2.1 million) of all 5- to 13-year-olds with working parents were found to be "unsupervised." Moreover, white

15

families (7.8%) were more likely to have "latchkey" children than black families (4.3%).

4. Informal Adoption Patterns

Several sources of data indicate that extended families continue to provide vital child care support to black families (McAdoo, 1983; Malson, 1983a, 1983b, 1986; Stewart, 1981a, 1982, 1983; Taylor, 1985, 1986). While much attention is focused on the alarming increase in adolescent pregnancies among blacks, the fact that nine out of ten out-of-wedlock black babies live in three-generational households with their teen mothers and grandparents (or other relatives) is invariably omitted (Hill, 1977, 1981).

Moreover, economic hardships and the lack of housing contributed to a surge in "doubling-up" with kin during the 1970s and 1980s. During the 1974-75 recession, the proportion of black children living with their mothers in the households of relatives rose from 30% to 39% (Hill, 1975, 1977). Furthermore, the number of informally adopted black children living with relatives increased from 1.3 million to 1.4 million between 1970 and 1979, and the proportion of black children in informally adoptive families rose from 13% to 15%.

5. Foster Care Patterns

Although the total number of children in foster care declined sharply after 1977, the proportion of black foster children increased. The number of children in foster care fell from 500,000 in 1977 to 300,000 in 1979 and to 250,000 in 1983. As the proportion of white foster children fell from 62% to 53% between 1977 and 1983, the proportion of black foster children rose from 28% to 34%, and the proportion of Hispanic foster children rose from 5% to 7%. Although black foster children are less likely than white foster children to have physical or mental disabilities, they remain in foster care much longer. According to a 1982 study, 56% of black children had been in foster care two or more years, compared to only 36% of white children. Many studies have revealed that long-term foster children have a high risk of becoming delinquents, incarcerated felons, mentally ill, prostitutes, drug addicts, alcoholics, welfare recipients, and homeless (Billingsley & Giovannoni, 1972; Hill, 1977; Gurak, Smith & Goldson, 1982).

The number of children in foster care has risen steadily since 1983. Traditionally, most children were placed in foster care by the courts because of child abuse or neglect. But the current surge in foster care children, especially among blacks and Hispanics, is largely due to voluntary placements by low-income parents who are unable to obtain affordable housing (Children's Defense Fund, 1984, 1986). There has also been a sharp increase in the foster care placement of babies born to alcohol-addicted, drug-addicted, and AIDS-infected mothers (National Urban League, 1987a, 1988).

16

6. Formal Adoption Patterns

While blacks are more likely than whites to be among the one-third of foster children freed for adoption, black children are less likely to be adopted than white children. Blacks comprised two-fifths (37%) of the 50,000 children freed for adoption in 1982, but accounted for only one-fifth (22%) of those actually adopted.

Although it is frequently stated that black families are not as interested as white families in legally adopting children, research studies have revealed that the rates of formal adoption are higher among black than white families of comparable economic status (Gurak, Smith & Goldson, 1982). Moreover, the National Urban League's Black Pulse Survey revealed that three million (or one-third of) black household heads were interested in formally adopting a black child (Hill, 1981).

7. Child Abuse Patterns

According to the National Study of the Incidence and Severity of Child Abuse and Neglect conducted by the U.S. Department of Health and Human Services between 1979-1980, 652,000 children under 18 years old were identified as abused or neglected for a national incidence rate of 10.5 per 1,000 children. The incidence rates for abuse and neglect were similar: 5.7 per 1,000 children for abuse and 5.3 per 1,000 children for neglect.

Blacks had lower incidence rates for child abuse and neglect than whites for all form of abuse (i.e., physical, sexual, and emotional) and neglect (i.e., physical and emotional), except for educational neglect. Similarly, incidence rates for blacks for all types of child abuse and neglect–except for educational neglect–were under 15%, while the rates for whites in most forms of child abuse and neglect were 83%. Studies have found the lowest levels of child abuse and neglect in families with strong kin-ship networks (Hill, 1977).

8. Housing Patterns

Adequate and affordable housing is becoming increasingly inaccessible to middle-income and low-income families. Soaring housing prices and rent have out-paced increases in family incomes, and there has beeen a sharp decline in low-income housing.

The housing crisis is most severe for low-income families. According to a recent MIT study, the number of poor households is expected to jump from 11.9 million to 17.2 million between 1983 and 2003. Over that same 20-year period the number of low-income housing units is expected to shrink from 12.9 million to 9.4 million. Currently, about half a million low-income units are disappearing each year, largely due to widespread displacement of poor families through urban renewal, abandonment, gentrification, and condominium conversions. Furthermore, the expiration of subsidies for 57% of the 581,330 rental-assisted private units over the next 12 to 15 years could remove about 334,000 units from the low-income housing market. One million black households (including one-third of all poor blacks) in subsidized or public housing would be acutely affected by subsidized rent expirations.

The worsening housing shortage for the poor is directly responsible for the sharp increase in the number of homeless individuals and families across the nation. While HUD estimated the homeless population in the United States at 250,000-300,000 in 1984, advocates for the homeless contend that a more accurate count is closer to 2 to 3 million. One-third of the homeless consists of families, involving about 500,000 children. Since two-thirds of the shelters do not accommodate families, they are often placed in "welfare hotels." In addition, there are hundreds of thousands "couch people," families who double-up with relatives or close friends for varying periods of time. In New York City, this "hidden homeless" situation is estimated to comprise about 100,000 families, including 200,000 children. Insensitive public and private housing policies ensure that the problem of homelessness will become even more severe in the near future (Children's Defense Fund, 1984, 1986; Cazenave, 1988).

III. A HOLISTIC PERSPECTIVE ON BLACK FAMILIES

A. COMPREHENSIVE FRAMEWORKS

One of the most significant efforts to adapt DuBois' holistic framework to the study of black families was undertaken by Billingsley (1968). Based on the structural-functional theory of the family posited by Parsons and Bales (1955), Billingsley (1968) developed a conceptual paradigm that characterized black families as a social subsystem mutually interacting with subsystems in the black community and in the wider (white) society. Schematically, black families are depicted by a circle embedded within concentric circles of the two larger systems. According to the systems framework, an adequate understanding of black families requires assessing the separate and combined effects on family functioning of:

- External subsystems in the wider society, such as societal forces and institutional policies in the area of economics, politics, education, health, welfare, law, culture, religion, and the media;

- External subsystems in the black community, such as schools, churches, peer groups, social clubs, black businesses, neighborhood associations, etc;

- Internal subsystems in families, such as intra-household interactions involving husbands and wives, parents and children, siblings, other relatives, and nonrelatives.

Billingsley's formulation is one of several efforts by social scientists to use ecological and systems frameworks for examining family functioning. Brim (1957) offered a social systems approach for assessing patterns of child development, and a comprehensive literature review by Hill and Hansen (1960) highlighted several studies that used a "systems perspective" to examine American families. Bronfenbrenner (1979) also advocated the use of ecological frameworks for studying child and family development. But Billingsley was the first scholar to adapt the systems framework explicitly for the study of black family life.

To broaden the perspective of black family research from its traditional "male-headed/female-headed" dichotomy, Billingsley (1968) systematically identified the structural diversity of black families by developing a typology depicting 32 different kinds of nuclear, extended, and augmented family households. This typology underscores the fact that the structure, functioning, and needs of black families may change significantly as family members pass through various stages of their life cycles. Unfortunately, the important research and policy implications of Billingsley's systems framework and family typology have not been adequately explored by social scientists over the past two decades (Williams and Stockton, 1973).

Allen (1978) evaluated the relative merits of several conceptual frameworks for studying black families. He felt that a major weakness of the structural-functional systems model was its "static" character. Accordingly, he urged that developmental concepts be incorporated into the ecological systems framework. Allen contended that the developmental approach was dynamic since it viewed families and family members as moving through a life cycle characterized by a series of developmental stages. At each stage of the life cycle, families (due to compositional, positional, and individual changes) are confronted by different demands and varying resources to meet those demands. On the other hand, he viewed the systems paradigm as more effective in linking family members to the demands and resources of external subsystems in the black community and in the wider society. Consequently, Allen felt that the ecological and developmental approaches were complementary in enhancing the understanding of black family life.

As noted above, Peters and Massey (1983) were critical of the failure of family researchers in the field of stress and coping patterns to explicitly incorporate black individuals and families in their theoretical and methodological analyses:

> This non-inclusion of the special needs, problems, and stresses of black families in the conceptualization of stress-related research is one example of the subtle and elusive nature of institutional racism within American culture. As an outgrowth of the prevailing negative approach implicit in the omission of blacks from many normative studies, observations and considerations of behavior in black families have rarely been examined within the concepts of family stress theory.

> [There is a need] for analysis of those coping behaviors in black families that can be viewed as a combination of adaptation and response to the continuing stress of perpetual and pervasive racism in people with an African heritage that demands and respects family survival. By examining intra-family, inter-family, and family community relationships, interactions, and processes, the various strategies which allow racism to be absorbed, deflected, combatted, succumbed to and/or overcome by particular black families and individuals can be studied. (p.199)

One theoretical perspective that many scholars (Willie, 1976, 1985; Taylor, 1981; Cazenave, 1981) have found useful for explaining stress and coping behavior among blacks is Merton's theory of anomie and deviance, which is also popularly known as the "blocked opportunity" theory. According to Merton's thesis (1957), high rates of deviant behavior are expected among groups in American society who are frustrated in achieving societal goals such as monetary success through legitimate means (such as obtaining quality education and employment) because of their disadvantaged position in the stratification hierarchy.

Moreover, Merton stipulated that such frustrated groups were likely to be highly concentrated among the four deviant role adaptations: innovation, ritualism, retreatism, and rebellion. In fact, Willie (1976) found Merton's role types to be very useful in his analyses of black families. In a subsequent article, Merton (1964) elaborated his original formulation by setting forth an ecological paradigm of deviance that required assessing the separate and combined effects of factors at the societal, community, group, and individual levels on rates of deviance among various groups in society (Hill, 1980). Clearly, Merton's blocked opportunity paradigm enhances our understanding of black families when it is combined with Billingsley's systems framework and Allen's developmental approach.

Many other scholars (Nobles, 1974a, 1974b, 1981; Hare & Hare, 1984; Kunjufu, 1984, 1985, 1986a, 1986b; Aminifu, 1985) have offered useful Afrocentric frameworks for understanding black families. For example, Nobles has consistently argued that no significant advance in our knowledge of black families will occur until social scientists recognize them as African-American families (Nobles, 1974a; Nobles and Goddard, 1984). Moreover, the works of Karenga (1982, 1986) have made a persuasive case for placing analyses of black families within a cultural framework. For example, Karenga (1986) contends:

Any serious solution to the crisis of the black family must recognize its dual rootedness and heritage in both the Afro-American community and culture and the U.S. society and culture. The black family unfolds or withers in a real world, the world of U.S. society and culture with its major contradictions of race, class and sexual oppression and a host of secondary ones....

Culture is key to understanding and solving the crisis in the black community and family.... [W]e must totalize the approach and that means taking a cultural approach. This approach not only includes stress on social ethics, but offers critique and correctives in the seven basic areas of culture–religion, history, social organization, economic organization, political organization, creative production (i.e., art, music and literature), and ethos–the collective self-consciousness achieved as a result of antiquity in the other six areas. (pp. 50,51)

The several conceptual frameworks described above have improved the quality of research on black families and have facilitated the development of more relevant, sensitive, and effective public policies and programs for ameliorating their social and economic problems. Unfortunately, only a small number of social scientists have used them systematically in their studies (Allen, 1978; Engram, 1982). There is a vital need for more research on the relative merits of these various paradigms in addressing various issues about the separate and combined effects of societal forces, social policies, and factors at the community, family, and individual levels on black family structure and functioning.

B. KEY THEMES

The holistic framework that we recommend to guide research and policy development related to black families is one that places a major priority on the following themes: diversity, dynamic, balance, solutions, and empiricism. We shall now illustrate how each of these dimensions can enhance significantly the nation's understanding of the problems and solutions related to the functioning of black families.

1. Diversity

A major shortcoming of the conventional approach to examining black families is its monolithic assumptions. For example, numerous assertions are made about the homogeneity of "underclass" values and life-styles of individuals and families in the same low-income strata without presenting any empirical evidence (Murray, 1984; Loury, 1984; Lemann, 1986). Yet, over two decades ago, the pioneering studies of child-rearing among poor urban blacks by Hylan Lewis (1967) effectively documented the fact that there is much heterogeneity in values, attitudes, and socialization practices among poor black families.

Research by other urban ethnographers (Liebow, 1967; Valentine, 1968; Ladner, 1971, 1973; Stack, 1974) also found diverse values and behavioral patterns among low-income black families. The popular practice of defining the "underclass" as welfare recipients obscures the fact that the long-term poor comprises heterogenous groups (e.g., the elderly, the disabled, the mentally ill, foster children, welfare recipients, prisoners, ex-offenders, and the homeless) that require different policy prescriptions (Coe, 1978, 1982; Danziger & Weinberg, 1986).

In contrast to the deficit perspective's fixation on the "underclass" or "lower-class," the holistic approach underscores the importance of examining working-class, middle-class, and upper-class blacks as well (Willie, 1976; 1985; Danziger & Gottschalk, 1986; Landry, 1987). In fact, a basic tenet of the holistic paradigm is that effective policies for remedying the crisis among black families cannot be developed without sufficient knowledge of their structural, class, ethnic, regional, religious, attitudinal, and behavioral diversity (Engram, 1982).

2. Dynamic

Traditionally, black families are viewed from a static perspective. All black families receiving welfare at one point in time are automatically presumed to be long-term recipients (without presenting any length of time data) and are assumed not to experience any upward mobility (Wilson, 1978, 1987; Murray, 1984; Loury, 1984). Similarly, families that are "middle class" at one point in time are assumed to continually maintain that position and not experience any downward mobility. However, such presumptions have been strongly contradicted by major panel studies (Coe, 1978; Duncan, 1984; Bane, 1986; Levy, 1987) that reveal continuous and extensive vertical mobility between class strata among black and white families.

The static character of most analyses of class strata in America is mainly due to the historic dependence of social researchers on cross-sectional data–especially the surveys and censuses conducted by the U.S. Census Bureau (Hill, 1981; Duncan, 1984). Since cross-sectional data only measure social attributes at one point in time, they are not useful in systematically determining (a) the nature and degree of changes in characteristics for the same individuals or families at different points in time and (b) the temporal sequence of factors and processes that contributed to those changes (Elder, 1985a, 1985b).

In fact, it was to obtain more accurate knowledge about the factors responsible for families falling into and rising out of poverty that the U.S. Office of Economic Opportunity (OEO) contracted with the University of Michigan in 1967 to initiate a longitudinal survey of 5,000 American families. This survey, known as the Panel Survey of Income Dynamics (PSID), has significantly enhanced the state of knowledge about the dynamics of family structure, functioning, and mobility among black and white families.

One of the major findings of the PSID is that, contrary to popular belief, there is extensive turnover and mobility among the poor and welfare recipients (Coe, 1978, 1982; Duncan, 1984). For example, although two-thirds (66%) of blacks were poor during one year between 1967 and 1975, less than one-tenth (7%) remained poor throughout those nine years (Coe, 1978). And, based on PSID data from 1968 to 1979, Hofferth (1985) strongly reinforced Stack's (1974) ethnographic findings about the extensive changes in the household composition and living arrangements of black children during their childhood. Thus, social policies designed to reduce poverty and welfare dependence will not be effective if they are based on the erroneous premise that low-income families are static and monolithic.

3. Balance

Although the conventional perspective focuses primarily on the negative attributes of black families, it is equally unproductive to react to this practice by focusing solely on positive characteristics. The holistic framework underscores the importance of balanced analysis: examining both weaknesses and strengths. Over a decade ago, Hare (1976) properly cautioned against romanticizing black family strengths. And Karanga (1982, p. 213) underscored the dilemma of trying to maintain a proper balance between deficits and assets in analyses of the black community:

How does one prove strength in oppression without overstating the case, diluting criticism of the system and absolving the oppressor in the process? Moreover, "the parallel dilemma" is how does one criticize the system and state of things without contributing to the victimology school which thrives on litanies of lost battles and casualty lists while omitting victories and strengths and the possibilities for change inherent in both black people and society?

Traditionally, "balanced" treatment of black families has meant emphasizing the positive characteristics of the black "middle class," while stressing the pathology of the black "lower class" or "underclass" (Wilson, 1978, 1987; Lemann, 1986). We strongly reject this practice and contend that the strengths and weaknesses of both middle-income and low-income blacks should be assessed.

4. Solutions

While encouraging relevant analyses of the severity of the problems impacting black families, the holistic approach places even greater emphasis on conducting studies that identify solutions to those problems (Billingsley, 1968; Engram, 1982). Thus, it places high priority on answering such questions as: (a) What factors are responsible for the ability of the majority of low-income black youth to achieve against adversity? and (b) What strategies are successful in overcoming many intractable problems in the black community? A strong case for solution-oriented research was made by Robert Woodson in an interview by William Raspberry (*Washington Post*, March 10, 1986):

> The only reason to spend your time studying failure is if you want to produce more failure. You cannot learn to produce success by studying failure. Every school, every neighborhood, no matter how dismal its circumstances, has successes. It's a mystery to me why we spend so much time crying over our failures and so little time trying to learn from our successes.

As Hill (1971) contends, a major reason for focusing on black family strengths is to identify coping behavior, assets, resources, support networks, and self-help strategies that have been successful in helping disadvantaged black children and their families to overcome problems. In recent years there has been a sharp increase in research on well-functioning low-income and middle-income black families (Cazenave, 1979; Lewis & Looney, 1982; McAdoo, 1983; Willie, 1985; Thompson, 1986; Landry, 1987), highlighted by a series of notable studies conducted by Howard University's Institute for Urban Affairs and Research (Gary, et al, 1980, 1983, 1984, 1985). This solution's perspective also promotes analyses that assess the relative effectiveness of a broad range of public and private policies for enhancing the functioning of black families. In short, it places a premium on studies that have implications for action both inside and outside the black community (Woodson, 1981a, 1981b, 1987).

5. Empiricism

An overriding objective of the holistic framework is to produce generalizations and propositions about the nature, causes, and cures of problems confronting black families that are supported by empirical evidence. Our conception of "empirical" is not restricted to quantitative data, but includes scientific evidence derived through qualitative methods as well (Lewis, 1967a, 1967b; Ladner, 1971; Stack, 1974; Ogbu, 1981). The methods used should be determined by the nature of the questions to be answered. For example, ethnographic case studies and large-scale surveys (or a combination) should be used to address issues for which those methodologies are suited.

Furthermore, we think that greater utilization of longitudinal data is needed to make more reliable and valid generalizations about the nature of change among black families in various socioeconomic strata at different stages of their life cycles (Kellam, et al 1977; Coe, 1978, 1982; Malson, 1983a, 1983b; Elder, 1985a, 1985b; Hofferth, 1985). Finally, greater caution should be taken to avoid sweeping generalizations about changes (or the lack of changes) among families based solely on cross-sectional data.

C.   KEY ISSUES ABOUT BLACK FAMILIES

We shall now illustrate how the holistic framework facilitates the identification of important issues that need to be addressed to increase our understanding of the nature, causes, and remedies of key problems experienced by black families. Most of these issues are either ignored or deemphasized by the deficit perspective because of its superficial and fragmented orientation. Integrating concepts from the systems, developmental, and blocked opportunity paradigms, the following two operational questions will guide the presentation of this report:

1. What do we know about the extent to which societal forces, social policies, community subsystems, family subsystems, and individual factors impede or facilitate the functioning of black families?

2. What implications does this knowledge have for developing policies in the public and private sectors, as well as self-help strategies in the black community, that will significantly improve the social and economic well-being of low-income and middle-income black families?

The first query seeks to synthesize research on factors at the societal, community, family, and individual levels that contribute to functional as well as dysfunctional patterns among black families. The second question is action-oriented: it focuses on innovative strategies that can take advantage of the knowledge we have acquired about the causes and cures of major problems affecting black families. We shall first

25

examine the negative and positive effects of societal forces and social policies at the community, family, and individual levels on black families Then we shall suggest action strategies for public and private policymakers, service providers, and self-help institutions in the black community for strengthening black families.

IV. IMPACT OF SOCIETAL FORCES

A. CLASS STRATIFICATION

One of the forces in American society that is a major determinant of the life chances of black families and their members is classism, i.e., the ranking of individuals and groups in a stratification hierarchy on the basis of their socioeconomic resources, their power, wealth, and prestige. Since it distributes these resources unequally, class stratification is a form of institutionalized inequality (Merton, 1957; Hare, 1982, 1988; Hill, 1988a). Most analysts have worked within four basic class strata: upper-class, middle-class, working-class, and lower-class. The most popular class criteria that social scientists use are income, occupation, and education. According to Merton's thesis, opportunities to achieve societal goals decline markedly the lower the position one occupies in the class hierarchy. Consequently, groups occupying disadvantaged class positions are more constrained to resort to nonconforming adaptations than groups occupying advantaged positions. How is it that blacks occupy fewer advantaged class positions than whites? This brings us to the predominant societal force affecting black individuals and families–racism.

B. RACIAL STRATIFICATION

Racism refers to attitudes, actions, norms, or processes by individuals, groups, or institutions that keep groups in subordinate positions because of their racial or ethnic characteristics (Marrett & Leggon, 1979; Feagin, 1978). This subordination is institutionalized by the society through racial stratification, i.e., the ranking of groups in a hierarchy on the basis of their racial-ethnic background (Wilson, 1973). In the United States, four major rankings of racial/ethnic groups–in order of increasing disadvantage–can be identified: (a) white Protestants ("WASPs"); (b) white Catholics and Jews ("white ethnics"); (c) Asians and white Hispanics; and (d) non-Hispanic blacks, Hispanic blacks, and Native Americans (Hill, 1988a). The ranking of these racial/ethnic strata is directly related to their differential power, prestige, and wealth. The greater salience of race over ethnicity is reinforced by studies (Massey & Denton, 1987) that consistently reveal the social and economic advantage of "white" Hispanics (particularly from Cuba and Mexico) over "black" Hispanics (particularly from Puerto Rico). The reason blacks occupy more disadvantaged class positions than whites is because of their disadvantaged position in the racial/ethnic hierarchy. Thus, the overall position of blacks in American society is a function of their degree of subordination in two structural hierarchies. This is manifested by the "truncated" class structure in which blacks with similar income, education, or occupations as whites do not have the same social status because of their differential positions in the racial hierarchy (Landry, 1987).

Consequently, analysts must move beyond their sole preoccupation with the individual characteristics of race and class and focus on the societal attributes of racial and class stratification. Ogbu (1981) contends that racial stratification should be used systematically as an institutional variable in analyses of the black community in the same way that race and class measures are used for individuals. Such an approach would significantly enhance our knowledge of how institutionalized mechanisms sustain racial inequality by having differential impact on the functioning of black and white families.

C.   SECTORAL STRATIFICATION

A third form of social stratification that has a significant effect on black family life is sectoral stratification, i.e., the differential ranking of subsectors within major institutional areas, such as employment, housing, education, health, administration of justice, etc. (Hill, 1988a). The most widely-discussed form of sectoral stratification has been the notion of "dual labor markets" (Baron, 1969). According to this thesis, labor markets are divided into two sectors–primary and secondary. Primary labor markets are characterized by stable employment, full-time work, high-paying jobs, salaried occupations, excellent fringe benefits, and safe working environments. Secondary labor markets are characterized by irregular employment, part-time jobs, poverty-level wages, hourly wages, poor fringe benefits, and hazardous working conditions (Wilson, 1978; Collins, 1986).

In the area of housing, primary markets are characterized by owners, single-family homes, and suburban residence, while secondary markets are typified by renters, multiple-dwellings, and central city residence. Similarly, in the area of health, primary markets are characterized by private health facilities, personal physicians, and excellent health insurance coverage, while secondary markets are characterized by public health facilities, clinic physicians, and no health insurance coverage. Because of the cumulative effects of racial and class stratification, blacks are disproportionately concentrated in the secondary sectors. More attention should be given to examining the impact of sectoral stratification on the functioning of black families.

D.   INDIVIDUAL RACISM

Currently there is much debate about the extent to which race has declined in significance. Some scholars (Wilson, 1978; Kilson, 1981) who contend that class is now a more important determinant of black life assert that race continues to be a fundamental barrier to the advancement of black Americans (Pinkney, 1984; Willie, 1985; Cazenave, 1988). One major reason for widespread disagreement about the significance of contemporary racism is the failure to distinguish between its two basic components–prejudice and discrimination. Although these terms are often used interchangeably, they differ substantively from each other. Prejudice involves negative or unfavorable attitudes or beliefs about racial and ethnic minorities, while discrimination involves negative or hostile treatment of them.

To what extent has racism declined in this country? According to opinion polls and surveys, there has been a dramatic decline in prejudice toward racial minorities over the past 40 years. Between 1942 and 1984, for example, the proportion of whites favoring integrated schools soared from 30% to 90% (Smith & Sheatsley, 1984). Similarly, the proportion of whites who believe that blacks are inferior to whites fell from 31% to 15% between 1963 and 1978 (Pinkney, 1984).

Many analysts caution against misconstruing these poll trends as reflecting a sharp increase in racial tolerance (Jackman, 1973; McConahay, Hardee & Batts, 1981). In fact, proponents of "modern" or "symbolic" racism contend that racial prejudice is still pervasive in America (McConahay & Hough, 1976), and that socially undesirable "redneck" hostility to blacks per se has been replaced by hostility to busing, affirmative action quotas, open housing, welfare, and immigration—hostility that can be justified on nonracial grounds (Kinder & Sears, 1981). Such contemporary racism is difficult to measure by conventional opinion polls, since it is often disguised or unconscious (Sighall & Page, 1971).

The continuing significance of racism is also manifested in the widespread discrepancy between support for abstract goals of racial equality and opposition to specific measures to achieve them (Schuman, Steen & Bobo, 1985). For example, 9 out of 10 whites favor integrated schools, but only one-fourth support busing to attain that end (Smith & Sheatsley, 1984). Although 93% of whites support the right to vote, only 57% approve of federal voting rights legislation. And 88% support equal employment opportunity, but only 62% approve of federal fair employment legislation (Austin, 1976).

More importantly, a sharp decline in prejudicial attitudes does not necessarily mean that there has been a marked drop in discriminatory behavior (Wicker, 1969). Unfortunately, since pollsters concentrate on monitoring intolerant attitudes, national trend data on intolerant behavior are virtually nonexistent (Hill, 1984). Thus, even if one concedes that prejudice may have declined, opinion polls provide no evidence that discrimination has also fallen. On the contrary, the recent surge in racial hostility across the nation (such as continuing attacks against blacks living in or passing through predominantly white communities, numerous racial incidents on college campuses, and repeated racial slurs by high-level public and private officials) suggests that racism is still widespread in America (Farley & Allen, 1987; National Urban League, 1989).

E.   INSTITUTIONAL RACISM

Yet even if there were strong empirical evidence of a sharp decline in prejudiced attitudes and discriminatory behavior among white individuals, it is still possible that institutional racism might not have abated and could even be on the rise. The fundamental weakness of the declining racism thesis is its sole focus on individual racism, its failure to systematically assess the role of institutional racism.

Institutional prejudice (or "cultural racism") refers to the norms, values, beliefs, or customs of the dominant society that are deemed superior to those of racial and ethnic minorities (Jones, 1972). The stereotypical portrayal of black families by the media is an example of institutionalized prejudice. Institutional discrimination refers to laws, regulations, policies, and informal practices of organizations or institutions that result in differential adverse treatment or subordination of racial and ethnic minorities. Moreover, as Carmichael and Hamilton (1967) observed, institutional prejudice and discrimination can be unintended as well as intended.

Intentional institutionalized discrimination may be overt or covert. Overt discrimination refers to the deliberate mistreatment of minorities by organizations or institutions based on explicit racial or ethnic criteria. Examples include slavery, the passage of the Black Codes after emancipation, and the imposition of de jure segregation in the North and South. Covert intentional discrimination refers to the deliberate mistreatment of minorities by organizations or institutions based on nonracial criteria that are strongly correlated with race. Covert discrimination is also known as "patterned evasion," the deliberate use of proxies for race in order to deny equal opportunities to racial minorities. The grandfather clauses, literacy tests, and poll taxes are early examples of patterned evasions in the area of voting rights (Feagin, 1978).

Recent examples of intentional institutional discrimination are: (a) public and private urban renewal that displaces working-class and poor black families from their homes and communities in order to construct housing for middle- and upper-income whites; (b) the refusal by banks, insurance companies, etc., to grant home mortgage loans, commercial credit, and insurance for fire, property, and automobiles to minority families living in "red-lined" neighborhoods; and (c) zoning that disproportionately excludes black families from white communities by prohibiting low-income and multi-family dwellings (Newman, et al., 1978).

F.   STRUCTURAL DISCRIMINATION

A major impediment to the development of strategies to counteract the effects of institutional racism on black families has been the failure of many policymakers, scholars, and civil rights leaders to recognize or acknowledge the role of "unintentional" or "structural" discrimination. According to Downs (1970):

Racism can occur even if the people causing it have no intention of subordinating others because of color, or are totally unaware of doing so. Admittedly, this implication is sure to be extremely controversial. Most Americans believe racism is bad. But how can anyone be "guilty" of doing something bad when he does not realize he is doing it? Racism can be a matter of result rather than intention because many institutional structures in America that most whites do not recognize as subordinating others because of color actually injure minority group members far more than deliberate racism. (p. 78)

Unintentional institutional discrimination refers to societal forces or policies that have adverse effects on racial and ethnic minorities–although these actions were not designed to be discriminatory (Friedman, 1975; Feagin, 1978; Hill, 1988a). Society-wide trends such as recessions, inflationary spirals, the closing of plants in inner-cities, automation, and the shift from manufacturing to high-tech and service industries, etc., have had unintended, discriminatory effects on black families (Bluestone & Harrison, 1982). Such structural discrimination has contributed to persistently high rates of "structural unemployment" among young and adult workers in black families (Randolph, 1931; Killingsworth, 1966).

An example of unintentional discrimination in the area of social policies is manifested in recent changes in eligibility for retirement benefits. To enhance the solvency of the Social Security Trust Fund, in 1983 the 98th Congress raised the eligible age for retirement at full benefits to 66 and 67 years old between 2000 and 2022. This policy change, although not intentionally racially discriminatory, will have differential consequences for whites and blacks because of their different life expectancies. Black males, in particular, will be affected adversely, since their current life expectancy of 65 years insures that most of them will not live long enough to collect full benefits. Moreover, this increase in the eligible age for retirement benefits may have devastating effects on the families of thousands of black men and women who are forced into early retirement at reduced benefits because of ill health resulting from years of working in physically debilitating and hazardous jobs and industries. (Hill, 1983a).

According to Gurak, Smith, and Goldson (1982), examples of structural discrimination against minority families can also be found in the area of foster care and adoption:

...the increasing interest in analyzing the impact of the social systems upon persons...indicated the incompleteness of reducing all discriminatory practices to individually held attitudes of prejudice. It also has roots in the very character of institutional structures such as the criminal justice system, the system of education, the health delivery establishment, and in agencies delivering other services such as foster care for children. Even when revered by the public at large for their altruism and charitable work, even when staffed by essentially "non-prejudiced" persons, such structures can systematically produce discriminatory results affecting the lives of minority persons. (p. ix)

Many private agencies still require potential adoptive parents to meet the following criteria: (a) husband-wife couples; (b) middle-income; (c) able to afford various agency fees; (d) no children of their own; and (e) less than 45 years old. The black families that are most interested in adoption tend to be one-parent, low-income, over 45 years old, with children of their own (Hill, 1977). Because of such insensitive eligibility criteria, hundreds of black children are shunted from one foster care facility to another and upon reaching the age of 18 are discharged without having acquired adequate educational and vocational skills for productive lives as adults (Billingsley & Giovannoni, 1972; Hill, 1977; Gurak, Smith & Goldson, 1982). Hare (1988) describes structurally discriminatory processes in the field of education:

> This writer further agrees in what he terms a 'class-plus' analysis, with classism as the engine and racism as the caboose, that black Americans have simply been chosen to absorb an unfair share of an unfair burden in a structurally unfair system.

> ...our structural determination approach assumes that the character of the social system is preponderant as the determiner of the hierarchical arrangement of people within it, either their biological or cultural dispositions. It is further argued that, in addition to the inherent intergenerational inequality caused by inheritance, the education system through its unequal skill-giving, grading, routing and credentialing procedures, plays a critical role in legitimating structural inequality in the American social system...The structural argument... charges that the social system needs people to replenish its ranks at all levels of skills and credentials, and that in producing such differences the schools respond to structural needs rather than innate differences. (p. 83)

G. SEXISM

Sexism refers to differential adverse attitudes toward women because of their sex. It is a major societal force for perpetuating the subordination of women to men. Although white women also persistently encounter sexism, such experiences by black women have more devastating effects on black families. For one thing, black women are much more likely than white women to head single-parent families and to be the primary breadwinners in those families (Pearce and McAdoo, 1981; Malson, 1986).

Since black families headed by women are popularly characterized as "matriarchal," "vanishing," "nonfamilies," "pathological," and "broken," they experience discrimination because of race and sex in many areas, such as employment, housing, bank loans and credit, health, adoption and foster care, social welfare, the administration of justice, etc. (Rodgers-Rose, 1980; Harley & Terborg-Penn, 1978). Wives in black families are more likely than wives in white families to experience sexual discrimination in the labor market because of their higher labor force participation (Simms, 1985-86). Black women are also more likely to be concentrated in low-paying "traditionally female" occupations than white women (Malveaux, 1985; Burbridge, 1985-86; Collins, 1986). Finally, black women experience disproportionate levels of mental and physical abuse from black men because of the more frequent institutional barriers and frustrations experienced by black men relative to white men (Sizemore, 1973; Jewell, 1988).

Pearce and McAdoo (1981) underscore several sex-specific reasons for the increased "feminization of poverty":

> Thus, women, especially minority women, may be poor for some of the same reasons as men, but few men become poor because of female causes. Men generally do not become poor because of divorce, sex-role socialization, sexism or, of course, pregnancy. Indeed, some may lift themselves out of poverty by the same means that plunge women into it. The same divorce that frees a man from the financial burdens of a family may result in poverty for his ex-wife and children. Distinct reasons for the poverty among women can be traced back to two sources. First, in American culture women continue to carry the major burden of childrearing. This sex-role socialization has many ramifications. For example, women tend to make career choices that anticipate that they will interrupt their participation in the labor force to bear children. The second major source of poverty is the limited opportunities available to women in the labor market. Occupational segregation, sex discrimination and sexual harassment combine to limit both income and mobility for women workers. (p. 17)

H.   BABY BOOM COHORT

A demographic trend that significantly affected the structure and functioning of black families during the 1970s and 1980s was the "baby boom" cohort, i.e., the record-level surge in birth rates in the U S. after World War II. Thus, during the first half of the 1970s, the number of adolescents between the ages of 16-19 reached record levels. However, during the same period, the number of children born to married women declined sharply, while the number born to unmarried women fell more slowly. Thus, these demographic shifts led to alarming increases in the number of out-of-wedlock births to adolescents among whites as well as blacks.

As the baby boom cohort reached adulthood by the 1980s, the proportion of out-of-wedlock births to teenagers steadily declined. Nevertheless, since black teenagers are still five times more likely than white teenagers to have out-of-wedlock babies, adolescent pregnancy continues to be a major contributor to black family instability. However, since 90% of black unwed teen mothers continued to live with their parents, adolescent parents were not the main reason for the surge in female-headed black families during the 1970s.

33

I.   SEX RATIO

As Jackson (1971) effectively documented, a demographic factor that contributed markedly to the sharp increase in black female-headed families over the past decade and a half was the shortage of males relative to females. Although single-parent
families grew at about the same pace among blacks and whites during the 1970s,
black women had much lower remarriage rates than white women because of the
lesser availability of marriageable black men. Among persons of all ages, there are
only 90 black men to 100 black women, while there are 95 white men to 100 white
women.

Among blacks, the sex ratio is widest among those in their prime working
years. Among persons 25-44 years old, there are only 85 black men for every 100
black women, while there are about equal numbers of white men and white women in
that age category. However, when one corrects for the disproportionate census under-
count of black men, the gap narrows markedly to about 96 black men for every 100
black women between the ages of 25-44 (U.S. Bureau of the Census, 1982). Yet, a
shortage of marriageable black men continues to exist because of a number of factors:
high rates of unemployment, underemployment, arrest records, incarceration, disability, drug addiction, homicides, and suicides (Swan, 1981b; McGhee, 1984). Stewart and Scott (1978) attribute this imbalance to "institutional decimation," i.e., the
disproportionate elimination of black men from productive sectors of the society by
"benign" processes in all American institutions.

J.   RURAL TO URBAN MIGRATION

The migration of blacks from rural to urban areas of the South and North had
positive and negative consequences for black families. In several works, Frazier
(1931, 1939) described the destabilizing effects of urbanization on black newcomers to
towns and cities. He identified several effects of the urban environment that undermined the stability of black families: pressures on breadwinners to travel long distances from their families in order to find work; pressures on wives to supplement the
low wages of their husbands by going to work and leaving their children unattended;
the diminished influence of religious institutions; and the lack of adequate facilities
and services in such areas as housing, health, and education.

As Frazier (1926) concluded, it should come as no surprise that black families in
cities are disproportionately characterized by high rates of family disruption, delinquency, crime, ill health, low educational attainment, and overcrowding. And Gutman (1976) and Furstenberg, Hershberg, and Modell (1975) effectively documented
the fact that female-headed black families are even more strongly associated with the
urban environment now than they were with the rural environment during slavery.

K. CENTRAL CITY/SUBURBAN MIGRATION

Between 1950 and 1970, the proportion of blacks living in central cities jumped from 41% to 58%, while the proportion of whites in central cities declined from 32% to 28%. By 1980, the proportion of whites in central cities fell to 25%, while the proportion of blacks remained unchanged at 58%. At the same time, the proportion of whites in the suburbs doubled from 25% to 48% between 1950 and 1980, and the proportion of suburban blacks also doubled from 12% to 23% (O'Hare et al., 1982).

While 2.1 million blacks left central cities between 1970-80, 1.4 million blacks moved in, for a net out-migration of 700,000. Concurrently, while 1.9 million blacks moved to the suburbs, 1 million blacks moved out, for a net in-migration of 900,000. Contrary to popular belief, poor blacks accounted for one out of every two blacks moving to the suburbs during the 1970s, since the proportion of poor blacks in the suburbs remained at one-fourth from 1970 (25%) to 1980 (24%). The proportion of poor blacks in central cities did increase from 26% to 32% between 1970 and 1980 (O'Hare, et al., 1982).

L. RETURN MIGRATION

The historic out-migration of blacks from the South not only slowed dramatically during the 1970s, but the South also attracted the largest number of black in-migrants. For example, 415,000 blacks migrated to the South from other regions between 1975 and 1980, compared to only 162,000 blacks between 1965 and 1970. Preliminary data suggest that similar numbers (411,000) of blacks continued to migrate to the South between 1980 and 1985 (Cromartie & Stack, 1987).

According to Census Bureau classifications, the overwhelming majority of black migrants to the South during the 1970s and 1980s were newcomers. Yet Cromartie and Stack (1987) contend that, by failing to take account of the birthplace, prior residence, and familial ties of all members in a migrating household, census data markedly understate the number of black migrants who are returnees. Consequently, they developed a new migration category called "homeplace movers," i.e., any migrant to a state who resides in a household that includes a native of that state, whether that native is a returnee or stayer (Stack, 1987).

By applying this concept to 326,000 blacks who moved to 10 Southern states between 1975 and 1980, 82,000 black "newcomers" were reclassified as homeplace migrants. Children (71%), retirees (72%), and nonmetro movers (85%) are more likely to be homeplace movers than adults (59%) and movers to metro areas (53%). Black migration to the South is mainly homeplace migration, which not only involves returnees to their state of birth, "but also thousands of nonnative children and adults, who either follow their relatives back home, or join already established households in the South" (Cromartie & Stack, 1987 p. 13).

M. IMMIGRATION

Immigration has had many adverse effects on black families. During slavery, employment opportunities for free blacks in the North were directly related to competition for those jobs from newly-arriving foreigners (Frazier, 1949). And, after emancipation, numerous race riots broke out between immigrants and blacks over perceived or actual job competition. Immigrants also adopted restrictive labor union practices in order to eliminate blacks from certain jobs and industries (Drake & Cayton, 1945). Consequently, blacks made their greatest occupational advances during both World Wars–when European immigration was curtailed.

Recent studies suggest that an increasing source of black unemployment may be competition from Hispanic and Asian immigrants–legal and illegal. For example, Hispanics obtained about the same number of the new jobs created between 1975 and 1980 as blacks, although they were only about half the size of the black population. And, Asians obtained about half as many of the new jobs created during that period as blacks, although they were only one-fifth the size of the black population (Hill, 1981). Moreover, an analysis by Stewart and Hyclak (1986) revealed that immigrants–other than those from Cuba or the West Indies–adversely affected the earnings of black men in central cities. Since most demographers predict that Asians and Hispanics will constitute the fastest growing groups in the United States into the 21st century, job competition between them and blacks is likely to become more acute in the near future.

N. INDUSTRIALIZATION

Industrialization has had both positive and negative consequences on black families. Industrialization has brought about structural transformations in (a) American industries, i.e., from agriculture to manufacturing or from manufacturing to services; (b) technology, i.e., automation from low-tech to high-tech or from labor-intensive to capital-intensive; (c) sectors, i.e., from public to private; and (d) occupations, i.e., from farm to factory work, from factory to clerical work, from self-employed to salaried (Bluestone & Harrison, 1982; Drake & Cayton, 1945).

Frazier (1931) describes at length how the shift from an agricultural to a manufacturing economy had destabilizing effects on rural black families between 1865-1925. Johnson (1932) also provides an in-depth analysis of how specific industrial changes undermined the economic well-being of blacks during that period. And several scholars (Randolph, 1931; Killingsworth, 1966) have identified technological change as a key source of "structural unemployment" among blacks and other minorities because of their disadvantage in respect to educational and work skills. On the other hand, industrialization has also had many positive effects, especially in raising the occupational and earnings levels of wage-earners in black families as they moved from farm to factory work or from lower-paying operational jobs to higher-paying clerical and technical jobs (Frazier, 1949).

O. RECESSIONS

Wage-earners in black families have been disproportionately affected by recessions or "cyclical unemployment" because of the seniority principle of "last hired, first fired" and because of their concentration in unskilled and semi-skilled jobs which are most vulnerable to economic slumps. As Frazier noted, black workers were laid off disproportionately during the depression of 1921 and the Great Depression of the 1930s. Although black workers were variously affected by each of the eight recessions between 1948 and 1982, the four most recent recessions–1970-71, 1974-75, 1980, and 1981-82–were the most devastating.

The tripling in unemployment of black family heads during these recessions led to alarming increases in family instability and poverty. Each one-percent increase in the rate of black unemployment during the 1970s was related to a two-percent rise in the proportion of single-parent black families (Hill, 1986; Blank & Blinder, 1986). And studies by Brenner (1979) have revealed that high levels of unemployment produce devastating social consequences, such as physical and mental illness, alcoholism, family violence, divorce, separation, homicides, and suicides. Although numerous other researchers (Moynihan, 1967; Hill, 1975; Wilson, 1987; Swinton, 1988) have found a strong correlation between black unemployment and family instability, there appears to be reluctance on the part of many analysts to assess in a serious and systematic fashion the impact of periodic recessions on the structure and functioning of black families (Gilder, 1981; Murray, 1984; Loury, 1984).

P. INFLATION

At the same time that black families were reeling from the effects of back-to-back recessions during the 1970s, they were subjected to double-digit inflation. Although economic theory held that it was impossible to have high levels of unemployment and inflation simultaneously, the U.S. economy rose and lowered itself to the challenge, out of which a new term was coined, "stagflation." Between 1969 and 1980, consumer prices soared at an unprecedented annual rate of 12%, compared to only 3% during the 1960s.

As Caplovitz (1979) has shown, black families were acutely affected by the price inflation of the 1970s. His study revealed that the incomes of three-fourths of black families had fallen behind rising prices, whereas the incomes of one-half the white families had been so affected. Moreover, between 1969 and 1982, inflation eroded the purchasing power of black families by 14%, compared to a 5% decline in white family income (Hill, 1986). Thus real income fell about three times as much among black as among white families. And overall, most studies suggest that blacks and low-income groups are even more adversely affected by unemployment than by inflation (Blank & Blinder, 1986).

V. IMPACT OF SOCIAL POLICIES

A. FISCAL AND MONETARY POLICIES

The four most recent presidents–Nixon, Ford, Carter, and Reagan–promised not to place the burden of fighting spiraling inflation on the backs of the unemployed. Nevertheless, the four back-to-back recessions during the 1970s and 1980s were induced by their respective fiscal and monetary policies; they were not "natural disasters." Traditionally, the Federal Reserve Board tries to stem inflation by keeping interest rates within predetermined ranges, while permitting the money supply to expand more freely. These restrictive fiscal policies induced the recessions of 1970-71 and 1974-75.

Although consumer prices declined somewhat after the 1974-75 slump, they began to climb to two-digit levels toward the end of the 1970s. Consequently, the Federal Reserve Board vowed to fight inflation with nontraditional policies. More restrictive targets were set on the money supply and interest rates were permitted to rise unfettered. The soaring interest rates led to the 1980 recession and similar tight money policies brought on the 1981-82 recession–the most severe decline since the Great Depression. These spiraling interest rates also contributed to the disproportionate failures of black businesses. In general, federal fiscal and monetary policies during this period had an acute adverse impact on black workers, families, and businesses (Swinton, 1988).

B. INCOME TAXES

Historically, the American income tax system has been progressive, i.e., tax rates were related to the income levels of individuals and corporations. However, during the 1970s and 1980s the tax burden was markedly shifted from the wealthy to working-class and middle-class individuals and families (Levy, 1987; Blank & Binder, 1986). While the proportion of federal income taxes from corporations dropped between 1950 and 1983, the proportion of taxes from individuals increased from 35% to 47%. The tax rates for families of four at the poverty line increased from 2.2% to 3.3% between 1965 and 1983, and the tax rates for "near-poor" families (i.e., those with incomes that are half of the U.S. median income) rose from 2.9 to 4.9. Since working-class black families are over-represented among poor and near-poor families, they were disproportionally affected by the regressive federal taxes.

C. PAYROLL TAXES

The IRS "balance of payments" not only shifted to the personal income taxes of middle-income and low-income Americans, but to their Social Security payroll taxes as well. While the combined payroll taxes of employees and employers rose from 3% to 13% between 1950 and 1983, the proportion of federal revenues from payroll taxes more than tripled from 12% to 38%. Consequently, the total tax rates (i.e., both income and payroll taxes) for families of four at the poverty level jumped from 4.9% to 16.5% between 1955 and 1983, while the rates for near-poor families soared from 4.5% to 18.3%. Although the average income of whites is about one-and-a-half times that of blacks, whites pay taxes only slightly higher than those of blacks (20%).

Because of the erosion in the personal exemption and standard deduction by inflation during the first half of the 1970s, more poor families paid both higher income taxes and higher payroll taxes. To correct for these inequities, the Earned Income Tax Credit (EITC) was enacted in 1975 to ensure (a) that no families below the poverty level paid income taxes and (b) that a portion of the Social Security payroll tax would be refunded to working poor families. Nevertheless, the value of the personal exemption, the standard deduction, and the EITC continued to be eroded by double-digit inflation. Thus, the tax burden for families of four at the poverty level rose from 1% to 10% between 1975 and 1985, while the tax rate for families with annual incomes over $250,000 in 1985 was less than 5% (Blank & Binder, 1986).

The Tax Reform Act of 1986 not only markedly raised the thresholds of the personal exemption, the standard deduction, and the EITC, it also for the first time indexed them so as to ensure that they are kept abreast of rising inflation. The personal exemption was to be raised from $1,080 to $2,000 by 1989, while the standard deduction (for nonitemizing taxpayers) was to be increased from $3,670 to $5,000 for a married couple filing jointly and from $2,840 to $4,400 for single household heads by 1988. The maximum EITC credit was raised from $550 to $800 for 1987, and for that same year the maximum eligible family income was raised from $11,000 to $15,432, to reach $18,500 in 1988. About 3 million working poor families (one-fourth of whom are black) may be removed from the income tax rolls as a result of the 1986 reforms. Nevertheless, the current gap between the poor and rich in America is the widest it has been since the 1950s, primarily because of regressive federal tax policies and disproportionate cuts in programs for the poor (Center on Budget and Policy Priorities, 1984a, 1984b).

D.   GREAT SOCIETY PROGRAMS

Many of the anti-poverty programs enacted by the Kennedy-Johnson administrations during the 1960s as part of the "Great Society" efforts were the first federal government initiatives specifically targeted towards racial minorities as well as towards the economically disadvantaged. These programs fell into four groups— employment and training, education, in-kind services, and area development. The main jobs programs were: the Manpower Development and Training Act (MDTA), the Community Work and Training Program, the Work Experience and Training Program, and the Work Incentive Program (WIN) for welfare recipients. The educational programs included Head Start, Compensatory Education, and Open Enrollment (Levitan, 1985).

The key in-kind programs enacted during the 1960s were Medicare, Medicaid, food distribution, school breakfast, school lunch, food stamps, subsidized rent, community health, maternal and child health, and Indian Health Services. And the main area development programs were the Social Impact Program, Model Cities, Appalachian Regional Development, Public Works, Operation Mainstream, the Economic Development Administration, and Rural Development. Between 1964 and 1969, when "War on Poverty" efforts were at their peak, unemployment and poverty rates among black families fell to unprecedented lows. Although most of these economic gains were due to a prosperous economy, the anti-poverty programs targeted to minorities and low-income groups were also important contributors to black progress during the 1960s (Levitan, Johnston & Taggart, 1975).

Conservative analysts (Gilder, 1981; Murray, 1984) tend to focus on the unintended negative consequences of the Great Society programs, while liberal analysts (Levitan, 1985; National Urban League, 1988) concentrate on their positive effects. Systematic studies of specific Great Society programs reveal that some of them have had positive consequences while others were not very effective. One must clearly distinguish between programs. Programs in the areas of health, nutrition, and education were much more effective than those in the areas of housing, employment, and business subsidies. Although only a fraction of the poor were reached by many of these programs, due to limited funding, the record shows that most of those who were reached benefited from them.

E. BLOCK GRANTS

Although block grants are invariably omitted from most policy analyses of black families, the transforming of categorical grants to block grants during the 1970s and 1980s contributed significantly to the shift in government resources from blacks and low-income groups to middle-income groups and communities. As a result of President Nixon's "New Federalism" efforts to give over the administration of federal social programs to states and localities, many of the social programs of the 1960s were combined into broad "revenue sharing" block grants. Model Cities was replaced by the Community Development Block Grant (CDBG), the Manpower Development and Training Act (MDTA) by the Comprehensive Employment and Training Act (CETA) manpower block grant, and Title IV-A by the Title XX social services block grant (Hill, 1981).

Since block grants have little federal oversight and do not distribute funds primarily on the basis of economic need, many suburban areas with low levels of unemployment, substandard housing, and poverty received sizable CETA, CDBG, and Title XX funds. Several high-level evaluations revealed that minorities and other economically disadvantaged groups benefited less from the decentralized block grants of the 1970s than they did from many of the centralized categorical programs of the 1960s. It was not until the Carter administration that CETA, CDBG, and Title XX were retargeted to poor individuals, families, and communities.

Subsequently, in 1987, the Reagan administration further diluted targeting to the poor by creating block grant programs–including Community Services; Maternal and Child Health; Preventive Health and Health Services; Alcohol, Drug Abuse and Mental Health; Low-Income Energy Assistance; and Social Services (which absorbed Title XX). Although CETA was replaced in 1982 by a larger manpower block grant, the Job Training and Partnership Act (JTPA), the Community Development Block Grant remains unaltered. Congress, as well as state governments, successfully opposed the Reagan administration's efforts to transform AFDC into a block grant. In exchange for giving the states greater flexibility in determining the target populations of the block grants, funding levels for programs consolidated into block grants were reduced by 20%.

F. REAGAN BUDGET CUTS

While funding for certain programs for racially and economically disadvantaged groups were reduced indirectly through block grants, funding for most other programs for the poor were reduced directly–although the cuts were not as deep as President Reagan had proposed. By FY 1985, annual AFDC funding was reduced by $1.4 billion (rather than the proposed $2.8 billion cut), to $8.4 billion; food stamps by $2 billion (rather than the $7.5 billion proposed cut), to $12.5 billion; low-income energy assistance by $.2 billion (rather than the $.9 billion proposed cut), to $2.2 billion; child nutrition by $1.4 billion (rather than the $2.3 billion proposed cut), to $10.9 billion; Medicaid by $.7 billion (rather than the $3.9 billion proposed cut), to $24.2 billion; compensatory education by $.8 billion (rather than the $2.5 billion proposed cut), to $3.3 billion; and Job Corps by $.5 billion (rather than the $3 billion proposed cut), to $6.5 billion.

Although the Reagan administration sought the total elimination of the Community Services Block Grant (CSBG) and the Work Incentive Program for employable welfare recipients (WIN), Congress kept them, though it reduced FY 1985 funding for CSBG by $.3 billion to $.4 billion and reduced funding for WIH by $.2 billion to $.3 billion. Congress did accede to the administration's request to eliminate the Public Service Employment program, one of the most effective components of CETA. Since black families are over-represented (between 30%-45%) in most programs for the poor, they were disproportionately affected by the wide range of budget cutbacks.

Most of the cuts in programs for the poor were achieved by tightening eligibility requirements for the working poor and reducing the value of cash and noncash benefits for the poor who continued to receive assistance. For example, the Omnibus Budget Reduction Act (OBRA) cuts in 1981 removed between 400,000 and 500,000 working poor families (about 11%-14% of the total AFDC caseload) from the welfare rolls and eliminated about one million persons from the food stamps program due to more stringent eligibility criteria. At the same time, about 300,000 working poor families that remained on AFDC experienced sharp reductions in cash and in-kind benefits because of increased work disincentives (Children's Defense Fund, 1984). According to a 1987 report prepared by the Physician Task Force on Hunger in America, the number of Americans experiencing hunger and malnutrition rose to 20 million, largely because of the $7 billion and $5 billion cuts, respectively, in the food stamps and school lunch programs between 1981 and 1985.

In one sense, the Reagan administration policies of excluding the working poor from its safety net for "the truly needy" did succeed in retargeting funds to the non-working poor. Yet, evaluations of those budget cuts revealed that savings from those reductions were not used to increase real (inflation-adjusted) benefits for the poor individuals and families that remained on the public assistance rolls. Consequently, even "the truly needy" experienced sharp declines in their standard of living as a result of the drastic cuts in cash and noncash programs for the poor.

G. SOCIAL SECURITY

The black aged made stronger economic gains during the 1970s than the black nonaged because of several improvements in the Social Security program (OASDI). Amendments in 1950 and 1954 extended coverage to farm operators, agricultural workers, and domestic workers—occupations in which blacks were over-represented. Amendments in 1965 and 1966 extended coverage to all persons 72 years and older who did not qualify for Social Security benefits because of lack of coverage in their prime working years or insufficient qualifying quarters of work. Moreover, the regular minimum benefit was established to provide livable income ($122 a month during the 1970s) for individuals who worked in covered jobs at wages too low to qualify for adequate benefits. Furthermore, cost-of-living adjustments (COLAs) were instituted in 1972 to insure that Social Security benefits would automatically keep even with rises in the Consumer Price Index (CPI) (Hill, 1983a).

All of these policy changes in Social Security disproportionately benefited the black elderly, since they were more likely than the white elderly to have worked in jobs or industries not covered by Social Security, to have worked at wages too low to qualify for OASDI, and not to have private pensions to augment their OASDI benefits. Thus, 90% of the black aged receive OASDI benefits today, compared to 93% of the white aged. But 51% of the black aged living alone depend on Social Security for three-fourths or more of their income, compared to 38% of the white aged living alone. On the other hand, only 30% of the black elderly living in families depend on OASDI for three-fourths or more of their income, compared to 23% of the white elderly living in families. Furthermore, Social Security benefits for black retirees are about 80% of the benefits for white retirees, since the former received much lower wages than the latter during their working years (U.S. Social Security Administration, 1986).

Consequently, the black elderly experienced sharp declines in poverty during the 1970s. While the proportion of black elderly who were poor dropped from 75% to 59% between 1969 and 1979, the proportion of black elderly families fell from 42% to 26%. However, although the percent of all black persons 65 years and older who were poor declined from 50% to 36% between 1969 and 1979, the number of poor black aged increased from 689,000 to 716,000. But the real family income of black elderly couples rose 17% between 1969 and 1979, compared to a 13% increase among all black couples. And while the real income of all female-headed black families declined by 1%, the real income of elderly female-headed black families soared by 41% over that 11-year span.

However, many of the economic strides of the black elderly during the 1970s were severely undermined by sharp cutbacks in social programs during the 1980s. Despite the Reagan administration's promises to spare Social Security beneficiaries from its budget cuts, low-income OASDI recipients were disproportionately affected. In addition to eliminating the minimum benefit for future retirees, eligibilty was tightened drastically for recipients who retired early because of disabilities (a group in which blacks are over-represented). Moreover, benefits were eliminated for college students and for the parents of children receiving survivor's or dependent's benefits when their youngest child became 16 years old.

Furthermore, the creation of block grants forced the aged poor to compete with the nonaged poor, the disabled, the handicapped, and racial and ethnic minorities for a shrinking pie. Moreover, to increase the solvency of the Social Security Trust Fund, Congress in 1983 raised the eligible age for full retirement benefits to 66 by 2009 and to 67 by 2027. Consequently, most black men will not be able to receive their full Social Security benefits since they only have a life expectancy of 65 years (Hill, 1983a). Such structurally discriminatory policies suggest that the economic well-being of the black elderly will worsen significantly in the coming decades.

H.   WELFARE POLICIES

The government policies most often cited as a major cause of black family instability are those related to welfare, especially the Aid to Families with Dependent Children program (AFDC). According to conventional wisdom, the surge in female-headed families and out-of-wedlock births among blacks during the 1970s and 1980s was caused mainly by the increasing availability of AFDC.

Numerous studies have been undertaken to test the validity of this belief and no convincing empirical support has been found. For example, after a rigorous test of the "welfare caused female-headed families" thesis, Ellwood and Summers (1986) concluded:

Between 1972 and 1980 the number of black children in female-headed families rose nearly 20%; the number of black children on AFDC actually fell by 5%. If

AFDC were pulling families apart and encouraging the formation of single-parent families, it is hard to understand why the number of children on the program would remain constant throughout a period in our history when family structures changed the most. (p. 94)

Similarly, in examining the relationship between AFDC and out-of-wedlock births among blacks, Ellwood and Summers (1986) noted:

What about the sharp rise in the fraction of all black births to unmarried women? The birth rate to unmarried black women fell 13% between 1970 and 1980, but the birth rate to married black women fell even more–by 38%; thus the fraction of births to unmarried women rose. During the same period the unmarried birth rate to whites rose by 27%. It seems difficult to argue that AFDC was a major influence in unmarried births when there was simultaneously a rise in the birth rate to unmarried whites and a fall in the rate for blacks. (p. 94)

Furthermore, comprehensive reviews of research findings by Wilson and Neckerman (1986), Ellwood and Bane (1984), and Darity and Myers (1984) also found no credible evidence for popular assumptions about welfare causality. Most of these reviews concluded that high unemployment and the shortage of black men were more strongly associated with black female-headed family formation than the "attractiveness" of welfare benefits.

I.   AFDC-UP AND GA

Another popular assertion is that unemployed black men must desert their families to make them eligible for public assistance–since no welfare is supposedly available for poor two-parent families. But there are two public assistance programs that aid poor two-parent families: AFDC-Unemployed Parent (ADFC-UP) and General Assistance (GA) (National Urban League, 1980). The AFDC-UP program (which is federally-reimbursed) has been in operation since 1961. However, unlike the mandatory AFDC-Basic program for single mothers, AFDC-UP is optional. Consequently, only half of the states (none in the South) have AFDC-UP. Because of very restrictive eligibility criteria, AFDC-UP rolls have consistently comprised less than 10% of all AFDC recipients. The requirements–that AFDC-UP recipients have stable prior work histories, be eligible for unemployment insurance, and not be disqualified for UI benefits–disproportionately screen out poor black families. Such structural discrimination explains why only 25% of poor two-parent black families were receiving AFDC-UP in 1984, compared to 40% of poor two-parent white families (Hill, 1987b). About 253,000 AFDC-UP families (or 1.1 million persons) received benefits averaging $507 per month in 1986.

General Assistance (GA), which is completely funded by states and counties, is a successor to the Mother's Pensions programs established by states prior to the Social Security Act of 1935. Since the GA program is designed to provide short-term aid to individuals and families that are not eligible for the regular federally-funded welfare programs, poor two-parent families are usually over-represented. About a million individuals in 41 states received GA benefits averaging $127 per month in 1980 (Hill, 1981).

J.   CHILD SUPPORT POLICIES

The family court is the basic governmental entity for providing child support to single parents. It establishes responsibility to pay child support, sets the amount to be paid, and attempts to enforce the obligation of the noncustodial parent to pay. Yet the family court has a number of deficiencies. First, it often fails to order any awards at all. Only three out of five mothers eligible for child support receive awards. Second, the probability of obtaining awards varies with marital status. Eight out of ten divorced mothers have child support orders, compared to less than half of separated mothers and less than one out of five never-married mothers. Third, the amount of child support awards varies widely from state to state and county to county and is often inequitable and regressive. For example, in the state of Wisconsin, noncustodial parents whose income was less than $5,000 were ordered to pay child support payments that were 41% of their income, while noncustodial parents whose income was $40,000 and over were ordered to make payments that were only 19% of their income (Garfinkel & Melli, 1987).

Welfare agencies became a major vehicle for obtaining child support for low-income single parents with passage of the Child Support Enforcement Program (IV-D) in 1975. This legislation required each state to establish an Office of Child Support Enforcement similar to the new office at the federal level to help obtain and enforce child support awards to AFDC families and to non-AFDC families on request for a fee. As a condition of AFDC eligibility, custodial parent had to agree to assist welfare authorities in establishing paternity and locating the absent father.

Several features of child support policies have adverse effects on custodial parents on AFDC. After working four months, their AFDC benefits are reduced a dollar for every dollar of earnings. Moreover, prior to 1984, there was little incentive for mothers to induce absent fathers to make support payments when none of the amount paid would go to the children. Thus, Stack and Semmel (1973) argue that these "support" payments are more accurately described as "state reimbursements." To provide some incentive, child support amendments in the Deficit Reduction Act of 1984 (P L. 98-369) permitted states to disregard the first $50 of each monthly child support collected for families on AFDC (Everett, 1985).

Other provisions of this act, however, may have severe destabilizing effects on many AFDC families. For the first time, the income of all household members (such

46

as grandparents and nonrelatives) who are not legally responsible for providing support to children in AFDC families will be included in determining the amount of the AFDC grant. This will pressure many AFDC mothers in extended families, especially among blacks, to move away from relatives into housing they cannot afford. Moreover, for the first time all child support payments for children who are not part of the AFDC unit are to be included in determining the AFDC grant. This may cause many fathers, who faithfully pay child support to prevent their children from going on welfare, to discontinue those payments.

K. FOSTER CARE AND ADOPTION

Foster care is another social welfare program that is invariably omitted in conventional studies of black families. Almost two decades ago Billingsley and Giovannoni (1972) documented in great detail the disproportionate negative impact of foster care and adoption policies on black children and families. Numerous subsequent studies have confirmed the findings of that pioneering work (Fanshel & Shinn, 1978; Festinger, 1983).

Nevertheless, many child welfare agencies continue to use the following criteria for potential adoptive parents: (a) two-parent families; (b) middle-income; (c) no children; and (d) under 45 years old. Such criteria structurally discriminate against minority families, since the families most interested in adopting children are likely to be one-parent, low-income, with children, and over 45 years old (Hill, 1977; Gurak, Smith & Goldson, 1982). Consequently, disproportionate numbers of black children are likely to spend their entire childhood in the limbo of foster care. And studies have shown that persons reared in foster care are over-represented among incarcerated felons, alcoholics, drug addicts, prostitutes, and the homeless. In short, well-intentioned foster care and adoption policies may be unwittingly incubating tomorrow's "underclass."

L. HEALTH POLICIES

Both liberals and conservatives agree that government health policies have had a strong positive impact on black families. The passage in 1965 of Medicare for all persons 65 years and over and Medicaid for low-income individuals and families, and in 1974 of Supplemental Security Income (SSI) for low-income elderly, disabled, and blind, provided a major impetus for initiatives to improve access to quality health care to the economically disadvantaged. Other key health programs targeted for low-income groups were Community Health Centers, Food Stamps, School Lunch, School Breakfast, School Milk, Food Commodity Distribution, the Supplemental Food Program for Women, Infants and Children (WIC), and the Maternal and Child Health program (Levitan, 1985).

While the impact on blacks of some of these programs (notably Medicaid) is inconclusive, their combined impact has improved the health status of blacks markedly. For example, between 1960 and 1981, infant mortality among blacks fell from 44.3 to 20 per 1,000 live births, while maternal deaths among blacks dropped from 103.6 to 20.4 per 100,000 live births. Moreover, the percent of low birthweight black infants declined from 14.1 to 12.5 between 1969 and 1980 (U.S. Public Health Service, Health and Human Services, 1985). Furthermore, while the gap in life expectancy from birth between whites and blacks was 7 (70.6 to 63.6) years in 1960, the gap between whites and blacks narrowed to 4.5 (74.8 to 70.3) years by 1981.

Despite this progress, infant mortality today is twice as high among blacks as it is among whites, while maternal mortality is three times as high among blacks. There is also increasing evidence that, because of recent cutbacks in health programs for the poor, the proportion of low-income pregnant women receiving prenatal care has declined sharply, and the rate of infant mortality among blacks has not only failed to decline, it has risen in many states (Children's Defense Fund, 1986). Moreover, among persons 25 to 64 years old, black women (18%) are twice as likely as white women (9%) to have work disabilities today, while black men (16%) are one-and-a-half times as likely as white men (11%) to have work disabilities.

M. EDUCATION POLICIES

Several educational policies have also had positive consequences for black and low-income students and their families. Since it was established as a "War on Poverty" program in 1964, Head Start has provided a comprehensive array of child development services to children aged 3-5 from low-income families. Unlike most programs for economically disadvantaged students, Head Start has been able to obtain the active participation of parents as volunteers and paid staff. Follow-up studies of this program continually document its outstanding successes. Children who had been in Head Start were found to have higher rates of high school completion, college enrollment, and employment, and lower rates of arrests and welfare dependency than children not exposed to such preschool programs (Levitan, 1985). Unfortunately, because of funding constraints, the 450,000 children served by Head Start in FY 1985 accounted for only one-fourth of the low-income children eligible for those services.

Title I of the Elementary and Secondary Education Act of 1965 was established to provide funds to local school districts to target special educational initiatives to minorities and low-income children in elementary and secondary schools. Although evaluations of Title I reveal that it had some impact on improving the educational attainment of low-income children, its block grant features impeded its ability to target resources to the economically disadvantaged. This was also true of its successor, Chapter I of the Education Consolidation and Improvement Act, which was enacted by the Reagan administration in 1981.

Thousands of black young people have been able to obtain a college education as a result of government scholarship and loan programs. About $9.5 billion in Guaranteed Student Loans (at an annual interest of 8% after graduation) currently aid about 3.8 million low- and moderate-income students, while $873 million in Perkins Loans (at an annual interest of 5% after graduation) currently aid 944,000 students. Moreover, about $700 million currently help 800,000 students under the College Work Study program. However, one of the most important programs for helping large numbers of low-income black students to attend college was the Basic Educational Opportunity Grant (BEOG) program instituted in 1972.

The BEOG or "Pell" grants authorize a maximum award of $1,900 or one-half the cost of attending college (whichever is less) to economically disadvantaged students. About 2.8 million students (about one-third of whom are black) received Pell grants in FY 1985 that averaged $1,230 per award. Prior to the budget cuts of the early 1980s, about half of black college students received Pell grants, leaving only one-tenth having to rely on Guaranteed Student Loans. However, the disproportionate cuts in scholarships have forced many black students either to increase their future indebtedness or to forego college (Jones, 1981). In fact, while the percent of white high school graduates going on to college rose from 51% to 59% between 1975 and 1985, the percentage of black high school graduates going on to college fell from 46% to 42% (Gibbs, 1988).

N. HOUSING POLICIES

Some public and private housing policies have had positive effects on black families; others have had devastating consequences. One of the early government housing policies responsible for opening the suburbs to low-income and middle-income whites, at the same time confining blacks–regardless of income–to central cities, was the Federal Housing Administration (FHA) mortgage program established in 1934, which insures mortgage loans made by private lenders. The lower down payments and easier terms with FHA financing significantly increased home-ownership opportunities for young and working-class families between the 1940s and 1960s. Unfortunately, since FHA procedures have promoted racial discrimination overtly and covertly, black families have been largely restricted to ghettos in central cities, while the "white flight" to the suburbs has been subsidized by white–and black–taxpayers (Newman, et al., 1978).

Working in concert with the government's (effectively racist) housing practices have been the private lenders (i.e., banks, savings and loans associations, and mortgage bankers), speculators, and real estate agents. Financial institutions are mainly responsible for "red-lining"–the refusal to grant home mortgage loans, commercial credit, and insurance for fire, property, and auto to minority families living in designated (or "red-lined") neighborhoods and communities. Although "racial steering" and "blockbusting" have been declared illegal, real estate agents continue to reinforce residential segregation through more subtle techniques. Suburban communities are able to maintain racial segregation through exclusionary zoning, i.e., prohibiting multiple-family homes, apartments, mobile homes, and public housing and reserving large lots for building only single-family homes.

Working-class and poor black families have been displaced from their homes and communities through urban renewal, highway construction, housing abandonment, escalating rents, excessive property taxes, condominium conversions, and gentrification. According to a 1979 HUD report, about 500,000 households (with an over-representation of black families) were displaced each year between 1974-76 (U.S. Housing and Urban Development, 1979). Most studies of black family instability invariably fail to underscore the fact that much of the "pathology" in inner-city ghettos can be traced to public and private disinvestment policies.

Several housing assistance programs have helped working class and poor black families. During the first decade of the public housing program (1937-48), it was mainly restricted to working-class white couples (Leigh and Mitchell, 1980). However, with the inception of federal urban renewal in 1949, displaced single-parent and two-parent black families were given priority on public housing waiting lists. Thus, the proportion of blacks in public housing rose from 38% to 47% between 1952 and 1973 (Newman, et al., 1978). Since the 1.3 million public housing units for 4 million persons comprise only a small fraction (8%) of the 13 million low-income housing units in the United States, they have very long waiting lists.

The Section 8 rental assistance program, instituted in 1974, accounts for 2 million of the 2.6 million private units subsidized by the government in FY 1985. It helps 5 million poor persons obtain decent private housing by subsidizing the portion of rent exceeding 30% of household income. Yet federal housing assistance programs for the poor reach only one-fifth of the eligible households.

Blacks have already been affected by sharp cuts in government housing assistance programs, and they will be more acutely affected as 20-year government contracts expire for 60% of the 600,000 subsidized private units over the next 12-15 years. The current housing shortage is responsible for thousands of poor black families "doubling-up" with relatives and friends, while thousands of other poor black families and individuals live in temporary shelters, hotels, parks, and on the streets. Thus blacks are likely to continue to be overrepresented among the "hidden" and "visible" homeless in the coming decades.

O. PLANT CLOSINGS

Many government trade policies have had adverse effects on black workers and their families. Several studies have revealed that the industries with the largest job losses due to imports have a higher representation of black workers than those industries with the largest job gains due to exports. Thus black men have been disproportionately displaced by imports in the auto, steel, and rubber industries, and black women have been disproportionately displaced by imports in the apparel and textile industries.

While blacks comprise only 7% of the work force in the 20 manufacturing industries that gained the largest number of jobs due to exports between 1964-75, blacks accounted for 11% of the work force in the 20 manufacturing industries that lost the largest number of jobs due to imports. Moreover, while blacks gained 229,000 jobs through exports in 1970, they lost 287,000 jobs because of imports–for a net loss of 58,000 jobs (National Commission for Employment Policy, 1978).

Between January 1979 and January 1984, 11.5 million workers lost jobs because of plant closings or relocation, abolition of positions or shifts, or slack work. The U.S. Bureau of Labor Statistics (BLS) has defined the 5.1 million workers who lost jobs held for at least 3 years as "displaced." Blacks, who accounted for 600, 000 (or 12%) of the 5.1 million displaced workers, were much less likely than whites to be reemployed. While three out of five (63%) displaced white workers were employed by January 1984, only two out of five (42%) displaced black workers were employed. Moreover, black workers (42%) were twice as likely as white workers (23%) to be unemployed by January 1984. Furthermore, about half of all reemployed workers earned less than their income from their prior jobs (Flaim & Sehgal, 1985).

According to Bluestone and Harrison (1982), private disinvestment policies related to plant closings in inner-cities can also structurally discriminate against wage-earners in black families:

> Blacks are especially hard-hit because they are increasingly concentrated within central cities and in those regions of the country where plant closings and economic dislocation have been most pronounced. Moreover, as the number of jobs grew rapidly in the South, whites moved in to take the overwhelming majority of them. How capital mobility can have a discriminatory impact, intentionally or not, is shown clearly. When a laundry located in St. Louis began to decentralize in 1964, its work force was 75% black. By 1975 after it had opened up 13 suburban facilities and reduced its downtown operation, its black work force was down to five percent. (pp. 54-55)

P.   EMPLOYMENT AND TRAINING PROGRAMS

The first comprehensive federal jobs program was the Manpower Development and Training Act (MDTA) of 1962, which was designed initially to provide retraining for adult workers who had been displaced by technological changes or had not recovered from the severe 1960-61 recession. However, as a result of accelerated economic recovery and passage of the "War on Poverty's" Economic Opportunity Act of 1964, racially and economically disadvantaged groups became the primary MDTA populations. The major employment and training programs instituted during the 1960s

51

Framingham State College
Framingham, Massachusetts

were: MDTA classroom (institutional) training, MDTA on-the-job training (OJT), Concentrated Employment Program (CEP), Neighborhood Youth Corps, Job Corps, Summer Youth Program, and Apprenticeship Outreach. The Work Incentive Program (WIH), enacted in 1967, is the only federal jobs program specifically targeted to welfare recipients.

The Comprehensive Employment and Training Act (CETA), the manpower block grant which replaced MDTA in December 1973, was the major jobs program established by the Nixon administration. Its primary emphasis was on Title I (modest funding was also allocated to Title II to provide comprehensive manpower services) to facilitate the employability of the "long-term" unemployed through subsidized public employment. However, because of the deepening 1974-75 recession, Title VI was added to CETA in December 1974 to provide public service employment (PSE) for the "short-term" unemployed. Prior to 1978, there were smaller proportions of black and economically disadvantaged participants in CETA than there had been in the MDTA programs (Mirengoff and Rindler, 1978). However, the Carter administration targeted CETA more on minorities and the poor through its 1978 amendments. In 1982, the Reagan administration eliminated the public service component and absorbed the remaining CETA programs into the Jobs Training Partnership Act (JTPA).

What impact did these federal jobs programs have on breadwinners in black families? In both MDTA and CETA, black adults were more likely than white adults to receive training in programs that led to lower earnings (such as classroom training or work experience) than in programs that led to higher earnings (such as OJT or public employment). For example, blacks comprised 39% of the adults in MDTA-classroom training, but only 28% of the adults in MDTA-on-the-job training. Similarly, blacks accounted for 33% of the adults in CETA-classroom training, but only 25% of the adults in CETA-OJT (Burbridge, 1985-86).

Among blacks and whites, adult trainees reported more significant post-program earnings gains from the MDTA programs than from CETA. In fact, most gains from CETA were insignificant for both black and white men. Although women tended to have greater earnings gains than men in both MDTA and CETA adult programs, white women had somewhat larger earnings gains than black women. Job Corps was the only ongoing MDTA and CETA program in which the gains were greater for males than for females. But even in Job Corps, white youth reported larger post-program earnings than black youth, regardless of sex. Similarly, white women had much larger earnings gains than black women in the WIN program for welfare recipients (Burbridge, 1985-86).

In general, women had larger earnings from the training programs in which they were underrepresented–OJT and Public Service Employment. While black women did somewhat better in CETA-OJT than white women, white women had larger gains in CETA-PSE. The overwhelming majority of women in government jobs programs were trained for "traditional female" occupations. Nevertheless, these programs have enhanced the economic well-being of many women by shifting them from low-paying service jobs to low-paying–but slightly better–clerical jobs that were in high demand (Burbridge, 1985-86).

Female heads of families, especially among blacks, not only are sharply under-represented in most government jobs programs, but are also likely to have the poorest outcomes. According to a recent study of the Job Training Partnership Act (JTPA), minority female family heads comprised only 3% of the total 350,000 persons terminated (i.e., completers and dropouts) during the transition year from October 1983 - June 1984. Most significantly, although black and Hispanic women account for 60% of all poor families headed by women in the nation, they comprised only 14% of the 75,100 JTPA terminees who were single parents (Harper, 1985-86). Overall, AFDC recipients comprise only one-fifth of the JTPA participants. Unless special efforts are made to target training of minority single parents for jobs at livable wages, rhetoric about the need for economic self-sufficiency and drastic welfare reform will continue for decades.

Q. JOBS TAX CREDITS

A major strategy to increase the demand for disadvantaged workers has been to provide wage subsidies in the public and private sectors, mainly through public service employment and on-the-job training. Jobs tax credits are also designed to provide private employers with incentives for hiring minority and low-income workers. The first tax expenditure jobs program was the Work Incentive Tax Credit, enacted as part of the WIN II program in the Revenue Act of 1971. The WIN tax credit tried to help AFDC recipients registered in the WIN program to obtain jobs in the private sector by providing tax credits up to 50% of the first-year wages, up to 25% of the second-year wages, and up to 50% reimbursement for on-the-job training costs. Between FY 1973 and FY 1974, the number of placements in jobs involving WIN tax credit rose from 25,000 to 40,000.

The next major employment tax credit was the Targeted Jobs Tax Credit (TJTC), enacted under the Revenue Act of 1978, which replaced the WIN Tax Credit and the Vocational Rehabilitation Tax Credit when they expired on December 31, 1978. Although the Carter administration originally limited the TJTC to disadvantaged youths, aged 18-24, and cooperative education students, its coverage was broadened widely by the Reagan administration. Consequently, employers can now obtain Targeted Jobs Tax Credits if they hire persons from one of nine groups:
(1) vocational rehabilitation referrals; (2) economically disadvantaged youths aged 18-24; (3) economically disadvantaged Vietnam-era veterans; (4) Supplemental Security Income (SSI) recipients; (5) General Assistance recipients; (6) economically disadvantaged cooperative education students; (7) economically disadvantaged ex-convicts; (8) AFDC recipients and WIN registrants; and (9) economically disadvantaged summer youths aged 16-17.

Evaluations of the Targeted Jobs Tax Credit have found that economically disadvantaged youths aged 18-24 have been its major beneficiaries. In fact, low-income youths accounted for three-fifths of the 622,000 workers qualified for the TJTC in FY 1985. AFDC recipients and WIN registrants were the second largest group of beneficiaries, accounting for 16% of all persons qualifying during FY 1985. Yet, these assessments also reveal that the risk of becoming stigmatized as a welfare recipient, ex-offender, etc., contributes to the underutilization of the TJTC by many disadvantaged workers.

Conservatives and increasing numbers of liberals argue that wage subsidies in the form of subminimum wage differentials are needed to induce businesses to hire more minority youth. Yet the subminimum subsidies that currently exist have failed to markedly increase the hiring of minority youth. Although disadvantaged youths comprise the largest number of TJTC beneficiaries, this tax credit as well as the Subminimum Wage Youth Certificates (instituted in 1961) are still sharply underutilized for hiring black and Hispanic youths. Moreover, the Youth Incentive Entitlement Pilot Project–developed by the Carter administration as a Youth Employment and Demonstration Project Act (YEDPA) experiment in 1977 to test the feasibility of providing various wage subsidies for hiring disadvantaged youth–had very disappointing results.

Eight out of ten firms were still not willing to hire inner-city youths, even when offered 100% wage subsidies. Furthermore, a nationwide survey of employers conducted by the National Urban League's Research Department in 1981 revealed that over half of the firms were not willing to hire more minority youths–whether they were offered wage subsidies of 50%, 75%, or 100% (Hill & Nixon, 1984). In short, firms that were committed to hiring minority youth did so, regardless of the wage subsidy. Increasing evidence demonstrates that subminimum wages are not the panacea for increasing job opportunities for black young people.

R. UNEMPLOYMENT INSURANCE

The Unemployment Insurance (UI) program is another important employment-related policy that is rarely assessed in conventional studies of black Americans. Yet UI has important positive and negative effects on the functioning of black families. Because of the devastating impact of the Great Depression of the 1930s on unemployed workers and their families, Congress enacted UI as an integral component of the landmark Social Security Act of 1935 to provide interim economic support to workers who became involuntarily unemployed. It is an optional federal-state system in which the federal government sets broad minimum criteria for financing and administration and the states determine eligibility and benefit standards. It is primarily financed from employer taxes which are collected by the states and deposited in the U.S. Treasury.

As a result of liberalizing amendments over the years, almost all (97%) wage and salary workers are in jobs covered by unemployment insurance. But coverage and eligibility are not the same. Although many unemployed persons may have worked in occupations or industries covered by UI, unless they were involuntarily separated or laid off, they may still be ineligible for jobless benefits. Three unemployed groups are generally ineligible for UI: (a) workers who voluntarily leave or quit their jobs; (b) persons re-entering the labor force (such as housewives); and (c) persons seeking work for the first time (such as recent school graduates or dropouts). Since blacks are overrepresented among the ineligible categories of the unemployed, they are less likely than whites to qualify for UI benefits.

Yet even being laid off does not automatically qualify one for UI. The involuntary unemployed worker must have worked a "sufficient" number of hours over the last 12 to 18 months and had earnings that were above a specified "minimum" standard to be eligible. Most states require that an unemployed person have sufficient earnings during a "base period" (usually the first 12 months of the last 15 months). Thus, thousands of workers in marginal, seasonal, or irregular employment may be ineligible for UI benefits—even if they have been laid off their jobs—because they are not regarded as having sufficient, regular, and recent attachment to the labor force (Blank & Blinder, 1986). The irregular work histories of many low-income black workers prevent them from qualifying for UI benefits even when laid off.

Even monetarily eligible laid-off workers may not be able to receive unemployment insurance if they have one or more of the following disqualifications: (a) voluntary quitting without good cause; (b) laid off because of misconduct or failure to follow orders; (c) refusal to apply for or accept suitable work without good cause; and (d) unemployment due to a labor dispute or strike. Furthermore, workers receiving UI benefits may be prematurely terminated if they are deemed not to be actively seeking work or to have refused a reasonable offer without good cause. Studies have revealed that blacks are more likely to have UI disqualifications than whites, especially for misconduct (Felder, 1979).

Moreover, black women are more likely than white women to be disqualified for voluntarily quitting related to pregnancy, caring for an ill child or relative, or for poor personal health, since none of these are considered to be "good cause" reasons for quitting a job. Thus, unemployed black women heading families are disproportionately denied jobless benefits because of such structurally discriminatory UI disqualification criteria.

Prior to the 1980s, about half of all unemployed workers and eight out of ten laid-off workers received jobless benefits. However, according to the NUL Black Pulse Survey, only one out of ten (10%) unemployed black household heads were receiving UI benefits in 1979, and 20% had exhausted them. Thus, 70% had never received them. More significantly, over half (56%) of the laid-off unemployed black household heads never received UI benefits, one-fourth (24%) had exhausted them, while only 20% were currently receiving them. However, due to the tightening of UI benefits for long-term unemployed individuals and communities by the Reagan administration in 1981, the proportion of all jobless workers receiving UI plummeted (Blank & Binder, 1986). Consequently, by 1987, only one out of four unemployed workers across the nation received UI benefits.

The decreasing availability of UI benefits for unemployed workers has had devastating effects on their families and has forced many working-class black and white families to resort to welfare–for the first time in their lives. This shift is reflected in the doubling of the number of families receiving AFDC-Unemployment Parent (AFDC-UP) assistance, from 141,000 to 261,000 between 1980 and 1985.

However, despite the fact that black family heads are twice as likely to be unemployed as white family heads, the former are less likely than the latter to be eligible for AFDC-UP benefits. Since AFDC-UP eligibility criteria rely mainly on UI qualifying standards, they disproportionately exclude poor two-parent black families. In short, breadwinners with any UI disqualifications are automatically ineligible for AFDC-UP. Such structural discrimination helps to explain why 40% of poor two-parent white families received AFDC-UP in 1984, compared to only 25% of poor two-parent black families (Hill, 1987b). Although the UI program enhances the economic well-being of the small fraction of unemployed blacks who qualify, it severely destabilizes working-class and poor black families whose breadwinners fail to meet its insensitive eligibility criteria.

S. AFFIRMATIVE ACTION

There is widespread disagreement about the impact of affirmative action policies on the black community. While some scholars (Jones, 1981; Pinkney, 1984) contend that these policies have enhanced equal opportunities for all blacks, others (Wilson, 1987) agree with the conservative position (Glazer, 1975; Loury, 1984) that affirmative action has helped mainly middle-class blacks.

A major reason for the continuing controversy over affirmative action is the inability of proponents and critics to agree on common definitions. Conservatives describe it as "reverse discrimination" against whites to achieve "equal results" for "unqualified" minorities, while liberals describe it as "compensatory" action to achieve "equal opportunities" for "qualified" minorities. Moreover, affirmative action standards are characterized as "quotas" by conservatives and as "goals" and "timetables" by liberals.

Both liberals and conservatives identify redressing past intentional discrimination as the overriding goal of affirmative action, thus underemphasizing the goal of eradicating unintentional discrimination as well. Yet the original Executive Order 11246, issued by President Johnson in 1965, was explicit about combatting current institutionalized discrimination, both intended and unintended:

[Nondiscrimination] requires the elimination of all existing discriminatory conditions whether purposeful or inadvertent. A university contractor must carefully and systematically examine all of its employment policies to be sure that they do not, if implemented as stated, operate to the detriment of any persons on grounds of race, color, religion, sex or national origin...

The premise of the affirmative concept of the Executive Order is that unless positive action is undertaken to overcome the effects of systemic institutional forms of exclusion and discrimination, a benign neutrality in employment practices will tend to perpetuate the *status quo ante* indefinitely. (Pinkney, 1984, p. 157)

Although numerical quotas receive the most widespread publicity, they constitute only a tiny fraction of all affirmative action remedies. The overwhelming majority of measures involve education, moral persuasion, voluntary compliance, negotiation, mediation, guidelines, and timetables. Courts have only required quotas as a *last* resort for employers who have failed to demonstrate good faith efforts to discontinue or redress discriminatory policies.

Moreover, many analyses suggest that working-class, rather than middle-class, blacks have been the major beneficiaries of most affirmative action orders and decrees. First, more black youths from poor and working-class families have been able to attend college as a result of affirmative action than blacks from middle- and upper-class families, since most of the latter would have gone to college anyway. Secondly, the bulk of court-ordered affirmative action decrees have involved back pay and promotion timetables for minority workers who had been confined to *low-wage* blue-collar service and clerical jobs because of discriminatory practices.

Statistical analyses consistently demonstrate that working-class and poor blacks benefited disproportionately from the educational and occupational gains of the 1960s and 1970s. For example, according to a study of occupational mobility of blacks during the 1960s by Levitan, et al. (1975), laborers, agricultural and domestic workers experienced more upgrading than "middle-class" workers:

Although the greatest attention has been focused on blacks moving into the professional, technical and managerial jobs, the more extensive gains during the 1960s came at the lower end of the labor market as blacks moved out of unskilled labor and farm work and into semi-skilled operative and clerical jobs. Upgrading at the bottom affected almost four times as many blacks as the entrance into upper echelon job classifications. (p. 189)

Similarly, Landry (1978) concluded that "over 80% of black middle-class males in both 1962 and 1973 had moved up from class origins lower in the hierarchy (p. 73)." In fact, three out of five (63%) middle-class black men came from either the working class (40%) or "underclass" (23%), compared to only 18% that came from middle-class backgrounds. Moreover, Hill (1981) revealed that black students from working-class and poor families went to college during the 1970s in higher proportions than those from middle-class families. While the proportion of black college students with parents who were high school graduates soared from 21% to 31% between 1970 and 1979, the proportion of students with college-educated parents declined from 26% to 24%. Clearly, Affirmative Action contributed markedly to the growth in the "new" black middle class (Landry, 1987).

On the other hand, many analysts (Jones, 1981; Pinkney, 1984) have revealed a declining commitment to affirmative action by universities, businesses, and the federal government. Consequently, the proportions of black college students enrolled at the undergraduate and graduate levels have steadily declined since the mid-1970s. Other analysts (Palmer & Sawhill, 1984) call attention to sharp cuts made by the Reagan administration in funds for government agencies responsible for enforcing affirmative action policies. Moreover, Burbridge (1986) found that the number of class action suits filed by the federal government plummeted from 326 in 1979-80 to 82 in 1984-85.

VI. IMPACT OF COMMUNITY SUBSYSTEMS

What consequences do various subsystems in the black community have for the functioning of black families? The following features of inner-city communities have a significant adverse impact on black families: persistent high rates of unemployment, crime, delinquency, gang violence, drug abuse, AIDS, and alcohol abuse. On the other hand, there are self-help institutions, such as churches, fraternal groups, voluntary associations, schools, neighborhood groups, and extended family networks that enhance the vitality of black families. We will now examine the negative and positive characteristics of black communities in greater detail.

A. NEGATIVE COMMUNITY INFLUENCES

1. Joblessness

Back-to-back recessions, the exodus of industries, technological shifts, and continuing job discrimination have contributed to depression-level unemployment among black youths and adults. For example, according to the U.S. Labor Department, 13% of all blacks and 36% of black teenagers were unemployed in 1987. Yet the official jobless figures exclude 1.4 million black "discouraged workers" outside the labor force who want to work, and also fail to take into account part-time workers who want full-time jobs. When these excluded groups are incorporated, according to the National Urban League's Hidden Unemployment Index, the jobless rates increase to one out of four for all blacks and to one out of two for black teenagers. Thus in many poverty areas of inner-cities between 30% to 50% of all blacks and 65%-85% of black teenagers who want work are unemployed.

Although joblessness is mainly concentrated among black teenagers, various groups of black adults also have alarming jobless rates. For example, while 12% of black adults were officially unemployed in 1987, black adults had a "hidden" jobless rate of one out of four–the level of unemployment during the Great Depression of the 1930s. Between one-third and one-half of all black adults in poverty areas of inner-cities are, in fact, unemployed.

Moreover, contrary to the popular thesis about the economic superiority of black women, their unemployment rates are often just as high, if not higher, than those of black men. Furthermore, black women who head families have the highest jobless rates of all black adults. While black husbands and wives had official unemployment rates of 6% and 7%, respectively, in 1987, the official jobless rate for black female family heads was more than twice as high (16%). Unofficially, about three out of ten black women heading families are out of work today.

This pervasive joblessness among black adults and youths has devastating ramifications throughout the black community. Not only is persistent unemployment likely to lead to poverty, but since most jobless black breadwinners are not eligible for unemployment benefits, they are often forced to turn to welfare, Moreover, as Brenner (1979) and other researchers (Hagen, 1983; Currie & Skolnick, 1984) have shown, high rates of unemployment are directly associated with high levels of alcoholism, wife abuse, child abuse, family break-ups, mental illness, physical illness, suicides, crime, and imprisonment.

Furthermore, research has revealed that a key contributor to dropout rates among minority youth is the need to work in order to help their unemployed or under-employed parents (Gary, 1981). According to Gibbs (1988), 27% of males and 11% of females who drop out of school do so to work. But the lack of a high school diploma forces many school dropouts to turn to illegal activities, such as numbers running, burglary, selling hot goods, pushing drugs, etc. Several studies have verified the obvious, that school dropouts are more likely to engage in criminal activities than students who remain in school (Viscusi, 1986).

2. Crime

As many classic studies of crime have shown, minorities with the highest rates of unemployment also have the highest rates of crime (Shaw & McKay, 1931, 1942). Consequently, blacks are overrepresented in arrests, convictions, and incarceration. While blacks comprise 12% of the U.S. population, they account for one-fourth of ar-restees and one-half of the state prisoners. This overrepresentation is at least due in part to differential treatment of blacks and whites at every phase of the criminal justice process. Blacks, especially males, are more likely to be stopped, questioned, detained, booted, jailed, convicted, imprisoned, and executed than are whites committing the same or more serious offenses (Marable, 1983).

Such disproportionate rates of arrests, convictions, and incarceration contribute to the formation of black single families. Male criminal offenders are less available as marriage partners. Their police records are major barriers to legitimate employment; their low educational skills preclude them from all but the most menial jobs; their periodic court appearances prevent them from obtaining or maintaining steady work; and incarceration at prison facilities keeps them from their wives and girlfriends for long periods of time.

Since males comprise the overwhelming majority of criminal arrestees and prisoners, the increasing numbers of female offenders are often ignored. The proportion of female arrestees rose from 16% to 17% between 1975 and 1983. Moreover, although blacks comprise 12% of all women in the United States, they account for over half (53% in 1978) of all women in state and federal adult prisons (McGhee, 1984). And female offenders are invariably sent to penitentiaries that are far away from their families. Most incarcerated black women must rely on extended family members to care for their children—those that have not already been placed into foster care.

Blacks are not only overrepresented among criminal offenders, but among the victims as well (Stewart & Scott, 1978). Over half of all murder victims in the United

States are black, and homicide is the leading cause of death among black men between 15 and 44 years old. Black men (64.8 per 100,000 in 1981) are six times more likely than white men (10.4 per 100,000) to die of homicide, while black women are four times more likely to be murdered than white women. And low-income black families have the highest rates of criminal victimization. Although all black households were burglarized at a rate of 115 per 1,000 households in 1978, black families with incomes under $3,000 reported between 129 and 155 burglaries per 1,000 households per year (Marable, 1983).

3. Delinquency

Because of the aging of the baby boom cohort, the proportion of arrestees under age 18 declined from 26% to 17% between 1975 and 1983. But there has been an increase in the proportion of black youths arrested and incarcerated, especially for violent crimes (Woodson, 1981a, 1981b). Although blacks comprise 15% of all juveniles in the United States, they account for 21% of all juvenile arrests (Swan, 1981a). Moreover, they are arrested for one-fourth of the property crimes and half of all the violent crimes committed by juveniles. Between 1960 and 1979, the proportion of blacks arrested for juvenile crimes rose from 19.6% to 21.4% (Gibbs, 1984).

Consequently, most inner-city black youths, especially males, are likely to have had some contact with the criminal justice system (Swan, 1981a). About 15% of all black males between the ages of 15 and 19 were arrested in only one year (1979). Most criminologists contend that about one-fourth (25%) of black men are arrested at least once by age 16. It has been estimated that between 50% and 90% of black male adolescents in poverty areas have arrest or "police contact" records (Fogelson & Hill, 1968).

What is even more alarming is that juvenile crimes are increasing in severity at the same time that the offenders are declining in age. Between 1978 and 1983, the rate of referrals to juvenile courts rose 38% for 12-year-olds, 37% for 13-year-olds, 22% for 11-year-olds, and 15% for 10-year-olds. Part of this increase is attributed to recent efforts by organized crime to recruit younger juveniles to sell and deliver drugs.

Homicide is the second leading cause of death among black youth 15 to 24 years old. More than 2,000 black youths 10 to 19 years old were murdered in 1980, most of them by other black teenagers. In Detroit, an average of one child was shot every day in 1983, and 43 children under age 17 were murdered. While gang activity is responsible for some of this increased youth violence in many cities, much of it also involves individual youths. As Gibbs (1984) observes, "Inner-city neighborhoods are increasingly becoming brutalized by youth who burglarize stores and homes, vandalize schools and churches, and terrorize those who are old, sick and vulnerable (p. 9)." Clearly, black-on-black crime, among both youths and adults, is having devastating effects on the entire black community.

4. Drug Abuse

Drug abuse has plagued the black community for quite some time. According to the 1982 National Survey on Drug Abuse, one-third of both blacks and whites had used drugs illicitly at some point in their lives, and 13% of blacks and 12% of whites indicated they were currently using illicit drugs. According to Client Oriented Data Acquisition Process (CODAP), about one-fourth (23%) of the clients admitted to federally-funded drug abuse treatment centers in 1983 were black. Older black clients (25 years and over) are overrepresented among heroin (92%) and cocaine (69%) users, while younger blacks are overrepresented among marijuana (69%) and PCP (47%) users. Similar patterns hold among whites: older clients are overrepresented among heroin (84%) and cocaine (55%) users, while younger clients are overrepresented among marijuana (76%) and PCP (63%) users (Primm, 1987).

Although black youths 18 to 25 years old have about equal rates of drug abuse as white youth, drug abuse has risen sharply among black youths over the past 20 years. Since 1973, the mortality rate from drug-related deaths has increased markedly in nine major urban areas, with about one-third of those fatalities occurring among black youths 15 to 24 years old (Gibbs, 1984). The increase in drug abuse among black women has led to a sharp rise in births of drug-addicted babies—many of them spending several years in hospitals, especially in New York City, as "boarder" babies.

5. AIDS

The most menacing consequence of extensive drug abuse in inner-cities has been the disproportionate spread of AIDS (Acquired Immune Deficiency Syndrome) among minorities. Blacks constituted 25% of the 24,500 AIDS cases reported in the United States between 1981-1986, while Hispanics comprised 14% (Primm, 1987). Although men account for 90% of the AIDS cases of all races, minority women comprise the overwhelming majority of female AIDS cases. While blacks and Hispanics comprise two out of five (37%) male AIDS patients, they account for 70% of all women who have contracted AIDS. The AIDS disease appears to be transmitted disproportionately among minorities through intravenous drug users and their sexual partners; homosexual or bisexual men with AIDS are disproportionately white.

Minority children have also been hit hard by AIDS. Blacks comprise over half (58%) of the 350 children under 15 years old with AIDS, while Hispanic children account for one-fourth (22%). Black children are 15 times more likely and Hispanic children 9 times more likely than white children to contract AIDS. Most of these children acquire the AIDS disease before or during birth from mothers who were intravenous drug users sharing contaminated needles or whose sex partners were drug users.

Not only are minorities overrepresented among AIDS patients, they are also more likely than white AIDS patients to die from the disease. Blacks account for three out of ten AIDS-related deaths in New York City, where, in contrast to trends at the national level, drug addicts (53%) outnumber homosexual and bisexual men (38%) in AIDS-related deaths. Unfortunately, the number of AIDS cases is expected to spiral among all racial groups in the coming decades. According to Primm (1987), blacks are expected to comprise about 12,000 of the 179,000 AIDS-related deaths predicted to occur in this country by 1991.

6. Alcohol Abuse

Interestingly, among all the "self-destructive" behavior cited in most conventional studies of black families, alcohol abuse is conspicuously omitted. Yet many analysts have found alcoholism to be strongly associated with wife abuse, child abuse, homicides, family break-ups, mental illness, and physical illness in black families (Harper & Dawkins, 1977; Brenner, 1979). Moreover, liquor stores appear to be as numerous as churches in many black communities. Harper (1976) summarizes drinking patterns among blacks as follows:

> Blacks tend to be group drinkers, drinking with friends and relatives as opposed to drinking alone. Blacks tend to drink more frequently and heavily during the weekends. Urban blacks tend to drink more than rural blacks. Black alcoholics tend to be younger than white alcoholics. Blacks tend to either drink heavily or not at all. Fifty-one percent of black women do not drink compared with 39% of white women. However, of the black women who drink, a larger proportion tend to be heavy drinkers.

> Black alcoholics come from various socio-economic backgrounds. There seems to be an association or correlation among problem drinking, health problems and social problems in crowded black communities. Blacks are less likely to view excessive drinking as a disease and slower to confront it as a problem requiring help. Blacks tend to be admitted less frequently to treatment centers than whites (Bell & Evans, 1981, p. 10).

Numerous health problems among blacks have been found to be associated with alcohol abuse (Jones & Rice, 1987). For example, while the rate of cirrhosis mortality is twice as high among black men as it is among white men nationally, in some urban areas the rates are 3 to 12 times higher than for white men. Moreover, the rate of cancer of the esophagus among black men 35 to 49 years old–which is closely linked to alcohol consumption and smoking–is several times higher than among comparable-aged white men.

Despite the severe destabilization in black families resulting from alcoholism, there appears to be no sense of urgency on the part of black leadership to develop comprehensive strategies to effectively combat this disease. Some contributors (Harper,

1976) contend that the financial contributions to black leaders and organizations from the liquor industry may be mainly responsible for this inaction.

B.   SELF-HELP INSTITUTIONS

There is currently widespread debate about the relative merits of self-help and government aid as viable strategies for improving the social and economic conditions of the black community. The question of self-improvement has faced blacks consistently from slavery to the present time. In fact, less than three decades after Emancipation, DuBois (1908) noted, "It is often asked, 'What is the Negro doing to help himself after a quarter century of outside aid?'"

DuBois conducted a large-scale survey of black self-help organizations to provide an empirical base for an 1898 Atlanta Conference on the topic, "Some Efforts of American Negroes for Their Own Social Betterment." The research findings and proceedings of that gathering were published as the third volume in the Atlanta University Publication Series. This monograph revealed that the black community has a distinguished tradition of self-help, especially among free blacks in the North and South, during and after 250 years of slavery. Moreover, DuBois (1896-1917) updated his surveys of black self-help groups and published his findings in subsequent monographs, notably, "Economic Cooperation Among Negro Americans" (1907) and "Efforts for Social Betterment Among Negro Americans" (1909). However, there have been few comprehensive studies of black self-help on a national scale. Notable among those that have been conducted are Inabel Lindsay's Ph.D monograph, "The Participation of Negroes in the Establishment of Welfare Services, 1865-1900," (1952) and Edyth Ross's book, *Black Heritage in Social Welfare Services, 1860-1930*, (1978).

A recent monograph that has contributed significantly toward underscoring how important self-help institutions are is "To Empower People" by Berger and Neuhaus (1977). According to these analysts, nongovernment support systems serve as "mediating structures" to help individuals and families to cope with and counteract adverse societal forces and social policies. These mediating structures include both formal organizations (such as churches, private schools, voluntary associations) and informal subsystems (such as social clubs, neighborhood groups, peers, friends, and extended family networks).

Numerous studies have found that mediating structures provide the bulk of the services received daily by most individuals and families. During a crisis, the overwhelming majority of black people are more likely to turn to members of their informal support network (such as relatives or friends) before turning to members of formal support systems (such as social workers, doctors, lawyers, etc). For example, since 85% of black teenage mothers live in three-generational households with their own parents, most of the social and economic support they receive each day is provided by their immediate family–and not by welfare agencies. We will now examine the impact of self-help institutions on black families.

1. Black Churches

The black church continues to be a major force in the lives of the overwhelming majority of black people in America. According to a Gallup survey conducted in 1984, three-fourths (74%) of black adults belong to churches, compared to two-thirds (68%) of white adults. And, according to the NUL Black Pulse, two-thirds of black adults attend church each week (48%) or several times a month (19%). Moreover, seven out of ten black parents send their children regularly to Sunday school. The Protestant denominations influence the lives of eight out of ten blacks, most of whom are either Baptists (56%) or Methodists (13%). Furthermore, while only 6% of all blacks are Catholics, about 5% of black parents–many of whom are not Catholics–send their children to parochial schools.

The overwhelming majority of blacks have positive attitudes toward the black church. According to the National Survey of Black Americans (Taylor, et al., 1987), eight out of ten blacks think that black churches have helped the condition of black Americans, while only 5% think they have hurt them and 12% think they have made no difference. While low-income blacks (86%) are somewhat more likely than middle-income blacks (80%) to have positive attitudes toward the church, the college-educated (85%) and those with less than a high-school education (85%) are equally likely to think the black church has been helpful to blacks. Moreover, elderly blacks (93%) are much more likely to have favorable attitudes toward the church than young adults aged 18 to 25 (76%).

A survey of 21 black churches in the Washington, D.C., area, conducted by Howard University's Institute for Urban Affairs and Research (Brown & Walters, 1979), reported the following: (a) two-thirds of the church members were women; (b) about half were married, 25% were single, and 20% were widowed or divorced; (c) almost half were over 50 years old (44%), one-third were between the ages of 31 to 50 (32%), and one-fourth were under 31 years old (24%); (d) over half had post-secondary education (29%) or were college graduates (27%), one-fourth were high school graduates, and one-fifth had less than a high school education; (e) their median annual income was $8,000, with 21% having incomes under $5,000, and 13% over $20,000; and (f) half of them were homeowners.

Two-thirds of the church member respondents had belonged to their churches for over 10 years, while less than one-tenth had been members less than a year. The primary reasons that they gave for attending church were: satisfying spiritual needs (72%), personal involvement and satisfaction (57%), spiritual doctrine of the church (53%), and the leadership of the pastor (50%). Although most church members felt that the primary mission of the church was spiritual, over nine out of ten felt that it should also be involved in community action and providing social services.

A sample of residents in the neighborhood of the churches were also interviewed to obtain their perceptions about the churches and their role in the community. Although over half of the residents belonged to some church, only one-tenth belonged to

the church in the study sample. Two-thirds of the residents were only slightly familiar with the church, with 14% not knowing about the church at all. Four out of five
residents were not aware of the church's involvement in specific community-related
activities. While three out of ten felt the church was involved in community leadership, four out of ten felt they were not involved (Brown & Walters, 1979).

When DuBois conducted his pioneering studies of black self-help about a century ago, a major social welfare function of black churches was to provide economic
protection to families, especially to widows and orphans, during crises brought on by
sickness and death. Many black benevolent societies and black businesses, particularly in the fields of insurance and banking, grew out of the savings plans and clubs
launched by the early black churches. Due to the widespread availability of life insurance today–from both black and white firms–most black churches no longer have
to play major roles in providing such protections.

Black churches currently provide a wide range of social services directed toward
strengthening families and enhancing positive development of children and youth.
Many of the founding churches still provide vital services to the black community,
such as New York City's Mother AME Zion, Abyssinian Baptist, St. Phillips Protestant Episcopal, Concord Baptist, and Bridge St. AWME; Chicago's Bethel AME and
Olivet Baptist; Petersburg's, Guilfield Baptist (Virginia); Detroit's Second Baptist,
and many others. To combat the deterioration of black families, increasing numbers
of black churches have set up Quality of Life Centers to address the needs of all family members from a holistic perspective. One of the most prominent centers is the
Shiloh Family Life Center of Shiloh Baptist Church in Washington, D.C. Some of the
comprehensive services provided by such centers include day care, preschool programs, nurseries, parenting, family counseling, remedial education, family planning,
drug abuse prevention, employment training, and recreational activities (Alexander,
1987; Brown & Walters, 1979).

Because of the persistent difficulty in attracting and retaining men, numerous
black churches have adopted aggressive efforts to reach adolescent males. United
Methodist Church in Chicago has established Big Brother/Male Mentors programs to
provide positive male role models, especially for young men growing up in female-
headed families. Others, like Union Temple Baptist Church in Washington, D.C.,
have a broad array of activities to appeal to young black males, including formalized
rites of passage to prepare them adequately for the transition to manhood and responsible fatherhood. Many Pentecostal and Christian Charismatic churches also have
effective programs for increasing the participation of black young males in productive pursuits. While such programs specifically targeted to unchurched young men
are relatively new, black churches across the nation have many other programs that
assist adult and adolescent women, especially those who head families.

Assistance to orphans and homeless children has been a historic concern of
black churches. Most of the early black orphanages were founded by black religious
institutions. Recently, the disproportionate numbers of black children under foster
care have alarmed many black ministers. The adoption of two adolescent males in

1980 by a black Catholic priest, Father George Clements of Holy Angels Church in Chicago, dramatized the plight of black children in foster care. Because of the widespread concern that his actions aroused, Father Clements founded the "One Church, One Child" program, in which each black church would make a commitment to the adoption of at least one black child by a member of that congregation. This program has been so successful that it is being replicated across the country. For example, a group called "Ministers for Adoption" has been set up in Jackson, Mississippi, and a consortium of black ministers in Virginia has launched an aggressive statewide adoption campaign under the slogan, "Claiming Our Own."

The declining availability of affordable housing in the black community has stimulated black churches throughout the nation to build housing complexes for low-income families and senior citizens. Examples of such churches include: Allen Temple Baptist Church in Oakland, California, Wheat Street Baptist Church in Atlanta, Georgia, Church of the Good Shepherd Congregational in Chicago, Antioch Missionary Baptist Church in Chicago, and United House of Prayer for All People in Washington, D.C.

To revitalize entire neighborhoods, black churches have formed community development corporations to stimulate the growth of black businesses as well as to increase the stock of affordable housing. For example, Zion Investment Corporation (ZIC), a development arm of Zion Baptist Church in Philadelphia, has built a shopping center and created small businesses in such areas as construction, real estate, and wiring. And Zion's 23-year-old Opportunities Industrialization Center (OIC)–founded by its pastor, Rev. Leon Sullivan–is a nationally-acclaimed employment program that has trained over 750,000 low-income residents for a wide variety of jobs. Similarly, in Washington, D.C., the United House of Prayer for All People has constructed McCullough Plaza–a huge complex of housing developments, shopping facilities and small businesses. The St. John Community Development Corporation, set up by St. John Baptist Church, is revitalizing Miami's Overtown section–a low-income community that has been devastated by periodic waves of rioting during the 1980s. Moreover, Allen AME Church in Jamaica, New York, has established a housing corporation, a 300-unit senior citizens complex, a 480-pupil elementary school, a health service facility, and a home care agency for the elderly and handicapped (Alexander, 1987).

To insure more effective use of the mammoth resources of the black church, often referred to as "the sleeping giant," the seven historic black denominations agreed to form the Congress of National Black Churches (CNBC) under the direction of Bishop John Hurst Adams in 1978. CNBC has started up an impressive array of activities in such areas as church leadership development, economic and community development, and the strengthening of black families (Alexander, 1987).

2. Fraternal Organizations

As DuBois' studies of self-help revealed, fraternal societies have played a major role in providing vital support to black families. Initially, these societies were mainly concerned with providing economic protection during sickness and death. Consequently, they set up burial and insurance mutual aid plans. They also established orphanages and nursing homes. Presently, most secret fraternal societies place major emphasis on educational excellence and on the economic development of inner-city communities.

Although fraternal organizations on black colleges continue to be criticized for placing undue emphasis on socializing, more and more of them are rendering important services to low-income blacks. For example, in 1984, Delta Sigma Theta Sorority launched Summit II, a comprehensive campaign to assist black single mothers through the nationwide network of Deltas. Similarly, Alpha Phi Alpha Fraternity formed "Project Alpha" to provide positive male role models for black adolescent males being reared in single-parent families. Zeta Phi Beta Sorority launched "Stork's Nest" to promote proper prenatal care to pregnant and nonpregnant adolescent females in inner-cities and "Project Zeta," a nationwide drug abuse prevention program. And "Project Assurance" was established by Sigma Gamma Rho Sorority to provide a broad range of important health and nutrition information to black children and their parents.

3. Voluntary Associations

Black voluntary associations have traditionally provided major services to the black community. And women's clubs, as DuBois noted, have been in the vanguard of such efforts. These groups set up orphanages, nursing homes, nursery schools, elementary schools, hospitals, and businesses. During World War I, for example, to counteract neglect of black servicemen, black women's clubs set up their own "Black Red Cross" across the nation. Over the years, women's organizations have placed major emphasis on strengthening black families, enhancing the development of black children and youth, and improving the social and economic well-being of black women.

National black women's self-help groups that perform important functions for the black community include National Council of Negro Women, National Association of Negro Business and Professional Women's Clubs, National Black Nurses Association, Jack and Jill of America, the Girl Friends, the Links, National Hook-Up of Black Women, the Coalition of Black Women, and the National Black Women's Health Project. On September 13, 1986, the National Council of Negro Women sponsored the first national Black Family Reunion Celebration, where more than 250,000 people gathered in the nation's capital to attend workshops and obtain information about strategies they might adopt to strengthen black families in their communities.

Vital assistance to black individuals and families has also been provided by numerous black national organizations that specialize in social welfare. The oldest and largest of these groups is the National Urban League, which was founded by black and white social workers in New York City in 1910. Since its inception, the NUL has facilitated the training of black social workers across the nation, enhanced scholastic achievement through numerous educational initiatives, increased job opportunities for thousands of low-income and middle-income blacks, increased housing options for blacks, and provided a broad array of social and economic services to blacks in need.

To mobilize the resources of black national organizations to address the crisis confronting black families, the National Urban League and the NACCP co-sponsored the Black Family Summit at Fisk University from May 3-5, 1984. Over those three days, more than 100 black organizational representatives developed a comprehensive agenda for strengthening black families. Subsequently, spin-off summit conferences on black families have been held by coalitions of black organizations at the state, county, and city levels.

The National Urban League currently has several programs to prevent adolescent pregnancy and to provide vital support to unwed adolescent parents. It has also launched a nationally-acclaimed media campaign to encourage greater responsibility on the part of adolescent males in their sexual relations with adolescent females. Many innovative programs in these and related areas are being implemented by Urban League affiliates in more than 100 cities. For example, comprehensive Black Family Resource Centers have been set up by UL affiliates in Baltimore, Maryland, and Columbus, Ohio. And special programs targeted to single black adolescent mothers and fathers are underway in UL affiliates in Chicago, Albany, and in many other cities. Other national black organizations that provide important services to black children and their families include National Black Child Development Institute, National Caucus and Center on Black Aged, National Association of Black Social Workers, and National Association for the Southern Poor.

4. Private Education

The poor quality of education in many inner-city public schools has spurred numerous self-help groups to develop a broad range of strategies to enhance the educational attainment and employability of black young people. One such strategy has resulted in a surge in the number of black independent schools. One of the most widely-acclaimed private black schools is Westside Preparatory in Chicago, founded by Marva Collins. Other exemplary independent black schools include Provident St. Mel in Chicago, the Chad School in Newark, N.J., Ivy Leaf School in Philadelphia, Lower Eastside International Community School in New York City, Randall Hyland in Washington, D.C., Red School House in St. Paul, Minn., and the W.E.B. DuBois Academic Institute in Los Angeles. Because of the mushrooming of these schools, national networks have been formed to enhance their collective influence, such as the

Council of Independent Black Institutions (CIBI) and the Institute for Independent Education.

To provide quality education to the "pushouts" of public schools, the New York Urban League established the Street Academy and Harlem Prep in Harlem during the late 1960s. By providing a broad range of supportive services (such as counseling, child care, and vocational training) these "academies of the street" have helped hundreds of black youth not only complete high school, but to go on to college as well. Street academies have been set up throughout the nation, in Washington, Oakland, Detroit, and South Bend, to name but a few. Some of these programs have been so successful that they have been "adopted" by local school systems, such as in Washington and in New York City.

One of the most innovative educational programs for black youth, developed by public housing residents, is "College Here We Come." This initiative was launched in 1974 by Kimi Gray and other residents of the Kenilworth-Parkside public housing complex in southeast Washington, D.C. Its goal was to raise the educational and occupational horizons and attainment of young people residing in public housing. By providing a broad range of social and economic support, this effort enabled more than 600 low-income youth to attend college. During semester breaks, these students would return home to serve as positive role models for other public housing youth. Other innovative grassroots programs to enhance the educational capabilities of black youth were developed by such groups as Complex Associates in Washington, D.C., Glenville Community Center in Cleveland, Urban Youth Action (UYA) in Pittsburgh, and the W.E.B. DuBois Learning Center in Kansas City.

Another self-help institution in the black community that is still a lifeline for thousands of black youths and their families is the Historically Black College (HBC) (National Advisory Committee on Black Higher Education and Black Colleges and Universities, 1980). Although only 17% of black college students attend these institutions, HBCs accounted for two-fifths (38%) of all baccalaureate degrees conferred on blacks in 1975-76, 22% of the master's degrees, 4% of the doctorates, and 20% of the professional degrees. Recent studies have revealed that black students in HBCs are more successful academically and socially than are black students attending other colleges. While 70% of blacks in HBCs complete their studies, 70% of blacks in other colleges drop out.

Despite the positive impact of HBCs on black upward mobility, some policymakers contend that these institutions have outlived their usefulness as separate entities and must be merged with white institutions or phased out. Indeed, such mergers and closings have been proceeding at a rapidly increasing pace (Swan, 1981b), and this dissipation of historically black institutions has consequences not only for black students and their families but for the entire nation as well.

5. Neighborhood Groups

Neighborhood self-help groups–not affiliated with national voluntary organizations–have become increasingly significant in addressing many of the social and economic ills afflicting low-income blacks. According to a 1981 self-help survey, two out of five black adults contribute money to self-help groups in the black community and one out of four actually participate in such groups (Evaxx, 1981). As might be expected, somewhat higher proportions of middle-income blacks (42%) than low-income blacks (32%) contribute money to self-help efforts. Similarly, middle-income blacks (31%) are more likely than low-income blacks (24%) to become involved in such activities. Nevertheless, contrary to popular belief, between one-fourth to one-third of low-income blacks contribute their time or money to grassroots efforts to improve conditions in their communities. This sizable participation of poor blacks in helping themselves is reflected in the sharp increase in the number of indigenous groups in inner-cities over the past two decades. These grassroots groups perform vital functions in strengthening families, facilitating adoption and foster care, reducing anti-social behavior, enhancing education and employment skills, promoting businesses, and developing the community.

One exemplary grassroots effort is the Sisterhood of Black Single Mothers, founded by Daphne Busby in the Bedford-Stuyvesant section of Brooklyn. Since its inception in 1973, the Sisterhood has demonstrated that the circumstances of low-income single mothers can be improved significantly by addressing their needs from a holistic perspective, by enhancing their sense of self-worth, and by developing their skills in such areas as parenting, male-female relations, education, and employment. To increase the involvement of unwed fathers in raising their children, the Sisterhood recently helped form the Black Fatherhood Collective. The House of Imagene, founded by Rev. Imagene Stewart in Washington, D.C., was one of the first shelters established for abused black women in this nation. The People's Busing Program in Cleveland maintains contacts between prisoners (both male and female) and their families by providing low-cost transportation to correctional institutions throughout Ohio. Other effective family-strengthening neighborhood groups include Baltimore Family Life Center, Teen Father Program in Cleveland, Teenage Parents Program (TAP) in Westchester, Pennsylvania, James E. Scott Community Association in Miami, and Parents and Youth on Family Functioning (PAYOFF) in Washington, D.C. (U.S. Executive Office of the President, 1986).

A nationally-recognized grassroots initiative in the field of adoption and foster care is Homes for Black Children (HBC), founded by Sydney Duncan in Detroit during the late 1960s. Alarmed by the large numbers of black children growing up in foster care, HBC was determined to demonstrate that there were more than enough families in the black community that were willing and able to provide wholesome environments for children who needed homes. Over a ten-year span, HBC found adoptive homes for over 700 black children. Spin-offs of HBC in other cities have also succeeded in finding black homes for black children. Mother Clara Hale founded Hale

71

House in Harlem which, since 1969, has provided interim care for over 500 children until their mothers were rehabilitated from alcohol or drugs. The Adopt-a-Family Endowment was founded by Dr. James Mays, a black politician in Los Angeles, to provide surrogate extended family support to troubled one-parent and two-parent black families. This successful program is being implemented in Washington, D.C. (e.g., by Lincoln Congregational Temple) and in many other cities.

A major objective of many neighborhood groups has been the reduction of gang violence and youth crime. An internationally-acclaimed self-help group in this connection is the House of Umoja, which was founded by Sister Falaka Fattah and her husband, David, in Philadelphia during the late 1960s. The Fattahs used the African extended family concept to provide constructive alternatives to gang violence. Umoja channeled the energies of former gang members to productive endeavors, such as helping to build Urban Boys Town, one of the largest community-based residential facilities for troubled black youth in this nation, and creating a variety of youth-operated small businesses. Other indigenous groups that have succeeded in reducing youth crime and gang violence are Inner-City Roundtable of Youth (ICRY) in New York City, Family Helpline in Los Angeles, Youth in Action (YIA) in Chester, Pa., and SAY YES–Youth Enterprise Society in Los Angeles (Woodson, 1981a, 1981b).

Neighborhood groups are using a variety of innovative strategies for the positive development of inner-city black youth. SIMBA ("Young Lion" in Swahili) is a comprehensive male socialization program developed by Jawanza Kunjufu (1984, 1985, 1986a, 1986b) to prepare black boys between the ages of 7 and 19 for the rites of passage to responsible manhood. SIMBA provides positive black adult male role models, develops life skills, enhances ethnic and cultural identity, and promotes healthy male-female relationships. Such programs have been formed by neighborhood groups in many cities, notably in Cleveland (the East End Neighborhood House) and in Chicago. The "Responsible African-American Men United in Spirit" (RAA-MUS) program was developed by Dr. Kenneth Ghee in Cincinnati to provide positive socialization for young black males. Other groups with programs for the development of black children and youth are Midtown Youth Academy, the Institute for Urban Living, and RAP, Inc., in Washington, D.C., International Youth Organization (IYO) in Newark, the Mustard Seed Learning Center in Harlem, the Berkeley Academy for Youth Development in California, and Concerned Black Men in Washington, D.C., Philadelphia, and several other cities.

To increase the stock of affordable housing for poor families, neighborhood groups have adopted many strategies. One popular approach is "sweat equity," through which low-income families handle down payments or lack of credit through their own labor. By participating in the construction or rehabilitation of their homes, low-income people build up equity credits which are used in lieu of cash, for down payments or towards the purchase price. Self-help housing efforts have been successfully implemented by urban and rural groups such as Jubilee Housing in Washington, D.C., Delta Housing Development Corporation in Indianola, Mississippi, the S.E. Alabama Self-Help Association (SEASHA) at Tuskegee Institute, Alabama, and

Flanner House Homes in Indianapolis. Other grassroots groups that have successfully converted declining neighborhoods and communities into thriving ones include Operation Better Block (OBB) in Pittsburgh, Eastside Community Investments (ECI) in Indianapolis, and Collinwood Community Service Center in Cleveland.

Some of the most spectacular accomplishments in community revitalization have occurred in public housing. Several resident management corporations have demonstrated that they can maintain safe, pleasant, and comfortable living environments more efficiently and cost-effectively than local public housing authorities. For example, after three years of tenant management in Kenilworth-Parkside in Washington, D.C., there were sharp declines in vandalism, welfare dependency, school dropouts, teenage pregnancy, and unemployment. Over the same period building repairs and rent collections rose sharply. Other successful resident management initiatives include Bromly-Heath in Jamaica Plains, Massachusetts, Cochran Gardens in St. Louis, B.W. Cooper in New Orleans, and A. Harry Moore Houses in Jersey City, New Jersey. One key to their success is the establishment of numerous resident-operated small businesses in such areas as maintenance, day care, laundry, tailoring, barbering, beauty care, catering, and thrift shops. Resident management provides firm behavioral and maintenance standards for residents and enhances the residents self-esteem and sense of personal efficacy by encouraging tenant involvement (Woodson, 1987).

Many grassroots groups are convinced that the conditions in black communities will not improve significantly until comprehensive economic development takes place. Some of the neighborhood organizations that have succeeded in developing businesses in low-income communities are Business Opportunities System (BOS) in Indianapolis, Bedford-Stuyvesant Restoration Corporation in Brooklyn, South Arsenal Neighborhood Development Corporation (SAND) in Hartford, and Jeff-Vander-Lou in St. Louis.

Increasing numbers of neighborhood groups focus on enhancing the entrepreneurial skills of minority youth. For example, the Educational Training and Enterprise Center in Camden, N.J., has helped hundreds of youths to create businesses in such areas as food vending and janitorial services. Several national organizations provide invaluable technical assistance to self-help groups in minority neighborhoods, notably the National Center of Neighborhood Enterprise (NCNE), founded by Robert L. Woodson, and the National Association of Neighborhoods (NAN), under the direction of Stephen Glaude, both of which are based in Washington, D.C.

6. Informal Support Networks

The continuing significance of informal support networks in the functioning of black families was documented by numerous studies during the 1970s and 1980s. Research by historians such as Genovese (1974), Gutman (1976), and Blassingame (1972), found mutual aid networks to be vital for the survival and advancement of black people during and after slavery. Moreover, studies by urban ethnographers such as Ashenbrenner (1973), Stack (1974), and Martin and Martin (1978) revealed that those mutual exchange systems were of special importance to low-income black families living in urban and rural communities during the 1970s.

These rich insights about black informal support patterns, drawn from historical and ethnographic research, were reinforced by surveys conducted at the national and local levels during the 1980s. One survey with national-level data on such patterns was the National Survey of Black Americans (NSBA) conducted in 1979-80 by the Institute for Social Research's Survey Research center at the University of Michigan. The NSBA comprised a nationally-representative sample of 2,100 blacks aged 18 years and over. The Black Pulse Survey conducted in 1979-80 by the National Urban League's Research Department was the second survey with national data on social support networks among blacks. The Black Pulse comprised a national cross-section of 3,000 heads of black households. Local surveys with in-depth data on informal support patterns among blacks were conducted by McAdoo (1981, 1983), Malson (1980, 1983a) and Howard University's Institute for Urban Affairs and Research (Gary, et al., 1980, 1984).

The findings from these surveys reinforced one another, whether they were conducted at the national or local levels. For example, all of these studies revealed that blacks lived in close proximity to most of their kin. Eighty-six percent of the respondents in the Black Pulse Survey reported that they had relatives living in the same city (but not in their households), compared to 80% of the respondents in the NSBA (Hill, 1981; Taylor, 1986). And, in McAdoo's 1983 study, 86% of the single black mothers had relatives living within 30 miles.

Not only do most blacks live close to their kin, they also have very frequent contact. Three-fourths of the Black Pulse respondents visited their relatives daily (39%) or several times a week (36%). Two-thirds of the NSBA respondents visited their relatives daily (37%) or several times a week (28%). Three-fifths of the single mothers in McAdoo's study visited their relatives at least several times a week.

Eight out of ten blacks in the NSBA survey indicated that they received some support from their kinship network (Taylor, 1986). What kind of support did they receive? According to the Black Pulse Survey, money (33%), child care (27%), and transportation (26%) were the most prevalent forms of support received. In McAdoo's 1983 study, emotional help, child care, and financial help were seen as the three most important categories of help.

According to ethnographic studies, such as Stack's (1974), "what goes 'round, comes 'round." To what extent do the survey data reveal patterns of reciprocity? The Black Pulse Survey documents extensive mutual exchange. Money (23%), transportation (21%), and child care (17%), were also the most frequent forms of aid provided to relatives (Hill, 1981). Similarly, McAdoo's study found emotional help, child care, and financial help to be the most frequent forms of assistance provided to relatives. The Howard University study (Gary, et al., 1984) found more reciprocity when advice or help other than money was exchanged.

There continues to be widespread disagreement as to whether mutual aid networks are compensatory mechanisms for those in economic need. According to one thesis, low-income blacks are more likely than middle-income blacks to have closer ties to kin and to belong to informal support networks. The findings from all of these surveys strongly contradict the compensatory thesis. Not only are middle-income blacks just as likely as poor blacks to have contact with kin, but they are also just as likely to receive assistance.

For example, 88% of middle-income blacks ($20,000 and over) in the NCBA survey reported receiving help from kin, compared to 74% of low-income blacks (under $5,000). And middle-income blacks ($20,000 and over) in the Black Pulse survey were just as likely (88%) as low-income blacks to receive child care help from kin. Moreover, although low-income blacks (24%) were somewhat more likely than middle-income blacks (19%) to receive money from kin, the differences were not statistically significant.

It should be understood, however, that many of the relatives that are part of the mutual aid networks are "fictive kin," that is, nonrelatives who are as close as, and sometimes closer than, blood relatives. For example, Malson (1983a) observes:

> The absorption of non-kin into the existing familial structure has long been an attribute of black life. These persons are usually referred to as "play sisters" or "cousins" to communicate the closeness of the relationship. Like other studies, McAdoo (1981) found that 71% of the subjects in her study had relationships with fictive kin. They took the roles of sisters, brothers, aunts, and uncles. (p. 42)

Fictive kin may also include nonrelated friends who have performed as mothers, fathers, grandparents, aunts, uncles, sisters, and brothers (Aschenbrenner, 1973; Stack, 1974; Martin & Martin, 1978). Some fictive kin are designated as godparents as well. Thus black extended families extend, in fact, to many nonrelatives as well as relatives. While half of the single mothers in McAdoo's study cited relatives as their "significant others," one out of three also mentioned friends. Manns (1981) has revealed that nonrelated "significant others" may hold such positions as teachers, scout leaders, playground instructors, ministers, etc., as part of informal support systems.

Contrary to the popular view of the "isolated" elderly, many studies reveal that the black aged are integral parts of black informal support networks (Hill, 1978b; Taylor, 1985). The black elderly are more likely to take others into their households than to live in the households of younger relatives. Only about 4% of black families headed by persons under age 65 have elderly persons living with them. Yet one out of three black families headed by women aged 65 years and over have informally adopted children, compared to only one out of ten white families headed by elderly women (Hill, 1981).

Moreover, according to the NSBA survey, not only did most black elderly live near kin, but two-thirds of them that needed help reported receiving it (Taylor, 1985).

Proximity to kin and having living children were important determinants of receiving help. Eight out of ten black aged who lived close to relatives received support from them, compared to only about half of those who lived far distances from kin. And three-fourths of black aged with living children received support, compared to only two-fifths of those without any children. On the other hand, low-income black elderly (under $3,000) were more likely *not* to receive support from kin than were middle-income elderly ($10,000), 40% to 29%.

VII. IMPACT OF FAMILY SUBSYSTEMS

The overwhelming majority of studies of black families have concentrated on the extent to which family characteristics–primarily structure and social class–enhance or detract from the well-being of black families. As Billingsley (1970, 1973) and other scholars (Herzog, 1970; Staples, 1971a) have noted, the focus on family structure has been dichotomous–one-parent or two-parent. The broad range of extended and augmented configurations in black families has been largely ignored in conventional analyses of black families. Similarly, the focus on social class has also been dichotomous–either "underclass" or "middle class." This simplistic dichotomy obscures the importance of understanding conditions among the black "working class"–the plurality of black families who are neither "middle class" nor "underclass."

Effective policies and strategies for aiding the black "underclass" will not be forthcoming until a fundamental understanding of the circumstances and dynamics of the black "working class" and "middle class" is achieved. Such policies will also require a proper understanding of the contemporary role of African-American cultural patterns. In short, there is a need for policy researchers to concentrate on the complex interactions among structure, class, and culture in the functioning of low-income and middle-income black families today.

A.   FAMILY FUNCTIONING

A widespread deficiency of most research on black families is the failure to clearly define and make operational the concept of family "functioning." Although three types of family functions–instrumental, expressive, and instrumental-expressive–were identified by Billingsley (1968), most conventional studies have ignored those distinctions and continue to (1) equate structure with functioning, (i.e., generalize about functioning based solely on family structure), (2) assume the homogeneity of functioning, (i.e., assume that inadequate functioning in one domain is generalizable to other domains), and (3) use static characteristics to generalize about dynamic processes.

1.   Equation with Family Structure

This practice involves generalizations about family "stability" or "instability" based solely on family headship. One-parent families are arbitrarily assumed to be "broken" and "unstable," while two-parent families are arbitrarily assumed to be "intact" and "stable," without providing for any independent assessment of the stability or cohesion of each type of family. Having one or two parents only describes the headship of that family; it does not describe how well that family functions in various domains. Since about one out of every two marriages today ends in divorce, it is obvious that thousands of two-parent families are not as "stable" or "intact" as is commonly believed. In fact, many studies have revealed that, in some areas, one-parent families function as effectively, and sometimes more effectively, as many two-parent families (Kellam, et al., 1977; Hill, 1981).

2. Assumption of Functional Homogeneity

There is an assumption that functioning is a homogeneous entity, that inadequate functioning in one domain affects other domains. It is often reflected in the assumption that because the incomes of single-parent families are usually much lower than those of two-parent families, the former are also deficient in all noneconomic areas as well, including child-rearing. But the family functioning is not unitary, it is multi-dimensional. There are many areas of functioning and most of them can vary independently from one another. Thus one must clearly specify the various domains that are being discussed and assess systematically the adequacy of functioning in each of them.

Geismar (1973) is one of the few analysts to assess empirically and systematically the functioning of black families. He developed a scale of family functioning that comprised eight major domains: (1) family unity and relationships; (2) individual behavior and adjustment; (3) care and training of children; (4) economic practices; (5) home and household practices; (6) health conditions and practices; (7) social activities; and (8) use of community resources. Measures of the adequacy of functioning were derived in each of the eight areas and correlated with various family characteristics, such as headship and social class. Geismar found that many low-income black families that functioned inadequately in some areas, such as economic practices, functioned very well in many other areas, such as child care and family relationships. Geismar's study was pioneering in another respect—it was longitudinal and thus was able to assess changes in various areas of black family functioning at different points in time.

3. Use of Static Characteristics

Unlike Geismar's life-cycle approach, most traditional studies of black families examine the issue of functioning from a static perspective. Descriptions of black family characteristics for one point in time are used to generalize about the adequacy or inadequacy of functioning at other points in time. This is the fundamental weakness in the critique of Billingsley's family typology by Williams and Stockton (1973) in their innovative assessment of the correlation between family structures and functions (instrumental, expressive, and instrumental-expressive). Williams and Stockton concluded that they found no evidence of "resiliency" among certain single-parent family structures, especially the extended attenuated households, since they ranked lower on functioning than two-parent families. However, since the concept of "resiliency" is dynamic and refers to functioning at more than one point in time, the cross-sectional data used by Williams and Stockton were inappropriate for such a test.

In fact, several research findings based on longitudinal data reinforce Billingsley's hypothesis of resilience. For example, Geismar (1973) found that poor families with low levels of economic functioning at the outset of the study showed greater economic gains five years later than low-income families that initially had high levels of economic functioning. A panel study by Kellam, et al., (1977) revealed that black children reared in three-generational households headed by their grandmothers (i.e., extended-attenuated) had as strong positive social-psychological outcomes ten years later as children reared in two-parent families.

This fallacy is most frequently manifested in generalizations about "long-term" or "inter-generational" welfare dependency that are based on data about the receipt of public assistance by single-parents at *one* point in time. Such inferences are usually derived without obtaining any data about the length of time that the family has currently been on welfare, whether the family had any prior experience with welfare, and the extent to which the family was dependent on welfare, (i.e., whether income from public assistance comprised over half of its total income). The 15-year Panel Study of Income Dynamics (Duncan, 1984) found no empirical evidence for extensive "inter-generational" welfare recipiency among poor families.

B. FAMILY STRENGTHS

In order to properly assess the functioning of black families, it is necessary to study their strengths as well as their weaknesses. Billingsley (1968) considered such traits as "religion, education, money or property, jobs, family ties, and other community-centered activities. . .(as) the chief ingredients of strong family life" (p. 98). Hill (1971) identified five factors that have been responsible for the survival, stability, and advancement of black families: strong kinship bonds, strong work orientation, adaptability of family roles, strong achievement orientation, and strong religious orientation.

To determine which attributes the black community identified as constituting family strengths, Royce and Turner (1980) interviewed a random sample of 128 blacks in Dayton, Ohio. Although their findings tended to confirm the strengths already identified by black scholars, other strengths were cited as well: teaching children to respect themselves, teaching children how to be happy, stressing cooperation in the family, and disciplining children. Moreover, a study conducted by Christopherson (1979) of rural blacks in Oklahoma cited this list of strengths: a love for children, a general acceptance of children born out-of-wedlock, and a resilience which allowed them to cope with negative forces that impact upon the family (Gary, Beatty & Berry, 1985).

One of the most comprehensive studies of strong black families was conducted by Howard University's Institute for Urban Affairs and Research. One key objective of the investigators (Gary, et al., 1983) was to identify factors that contribute to strong black family life. Fifty families, nominated as "strong" by groups in the Washington, D.C., area, comprised the study's sample—half were married couples and the remaining half were female-headed. The two attributes that were most often cited by the respondents—regardless of family structure—as common strengths of black families were family unity and religious orientation. Other strengths cited were love, effective coping strategies, support, and sharing responsibilities.

C. FAMILY STRUCTURE

Since most research on black and white families is based on the U.S. Census Bureau's definition of "family," it is important to examine the major dimensions of that classification. First, the bureau clearly distinguishes between "households" and "families." A household comprises "all related and unrelated persons who reside in the same dwelling unit." Consequently, a household may consist of one or more families. A family is defined as "a group of two or more persons living together in a household who are related by blood, marriage or adoption." "Primary families" are those in which one of the members is a household head, while "secondary families" (or "subfamilies") are those in which none of the members are household heads. According to this official definition, all three of the following characteristics are required to constitute a family:

- *Co-residence*—only related members who live in the same household. Kin living in separate households are not classified as part of the same family;

- *Minimum Size*—at least two related co-residents. Prior to 1947, one-person households were classified as "families."

- *Formal Kin Ties*—the co-residents must be formally related by blood, marriage, or adoption.

Billingsley (1968) used the Census Bureau's core definitions to derive three basic types of family households: (a) *Nuclear Families*—households comprising primary families with no other related or unrelated co-residents; (b) *Extended Families*—households in which at least one related child or adult lives with a nuclear family; (c) *Augmented Families*—households in which at least one unrelated child or adult lives with a nuclear family.

In order to underscore the diversity of structures among black families, Billingsley expanded each of the three core family types—nuclear, extended, and augmented—into three subgroups: (1) "incipient," households, comprising married couples with no children of their own; (2) "simple" (nuclear) households, comprising married couples with their own children; and (3) "attenuated" households, with single parents with their own children. Secondly, he added three combinations involving augmented families: incipient extended augmented, nuclear extended augmented, and attenuated extended augmented. These classifications yielded 32 types of black family structures.

The prevalence of extended family households increased among blacks during the 1970s while remaining unchanged among whites. The proportion of blacks living in extended family households rose from 23% to 28% between 1970 and 1980, while it remained at 11% among whites (Allen, 1979; Allen & Farley, 1986). Moreover, based on Billingsley's typology, Payton (1982) found that only half of all black single-parent households consisted solely of mothers and their own children, and that three out of ten black women heading families were rearing children other than their own. However, as Williams and Stockton (1973) observed, by using the Census Bureau definitions as its building blocks, Billingsley's typology omits a common residential type–children living in households headed by single relatives such as grandmothers or aunts. Johnson's (1934) comment about this family structure, written over 50 years ago, is applicable today: "The numbers of households with old women as heads and large numbers of children, although of irregular structure, is sufficiently important to be classed as a type" (p. 37).

Yet, another major contribution of Billingsley's typology is its life-cycle perspective. It underscores the fact the researchers must examine changes in various areas of family functioning, from the early stages of their life-cycle (incipient nuclear: newly-weds with no children), to the intermediate (simple nuclear: couples with children), to later stages (attenuated nuclear: single parents with children).

D. FAMILY CULTURE

1. Abuse of Culture Concept

Another concept that is widely distorted in most discussions of black families is that of culture. A fundamental problem is the widespread use of this term as synonymous with "society" and "class." This intermingling of concepts has resulted in general failure among Americans to recognize African cultural patterns among blacks, and in general acceptance of the term, "culture of poverty," as an operational definition of blacks that lumps all three–culture, society, and class–together.

a. **African Cultural Patterns.** Historically, there has been a continuing debate between two schools of thought: (1) Frazier's (1931, 1939) perspective, which holds that blacks in America have no distinctive culture of their own because 250 years of slavery virtually destroyed all vestiges of African culture, and (2) Herskovits' (1941) perspective, which holds that African survivals continue to influence American blacks. Herskovits argues strongly against the view that American blacks have no African cultural legacies:

> . . .a caution is in order concerning the degree of purity assumed to exist in the African traits to be reviewed. . . .Negroes in the United States are not Africans,

but they are the descendants of Africans. There is no more theoretical support for an hypothesis that they have retained nothing of the culture of their African forebears, than for supposing that they have remained completely African in their behavior (p. 145).

Numerous contemporary scholars (Young, 1970; Blassingame, 1972; Genovese, 1974; Gutman, 1976; Shimkin, et al., 1978; Sudarkasa, 1980) find Africanisms in many aspects of black life, such as the extended family, child-rearing patterns, religion, language, music, art, rituals, nutrition, health, etc. Nevertheless, it is the Frazierian perspective that is widely-accepted by American social scientists today. It is reflected in assertions by Glazer and Moynihan (1963) that "the Negro is only an American and nothing else. He has no values or culture to protect" (Blauner, 1970, p. 132).

   b. **Culture of Poverty.** The alleged absence of a distinctive culture among blacks leads to the explanation of black lifestyles in terms of class or socio-economic position (Berger, 1970). Consequently, the values and behavioral patterns of middle-class blacks are said to reflect those of middle-class white Americans, while the values and behaviors of poor blacks are said to be manifestations of an "underclass culture of poverty." Although this was coined by Oscar Lewis (1959) based on his studies of the rural poor in Mexico and Puerto Rico, it has been adopted by contemporary proponents of "underclass culture" among inner-city minorities.

   According to this thesis, the economic deprivation of the "underclass" is self-perpetuated by an extensive array of negative and "self-destructive" lifestyle (such as female-headed families, welfare dependency, lack of work ethic, negative self-concept, etc.) that is handed down from generation to generation. In short, poverty is intergenerationally transmitted as a cultural "way of life," rather than as a result of contemporary forces such as racism, classism, and sexism. Thus, the "culture of poverty" notion leads back to the "blaming the victim" syndrome of the deficit model.

   A basic flaw in the culture of poverty thesis is its failure to distinguish clearly between "situational adaptations" that are reactions to contemporary circumstances and "historical adaptations" that are proactive cultural patterns transmitted inter-generationally through socialization. It is to the latter that Valentine (1968) refers when he states that the concept of "culture" has been used by many anthropologists to refer to positive "formulas for living" that help groups to survive and advance—regardless of the specific contemporary circumstances. Slaughter and McWorter (1985) also underscore the importance of this distinction:

   In an otherwise informative volume, Martin and Martin's (1978) study of extended black families continues to espouse the idea that blacks lost their African heritage through slavery. The black extended family was viewed, not as a construction within the context of the African-American experience, but as a self-help or survival unit generated by an ahistoric group of people living in a rural or agricultural setting.

The distinction we make is important. If the black extended family is an American adaptation of a long-standing African tradition, then clear cultural links to the diaspora are implied and can be expected to continue. This would occur because of a people's thrust for cultural continuity, even in a changed geographical setting (i.e., urban by comparison to rural). If it is merely a self-help or survival unit, then the black extended family will wane in scope and influence in accordance with any societal change which heralds significant social and economic improvements for black people. (p. 16)

Boykin and Toms (1985) not only provide a useful conceptual framework for synthesizing the competing views of culture, but also facilitate the development of an operational definition of African-American culture. These scholars (1985) contend that "African-Americans simultaneously negotiate three distinctively different realms of experience. . .mainstream, minority and black cultural" (p. 38). Mainstream culture refers to the values, norms, and behavioral patterns of white society; minority culture refers to the adaptations that minorities make in reaction to racism and oppression; and black culture refers to the proactive and positive cultural continuities that are transmitted explicitly and implicitly through socialization from generation to generation–regardless of contemporary circumstances.

2. African Concept of Family

Comparative research on family patterns among West Africans and black Americans by anthropologists reveals that conventional definitions of American families differ markedly from the West African concept of family in the significance attached to three dimensions: co-residence, formal kinship relations, and nuclear families.

   a. Co-residence. The African concept of family is not restricted to persons living in the same household but includes key persons living in separate households. Contrary to the popular belief that most families are "isolated" from kin, numerous studies have shown that the overwhelming majority of black Americans live in close proximity to kin. As already indicated, 85% of all blacks have relatives that live in the same city but in separate households. These studies have also revealed the importance of interhousehold networks for enhancing the social and economic functioning of black families, especially those headed by women.

   b. Formal Kin Relations. The African concept of family is not confined to relations between formal kin, but includes networks of unrelated as well as related persons living in separate households. Although most instances of "informal adoption" and "informal foster care" among black families involve the rearing of related children by grandparents, uncles, aunts, and other formal kin, thousands of black children are also being informally reared by nonrelated godparents, "grannies," etc., who are as close as, or closer than, formal kin.

Since the Census Bureau does not define individuals living with nonrelatives ("fictive kin") as comprising families, children in informal or formal foster care families are excluded from the official statistics on families. For example, in the 1970 census, 434,000 (black and white) children under age 18 who lived in the households of nonrelatives were classified as "not in families"–a convention that continues to be used in census publications. Thus, the requirement that individuals be formally related to one another to constitute families results in a sharp misunderstating of the actual extent of persons living in family settings.

   c.   **Nuclear Families.** Herskovits (1941) observes that the African "nuclear" family unit is not as central to its family organization as is the case for European nuclear families: "The African immediate family, consisting of a father, his wives, and their children, is but a part of a larger unit. This immediate family is generally recognized by Africanists as belonging to a local relationship group termed the "extended family" (p. 182). According to Sudarkasa (1975), unlike the European extended family in which the conjugally-based family (i.e., husband, wife, and children) is the basic building block, the African extended family is organized around consanguineal relations (blood) rather than conjugal relations (marital). Consequently, Sudarkasa (1980, 1975) urges a reformulation of the classic dichotomy between nuclear families and kinship networks:

> The question of the relationship between consanguinity and conjugality in black families is not to be broached in terms of the prevalence of one *or* the other. . . .it becomes apparent that the old debate (enjoined most recently by Gutman) as to whether historically blacks lived mostly in one-parent or two-parent families requires reformulation. Virtually all of Gutman's extraordinary data should be evaluated from another perspective. He was concerned with proving the antiquity of "the nuclear family" among blacks; this he considered to have been accomplished by his abundant documentation of the stability of conjugal unions over time.

> From the data we presented on African families, it should be clear that stable conjugal unions are not to be taken as necessary indicators of the prevalence of nuclear families of the Western type. What is crucial to investigate are the ways in which and the extent to which the conjugally-based groupings described by Gutman were embedded in or articulated with the wider kin networks also described by him (1980, p. 55). . . .

> When this fact is understood, it becomes clear that the instability of conjugal relations cannot be taken as the sole measure of the instability of the family. That black families exhibit considerable stability over time and space is evidenced by the enduring linkages and bonds of mutual obligations found among networks of consanguineal kin (1975, p. 238).

84

3. Extended Family Networks

Many scholars (Nobles, 1974a, 1974b; Shimkin & Uchendu, 1978; King, 1976; Foster, 1983) have documented African cultural continuities in the extended family networks of black Americans. For example, King (1976) observes:

> The Afro-American extended family tends to follow the pattern of African extended families and include all of the relatives, both legal and biological. The black family is not to be confused with that concept of family which limits it to only the biological parents. The extended family in Black America, as in Africa, has given black people much security in times of need.

Harvey (1985b) also emphasizes the importance of kin networks:

> The deep sense of kinship has historically been one of the strongest forces in traditional African life. Kinship is the mechanism which regulates social relationships between people in a given community; almost all of the concepts pertaining to and connected with human relationships can be understood and interpreted through the kinship system. (p. 13)

Sudarkasa (1980) further underscores these continuities:

> As a student of continental African societies, it is not surprising to me that contemporary writings on Afro-American history, most notably those of Blassingame (1972), Genovese (1974) and Gutnan (1976), reveal the presence of African patterns in Afro-American consanguineal kin groupings ("kin networks"), husband-wife relations, sibling bonds, socialization practices, patterns of exogamy, marriage rules and rituals, naming practices, relationships between alternate generations (i.e., grandparents and grandchildren), patterns of respect and deference, and the extension of kinship terminology to elders throughout the community (p. 52).

Some writers (Pleck, 1979) contend that extended family networks are a hindrance to upward mobility among blacks. Consequently, middle-class blacks are reputed to be less involved in kin networks than lower-class blacks. To empirically test this thesis, McAdoo (1981) conducted an in-depth study of middle-income blacks living in urban and suburban areas of Washington, D.C., and reached these conclusions:

> The hypothesis that families would be involved in the kin-help exchange network, even after obtaining middle-class status status, was supported: Parents indicated an extensive and intensive involvement with the network. The ma-

jority tended to live within 30 miles of their family members, a fact that facilitated interaction. . . .

Family members were seen as the most important source of outside help. Eighty percent of the families had a reciprocal involvement with their kin. They gave and received help with child care, financial aid and emotional support. The reciprocal obligations that were involved with the support network were not felt to be excessive and were part of everyday life. . . .

The examination of upwardly mobile patterns in black families has indicated that the education and achievement of the individuals were often impossible without the support of the extended family. . . .The continuation of the extended family support systems reflects continued cultural patterns, and is a factor of the vulnerability of the black middle class. . . .The kin support network is still as essential now as it was in earlier generations, for it involves cultural patterns that were created and retained from earlier times that are still functional and supportive of black family life (pp. 163, 167).

McAdoo's findings are reinforced by results from national surveys, such as the National Survey of Black Americans (Taylor, 1986) and the NUL Black Pulse Survey (Hill, 1981). Those surveys consistently reveal middle-class blacks to be as active, and sometime more active, in kinship networks as are low-income blacks. Thus, further empirical support is provided for the notion of cultural continuities that cut across social class.

4. Child-Centered

Another attribute of contemporary black families that has been characterized as part of an African legacy is the importance attached to children. Nobles (1974b) observes that it is "deeply rooted in our African heritage and philosophical orientation which. . .places a special value on children because they represent the continuity of life" (p. 15). And Kenyatta (1983) asserts:

I hold very strongly that black families are neither patriarchal nor matriarchal nor even matrifocal *per se*. Rather, the black family is best understood as child-centered, as oriented toward reproduction and sustenance of black life in the context of a racist society, mindful of the genocidal potential of the dominant culture. (pp. 20-21)

King (1976) also underscores this emphasis on children.

If one considers that every child in the black community belongs to the entire black community, then it will be easier to grasp the importance Black Americans give to black children. How often has one heard that black women have too many illegitimate babies? How often has one heard that black women should be forced to practice birth control? What such questions overlook is the fact that in the black community there is no such thing as an illegitimate child. The children are loved and cared for by the entire community.

The greater reluctance of black woman to have abortions compared to white women has been attributed to a cultural legacy that values children highly–whether in wedlock or out of wedlock. Moreover, the steadily increasing informal adoption of black children reinforces this cultural continuity (Foster, 1983). Between 1970 and 1979, the number of black children living in the households of relatives jumped from 1.3 million to 1.4 million, raising the proportion of informally adopted black children from 13% to 15% (Hill, 1981).

To understand the contemporary magnitude of informal adoption, it should be noted that only 10% (100,000) of the one million black children living in families without their parents today are in formal foster care homes. Consequently, the black extended family network has succeeded in finding informal adoptive homes for 90% (900,000) of them. Put another way, black extended families place nine times more black children in homes than do foster care and adoption agencies. Yet these agencies are more likely to "screen out" such families as formal adoptive families, despite the fact that the lowest rates of child abuse are found among informally adopted children (Hill, 1977).

The disproportionately lower rates of child abuse among black families relative to white families in the same socio-economic status also suggests a cultural legacy of high evaluation of children. Billingsley (1973) highlighted this pattern as follows:

It is not generally appreciated, for example, that child neglect and abuse are much more common in white families than in black families. Child neglect is much more common among lower-class white families than among lower-class black families. Child abuse is much more likely to occur in white families than in black families who live in similar, or even worse, economic circumstances. (p. 310)

Although black families are overrepresented in the official statistics of child abuse and neglect, national surveys have consistently revealed relatively low incidences of child abuse among blacks. For example, a national survey conducted in 1979-80 by the National Center on Child Abuse and Neglect (1981) found as follows:

In general, incidence rates seem to be about the same for white and nonwhite children. For white children, incidence rates for all forms of maltreatment were much higher in low-income groups than in the higher income groups. For non-white children, incidence rates for neglect were higher in low-income groups and incidence rates for abuse were low and constant across income levels. (p. 2)

Billingsley and Giovannoni (1972) found the degree of church involvement to be inversely correlated with the risk of child abuse:

> Although the church is a formal community structure, church activities often bring members into closer informal contacts. This was so of many of the women, particularly the black mothers who reported attending church functions other than worship service. In general, the adequate mothers were much more engaged with the church than were the less adequate. The church was probably a source of support to these women, and possibly an untapped resource of assistance for neglectful parents. (p. 201)

This child-centeredness is also reflected in the extensive social and economic assistance provided to unwed adolescent black mothers by kin network (Ladner, 1971; Stack, 1974; McAdoo, 1983). Based on five-year follow-up data on unwed black teenage mothers in Baltimore, Furstenberg (1981) concluded, "Adolescents who remained with their parents were more likely to advance educationally and economically than their peers who left home before or immediately after their child was born" (p. 141).

Other studies (Geismar, 1973; Stewart, 1981a, 1982) have also revealed that unwed adolescent mothers who continue to be assisted by kinship networks are more likely to complete high school, go to college, hold steady jobs, and not have to rely on welfare than teenage mothers who are separated or isolated from their parents and other relatives. For example, Stewart (1981b) found that mothers in extended family households are more likely to go to school and to work than young mothers in nonextended households.

5. Bicultural Socialization

Many scholars (Dixon & Foster, 1971; Valentine, 1971; Lewis, 1975; Hale-Benson, 1982; Pinderhughes, 1982; Boykin & Toms, 1985) contend that African cultural residues are transmitted inter-generationally by Black Americans through bicultural socialization. Such patterns of dual socialization facilitate the acculturation of blacks to mainstream and African-American cultural patterns simultaneously. DuBois (1903) highlighted this duality in the following classic statement:

> The Negro is a sort of seventh son, born with a veil, and gifted with second-sight in this American world—a world which yields him no true self-consciousness, but only lets him see himself through the revelation of the other world. . . .One ever feels his two-ness—an American, a Negro; two souls, two thoughts; two unreconciled strivings; two warring ideals in one dark body, whose dogged strength alone keeps it from being torn asunder.

According to many scholars, biculturation helps to explain the consistency of differences between blacks and whites regarding family organization, fertility patterns, child-rearing, learning styles, linguistic patterns, religious behavior, funeral rituals, nutrition, song, and dance. However, as Boykin and Toms (1985) note, African continuities are often transmitted unconsciously by black Americans as traditional or habitual values, beliefs, behaviors, and customs:

Of course we cannot rule out that black cultural values or beliefs are overtly taught per se. But if and when it happens, it typically is done without awareness that they are embedded within a comprehensive cultural complex of West African origins. . . .This, then, is a tacit socialization process. Tacit because, for all intents and purposes, black parents typically are unaware that they are transmitting cultural styles or even cultural values. (p. 42)

Yet, not all black families have the same ability to provide bicultural socialization (DeAnda, 1984). Pinderhughes (1982) observes:

Some Afro-American families are comfortable with biculturality; they are unusually strong, flexible, tolerant of ambiguity, and creative in dealing with the American and victim systems. Other Afro-American families are not comfortable with biculturality; for them, dealing with the two different values systems creates a conflict in values and a confusion about identity. (p. 94)

Increasingly, research (Dixon & Foster, 1971; Hale-Benson, 1982) demonstrates that bicultural socialization is facilitated among blacks because of the African cultural capacity to synthesize opposites or polarities. Lewis (1975) states the position as follows:

The Afro-American cultural orientation, the bringing together of polarities, stands in direct contrast to the Euro-American concern with dualities. Mainstream culture is understood in the setting up of linguistic, analytic, and moral dichotomies, such as subject/object; mind/body; good/bad; sacred/profane, etc. Afro-American culture, however, is characterized by unity and synthesis. Lerone Bennett (1964) notes that the black tradition affirms that good and bad, creative and destructive, wise and foolish, up and down, are in separable facets of existence. Therefore these polarities are not conceptualized as dichotomies. He finds that the existential unity expressed in "good is bad," is in conflict with the Euro-American dichotomy, "either good or bad." (pp. 225-226)

6. Role Flexibility

Black families have been found to manifest much flexibility and fluidity in such areas as household composition, marital relations, division of family roles, role of

89

women, and child-rearing. Stack (1974) underscores the elasticity of black families regarding child-rearing:

> People in The Flats often regard child-keeping as part of the flux and elasticity of residence. The expansion and contraction of households, and the successive recombinations of kinsmen residing together, require adults to care for the children residing in their household. As households shift, rights and responsibilities with regard to children are shared. Those women and men who temporarily assume the kinship obligations to care for a child, fostering the child indefinitely, acquire the major cluster of rights and duties ideally associated with "parenthood." (p. 62)

The disproportionate rearing of children by elderly black women reflects the greater role flexibility in aged black households than aged white households. Only one out of ten white families headed by women 65 years and over are rearing children today, compared to one out of three black families headed by elderly women. Although Herskovits, Sudarkasa and other scholars caution that the female-headed black family in America is not an African cultural pattern—since men were vested with the dominant authority in African family units and networks—the economic role of black women has been cited as an "African cultural legacy of role flexibility." For example, Herskovits (1941) contends:

> The open-air market is the effective agent in the retail distributive process, and business, as in West Africa, is principally in the hands of women. It is customary for them to handle the family resources, and their economic independence as traders makes for their personal independence, something which, within the family, gives them power such as is denied to women who, in accordance with the prevalent European custom, are dependent upon their husbands for support. (p. 180)

Numerous studies (Hyman & Reed, 1969; Jackson, 1971; Stone & Schlamp, 1971) have consistently found much flexibility and sharing of family roles among black men and women. Black women are more likely than white women to be breadwinners and black men are more likely than white men to perform household chores. Lewis (1975) attributes this flexibility to less sex-specific socialization patterns for male and female black children:

> In the community Young (1970) studies there is, from a Euro-American perspective, a remarkable degree of overlap in the behavior considered appropriate for men and women. Behavior which is associated with the male role in Euro-American culture is associated with both males and females in this community. For example, females as well as males are viewed as individualistic and nonconforming in their behavior. Both husband and wife have authority in the

home; both are responsible for the economic support of the family; both take the initiative in forming and breaking up a marriage and both may find separation to their advantage. . . .(pp. 229-230)

An examination of socialization patterns in the families studied by Young reveals the process by which children learn not only that certain traits are equally important for males and females, but that factors other than sex are a crucial basis of differential treatment and expectations of behavior.

We have already noted that black child-rearing techniques instill in both male and female infants similar traits of assertiveness, willfulness, and independence.

7. Religious Orientation

There appears to be much consensus that, if there is any area in which African cultural continuities are manifested by black Americans, it is regarding religious beliefs and behavior (Mbiti, 1970; Wimberly, 1979; Swan, 1981b; Harvey, 1985a; Sernett, 1985). Herskovits (1941) devoted an entire chapter to summarizing research related to "Africanisms in Religious Life." According to DuBois (1903), "The Negro Church of to-day is the social centre of Negro life in the United States and the most characteristic expression of African character" (p. 213).

Some of the religious expressions of black Americans that were identified by Herskovits as African residues include the hypnotic influence of the minister, the nature of sermons, belief in the supernatural, audience participation, hand-clapping, foot-tapping, the rhythm of songs, spirituals, dance, shouting, possession by spirits, body movements during possession, baptism by total immersion, voodooism, revivals, faith healing, and funeral rituals. Harvey (1985b) identified African survivals in black Christian churches as manifested in the role of the minister, rituals of holy communion, the symbol of the cross, the symbol of the snake, the black ministerial robe, the call and response, the singing of spirituals, shouting, and possession by the spirit.

Lewis (1955) provides a broader context for understanding various manifestations of spirituality among blacks:

To merely say "the Negro is deeply religious" is to be guilty of a bland oversimplification that obscures a wide variety of meanings and activities. . . . Salvation and forgiveness–the rewards of the Christian or of the 'saved'–are the central themes in local religion. . . .Religion is something of a reservoir; it is individually tapped and allowed to flow when needed or when ritual or the customary rhythm of life so demand. . . .

Within this general framework there are many belief and action patterns; characteristic variations are related to age, sex, denominations, and individual differences. In religious worship and ritual some persons and groups are active and highly emotional; others are restrained and passive. . . .

Religion appears to be a much more important aspect of the thought and behavior of older people. . . .To a large extent, church activities are oriented around the interests, support, and participation of these older people; effective control is in their hands. (pp. 131, 133)

In the past, most observations about the nature and degree of religiosity among blacks were mainly qualitative. However, over the past decade there has been an impressive array of empirical investigations of religious patterns among blacks at the national and local level (Nelson & Nelson, 1975; Sasaki, 1979; Brown & Walters, 1979; McAdoo, 1983; Taylor, 1986; Taylor, et al., 1987).

Once again, at the national level, findings from the NUL Black Pulse Survey and the University of Michigan's National Survey of Black Americans (NSBA) reinforce each other. According to the NSBA (Taylor, 1988), two-thirds of all blacks are church members, with 71% attending weekly (40%) or several times a month (31%). Based on the Black Pulse, three-fourths of blacks (76%) belong to churches, with 67% attending weekly (48%) or several times a month (19%). Furthermore, two-thirds of all blacks are either Baptists (56%) or Methodists (13%); 6% are Catholics.

Most studies comparing religious patterns between racial groups have usually found blacks to have higher levels of religiosity than whites. For example, Sasaki (1979) found blacks more likely than whites to: pray frequently, attend church, attach importance to their religious beliefs, have had a religious experience, have been "born again," feel the Bible is the word of God, and believe that God sends misfortunes as punishment for sins. The compensatory thesis has been the predominant explanation for the higher degree of religiosity among blacks relative to Whites (Taylor, 1988). Consequently, low-income blacks are expected to have higher levels of religious participation than middle-income blacks, since the former are more isolated from mainstream white institutions than the latter.

However, findings from several recent surveys tend to contradict the compensatory explanation. For example, according to the Black Pulse Survey, middle-income blacks were somewhat *more* likely than low-income blacks to belong to churches (75% vs. 71%) and to attend church each week (48% vs. 44%)–although the differences were not statistically significant. Similarly, the NSBA survey failed to find statistically significant differentiation between income and church membership or church attendance (Taylor, 1988). The NSBA survey went beyond traditional measures of religious participation to inquire about such practices as praying, reading the Bible, listening to religious programs on radio, watching religious programs on TV, and asking others to pray for them. Even these religious activities failed to yield statistically significant relationships with income.

Moreover, contrary to the compensatory thesis, levels of religious participation tended to be *higher* among better-educated and better-paid blacks, and among married as opposed to formerly or never-married blacks. (Taylor, 1988). Introducing another factor, the degree of religious participation increased with age. These findings suggest that the nature of religiosity among blacks is complex and cannot be adequately accounted for by traditional social class explanations. Thus, the significance of cultural determinants that cut across class strata needs to be more fully explored.

Since the black elderly are the most effective transmitters of cultural patterns, further insights might be obtained by examining their religious patterns. Based on the NSBA, Taylor (1986) focused on a sample of 581 blacks aged 55 years and over. In addition to obtaining data on church membership and church attendance, he also used a measure of "subjective religiosity," i.e., "How religious would you say you are—very religious, fairly religious, not too religious or not religious at all?"

Once again, contrary to the compensatory thesis, neither income nor education were significantly related to any of the three measures of religiosity. The strongest predictors were gender and marital status. Elderly women were more religious than elderly men and the currently married were more religious than the formerly or never married. However, religious participation was not related to health disabilities nor to the advancing age of the elderly–findings that suggest strong cultural underpinnings of religiosity among the black aged.

McAdoo's study (1983) of single black mothers provides further insights concerning the religious patterns of formerly or never-married women. Nine out of ten (94%) considered themselves to be very (19%) or fairly (75%) religious. One out of three (35%) attended religious services at least several times a month, while about half (52%) attended church only a few times a year (37%) or never (15%). Although most of them did not attend church frequently, three-fourths (72%) prayed frequently, while one-fourth (25%) prayed sometimes. Moreover, socioeconomic status was positively related to religiosity: middle-class mothers (27%) were more likely to be very religious than working-class mothers (16%) and grade-school educated mothers (30%) were more likely not to feel religious at all than high-school educated (3%) and college-educated mothers (6%).

8. Ethnic Subcultures

Another major deficiency of conventional studies of black families is the assumption of ethnic homogeneity. Most research investigations omit the broad range of cultural diversity among blacks from different states, regions, and countries. For example, despite the large-scale northern migration of blacks from the South since the early 1900s, there have been few comparative analyses of subcultural variations between northern and southern blacks.

When southern black newcomers to the North have been the focus of inquiry, their "culturally deficient" lifestyles have been blamed for the surge in rioting (McCone Commission, 1965; Fogelson & Hill, 1968), welfare dependency, unemployment, and female-headed families among northern blacks (Glazer & Moynihan, 1963; Lemann, 1986). However, the few systematic studies in this area reveal that southern-born blacks in the North have higher levels of employment, earnings, family income, and two-parent families than northern-born blacks (Long, 1974). Valentine (1971, p. 140) identified the following 14 subcultures among blacks in the United States:

A. Afro-English:

   1. Northern-urban U.S. blacks
   2. Southern-rural U.S. blacks
   3. Anglo-African West Indians
   4. Guyanese
   5. Surinam Takitaki
   6. West Africans

B. Afro-French:

   7. Haitian Creoles
   8. Other French West Indians
   9. French Guianans
   10. Louisiana Creoles

C. Afro-Spanish:

   11. Black Cubans
   12. A-B-C Islander *Papiamento*
   13. Panamanians
   14. Black South Americans

Most studies of immigration to the United States do not take account of blacks because of the widespread belief that virtually all blacks came to America as slaves. Despite the fact that persons of African descent comprise sizable proportions of the population of many Latin American countries (DuBois, 1915; Toplin, 1974)–e.g. Cuba, Puerto Rico, the Dominican Republic, Brazil, Venezuela, Panama, Colombia–Hispanic immigration is depicted as overwhelmingly "nonblack." Popular assertions that "Hispanics will soon outnumber blacks" imply–incorrectly–that blacks account for an insignificant fraction of the Hispanics immigrating to the United States. There is much support for Bryce-Laporte's (1973) contention that black immigrants are doubly victimized, as blacks and as black foreigners:

The black immigrant is perhaps the least visible. . . .On the one hand, as blacks, their demands and protests as a constituent group receive the same basic disregard and neglect that the larger society and its leaders display toward the efforts of native Black Americans to improve their positions in American society. . . . [T]heir cultural impact as *foreigners* has generally been ignored or barely mentioned in American social and cultural history. The point is that they suffer double invisibility on the national level–as blacks *per se* and as black foreigners as well. (p. 44)

This "invisibility" of black immigrants is reinforced by U.S. Census Bureau practices that obscure or understate their real numbers. First of all, census publications provide information on country of birth for white immigrants but not for black immigrants. Secondly, the 1980 census only has data for first-generation immigrants–whether white or black. Consequently, according to the 1980 census, the number of foreign-born blacks in the United States is 816,000 or 3% of the total black population. In prior censuses, data were also available for second-generation immigrants–American-born persons whose parents were born abroad. However, since West Indian blacks have been immigrating to the United States since the early 1900s, even data on both the first and second generations would continue to understate the actual number of blacks of Caribbean origin in the United States.

In order to obtain more accurate national-level data on Caribbean blacks, the National Urban League's Research Department placed an ethnic origins question directed to Caribbeans on its Black Pulse Survey of a nationally representative sample of 3,000 black households in the fall and winter of 1979: "Are you of West Indian or other Caribbean descent?" The Black Pulse Survey obtained the same proportion (3%) of foreign-born blacks as did the 1980 census. But it also revealed that 10% of the blacks in the United States–not 2% or 3%–were of Caribbean descent. Consequently, Hill (1983b) estimated that the Caribbean black population in the United States is actually about 2.5 million–more than three times larger than their numbers in the 1980 census. Three-fourths of these Caribbean blacks live in the state of New York.

Moreover, as Bryce-Laporte also observed, on the few occasions that American social scientists (Glazer & Moynihan, 1963; Sowell, 1978) have focused on West Indian blacks, the emphasis has been on their social and economic "superiority" over native-born black Americans. Rarely are Caribbean blacks examined as an ethnic group of inherent value and interest. It is for this reason that the pioneering study, *The Negro Immigrant,* by Ira D. Reid (1939), has continued for half a century to be the definitive assessment of the social and economic characteristics of black immigrants, though the insightful studies of nonwhite immigration (Bryce-Laporte & Mortimer, 1976; Bryce-Laporte, 1980; Mortimer & Bryce-Laporte, 1981), undertaken by the now-defunct Research Institute on Immigration and Ethnic Studies (RIIES) at the Smithsonian Institution, have contributed markedly to updating that classic work.

Several recent studies contradict some of the conventional wisdom about the higher social and economic attainment of black immigrants relative to native-born black Americans. Based on his analysis of 1970 census data, Sowell (1978) concluded that West Indian blacks not only had higher family incomes than black Americans, but that their incomes were comparable to white Americans. He also concluded that West Indians had higher levels of employment and family stability than black Americans.

However, based on their in-depth analysis of the 1980 census, Farley and Allen (1987) failed to find empirical support for Sowell's observations. Instead, these researchers found the family income, occupational attainment, family structure, and labor force patterns of foreign-born and native-born blacks to be comparable to one another. Only in the area of educational attainment were native-born blacks at a marked disadvantage to foreign-born blacks. Farley and Allen (1987) concluded, "Most claims concerning the achievements of West Indian blacks in the United States are greatly exaggerated."

Hill's (1983b) analysis of the Black Pulse data also revealed more similarities than differences in the social and economic status of Caribbean and non-Caribbean blacks. And, contrary to the conventional wisdom that West Indians are less discriminated against than American blacks, he found Caribbean blacks to be just as likely as non-Caribbean blacks to report recent experiences of racial discrimination in the United States.

Contemporary case studies of black immigrants (Bonnett, 1980; Johnson, 1981) continue to uncover considerable discrepancies between the lifestyles, values, and attitudes of the various Caribbean and African nationalities, as well as between them and native-born black Americans. These differences contribute to tension and hostility (Reid, 1939; Bryce-Laporte, 1973; Johnson, 1981). Since the number of black immigrants will continue to rise sharply in the coming decades, more research is vitally needed on the impact of these diverse ethnic subcultures on the structure and functioning of black families–both immigrant and nonimmigrant–and on the implications of black immigration for public policies (Austin, 1980).

E.   FAMILY CLASS

1.   Abuse of Class Concept

Class is the most overused–and misused–concept in studies of black and poor families. Conventional usage of this concept suffers from three fundamental weaknesses: (a) lack of any specific criteria for defining membership in different class strata; (b) failure to incorporate measures of vertical mobility in analyses of class strata; and (c) reifying class concepts, i.e., treating atypical abstractions of class strata as if they were typical in reality.

a.   Criteria. One of the most frequent abuses of the class concept, especially prevalent in the news media, is the failure to provide explicit criteria for membership in different class strata. Numerous references are made to such groups as "middle-class," "lower-class," and "underclass" without defining these terms, without specifying the composition of these class strata.

For example, most analyses of black families today contain references to a "growing underclass." Yet the data that are usually presented to support such assertions relate to increases in the proportion of all single-parent black families, to increases in the proportion of all poor black families, or to increases in poor single-parent black families. It is never made clear whether this "underclass" includes all one-parent black families, poor and nonpoor; all poor families, those on welfare and not on welfare; or all poor families, one-parent and two-parent. In short, no criteria are provided to specify the nature, size, and composition of the "underclass."

b. **Vertical Mobility.** One of the most persistent deficiencies of most analyses of stratification among blacks is the virtual absence of any systematic assessment of vertical mobility. This is most evident in the lack of any analysis of downward mobility among the "middle-class" and upward mobility among the "underclass," since both of these class strata are posited to perpetuate themselves. Yet numerous studies have shown that, over the past decade and a half, "middle-class" individuals and families experienced periodic recessions, inflation, marital instability, child abuse, family violence, delinquency, and substance abuse.

For example, the number of female-headed families rose ten times faster among college-educated than grade-school educated black and white women during the 1970s. Moreover, many investigations have revealed that the overwhelming majority of "middle-class" blacks came from lower socio-economic backgrounds. In short, one cannot adequately understand the functioning of black families in different socio-economic strata without also examining the nature and degree of mobility in and out of each stratum.

c. **Reification.** One of the most frequent flaws in discussions of stratification among minorities and low-income groups is the reifying of class prototypes. "Reification" refers to the fallacy of treating conceptual abstractions as if they existed in reality. Many commentators fail to realize that the number and composition of class categories, such as upper class, middle class, and underclass, are arbitrary in distinction and differ according to the objectives of the analysis. For example, Marx and Engels (1932) found it more expedient to use only two class strata (i.e., the bourgeoisie and proletariat), while Warner and Lunt (1942) found it more useful to employ six social classes (upper-upper, lower-upper, upper-middle, lower-middle, upper-lower, and lower-lower) in several of their community studies. Myrdal (1944) identified the fallacy of reification in his criticism of the Warner school for treating abstract prototypes as if they were real:

> In such an approach it is of importance to keep clear at the outset that our class concepts have no other reality than as a conceptual framework. . . .We must choose our class lines arbitrarily to answer certain specific questions. . . .

> The authors of the Warner group. . . often give the reader the impression that they believe that there are *in reality* clearly demarcated social classes. . . [and]

each of these classes has its distinctive patterns of familial, recreational and general social behavior. . . .

Because of this misconception. . .which is sometimes called reification. . .these authors become tempted to give us a somewhat oversimplified idea about social stratification in the Negro community. . . .[W]hat they are actually presenting is an ideal-typical–and, therefore, overtypical–description, based on much detailed observation which is all organized under the conceptual scheme applied. By unduly insisting upon the realism of this analysis, however, they come to imply a rigidity in the class structure which is not really there. (p. 1,130)

Reification is manifested in defining the "underclass" in terms of: (1) a female-headed family; (2) weak work ethic; (3) negative self-concept; (4) on welfare for many generations; and (5) chronically poor. Not only is this prototype atypical of most poor blacks, but no data is provided on the number of blacks that *simultaneously* have all five attributes. Such analysts fail to realize that the primary function of prototypes is not to mirror reality, but to abstract it.

We will provide two examples of reification in current discussions about the black "underclass." Since families on poverty and welfare are the most "typical" prototypes of inner-city families, the impression is conveyed that they constitute the majority of black families living in poverty areas (Wilson, 1987). Yet, according to the 1980 census, only one-third of black families living in poverty areas in the United States are poor and only one-fifth receive public assistance. Consequently, two-thirds of black families in poverty areas are not poor and four-fifths of them receive no welfare.

Secondly, "the poor female-headed family on welfare" is most often used to convey the impression that this prototype is "typical" of the majority of black female-headed families (Murray, 1984). Yet only one-third of all black families headed by women are poor and on welfare. Although this prototype conforms to an unrepresentative minority of female-headed black families, it is reified as constituting the majority.

2. Operationalizing Class Strata

At least five stipulations should be satisfied by a working definition of class strata for black families: (1) it should encompass all class strata; (2) the class strata should be mutually exclusive; (3) it should facilitate measuring changes in the composition and size of the different class strata over time; (4) it should permit comparisons with class strata among whites; and (5) it should enhance the targeting of specific strata for social action and policies. The class topology offered two decades ago by Billingsley (1968) meets all of these requirements. His topology identified five class strata in the black community: upper class, middle class, working nonpoor, working poor and underclass.

Our presentation will be organized around the following five groups: (1) upper-income ($50,000 and over–in 1983 dollars); (2) middle-income ($25,000-49,999); (3) working near-poor ($10,000-24,999); (4) the working poor (employed, below official poverty level); and (5) the nonworking poor (not employed, below official poverty level). We will highlight empirical studies that focus on each of these five groups. Although most of them examine several social classes, the studies will be referenced according to the group given the major emphasis or the one comprising the bulk of the study's sample.

What is the size of the various class strata based on our operational definition? According to 1983 Current Population Survey (CPS) data, 4% of black families are upper-income, 23% are middle-income, 36% are working near-poor, 14% are working poor and 23% are nonworking poor. If the working poor and near-poor are classified as "working class," this category would comprise half of all black families. And, if the nonworking poor are characterized as "lower-class," this category would comprise one-fourth of all black families.

How has the size of these various strata changed since 1969? Between 1969 and 1983 the proportion of upper-income black families rose from 3% to 4%, the middle-income edged down from 24% to 23%, the working near-poor declined sharply from 45% to 36%, the working poor remained at 14%, while the nonworking poor jumped from 14% to 23%. These findings suggest that the sharp increase in nonworking poor black families was primarily due to the marked decline in working near-poor families. They also underscore a major shortcoming of conventional studies that omit the black working class. The composition of each of these five class groupings will now be described in greater detail.

3. Nonworking Poor

Between 1969 and 1983, the number of nonworking poor black families increased from 716,000 to 1.5 million. Eight out of ten nonworking black families have children under age 18 (79%) and are headed by persons under age 65 (79%), while three-fourths are headed by women only. Only one-fifth of these families had one or more members working. Seven out of eight family heads gave one of the following three reasons for not working: keeping house, e.g., caring for dependent children (41%), disability (25%), and work discouragement (21%). Only one-fifth of nonworking black families have earnings; seven out of ten receive public assistance. One out of four (25%) receive Social Security, and one out of seven receive Supplemental Security Income (SSI).

The nonworking poor comprise four groups of families: (1) nonelderly families headed by women with children (57%); (2) elderly families with and without children (21%); (3) nonelderly families headed by men with children (11%), and (4) nonelderly families without children (11%). Fifty-seven percent of the nonelderly women heading families with children reported not working because of child care responsibilities,

23% indicated work discouragement, and 20% cited work disabilities. Eighty-five percent of the nonworking poor families headed by nonelderly women rely on welfare.

Forty-two percent of the nonelderly men who head families with children reported not working because of disabilities, 35% because of work discouragement, and 23% because of household responsibilities. Seventy-one percent of nonelderly heads of families without children were not working because of disabilities (43%) or discouragement (28%). Interestingly, only one-third of the elderly families with or without children reported not working because of retirement, while three out of five cited disabilities (36%) or household responsibilities (23%). Overall, disabled (25%) and discouraged (21%) workers comprise almost half (46%) of the nonworking poor. Moreover, this analysis reveals that the "typical" prototype of the "underclass"–nonelderly women heading families on welfare–comprises less than half of all poor black families.

Conventional studies of black families have placed most of their attention on the nonworking poor, and limited (and in some cases misleading) insight has come of this narrow approach. However, there are notable contemporary studies of black families that have examined the nonworking poor from a holistic perspective. Lewis' (1967c) pioneering study of child-rearing among the poor in Washington, D.C., is an outstanding example. Others include the in-depth studies of strategies for survival and advancement among the nonworking poor by Ladner (1971), Stack (1974) and Glasgow (1981). Analyses based on over 10 years of the longitudinal Panel Study of Income Dynamics survey (Coe, 1978) reveal that the nonworking poor are not static, and that they experience many transitions between welfare and work and between poverty and near-poverty.

4. Working Poor

Although the proportion of working poor black families remained at 14% between 1969 and 1983, their numbers rose from 668,000 to 963,000. Eighty-nine percent have dependent children and 95% are headed by persons under age 65, while 64% are headed by women. One-third of working poor black families have two or more earners. Earners in these families work disproportionately at low-paying jobs in industries with high turnover. Since all working poor families have some earnings, only one-fourth are on welfare. Moreover, one out of six of the working poor receive Social Security, while only one out of ten receive SSI.

Working poor black families comprise the following four groups: (1) nonelderly women heading families with childen (57%); (2) nonelderly men heading families with children (28%); (3) families headed by nonelderly persons without children (10%); and (4) families headed by elderly persons with and without children (5%). Three out of ten working poor families headed by women receive public assistance, compared to one-fifth of working poor families headed by men. While three-fifths of the heads of all poor black families have less than a high school education; the converse should also be noted, that two out of five are high school graduates. The working poor are concentrated in secondary sector service, their jobs characterized by low pay, high turnover, no fringe benefits, and poor working conditions.

Most studies of the black poor have focused on the nonworking poor rather than the working poor. Some notable exceptions to this are Liebow's (1967) study of irregularly employed black men; Stone and Schlamp's (1971) in-depth analysis of working poor fathers on and off welfare; Dill's (1980) life history study of elderly black women who had been household and domestic workers; Swan's (1981a) analysis of the problems faced by black ex-prisoners and their families in trying to achieve a productive reentry into society; Goodwin's (1983) study of the social and psychological functioning of employable mothers and fathers in the WIN program, and Clark's (1983) case study of family processes that facilitate or include academic achievement among poor children in one-parent and two-parent black families.

5. Working Near-Poor

Although the proportion of near-poor black families fell sharply from 44% to 36% between 1969 and 1983, their numbers rose from 2.1 million to 2.4 million. Nine out of ten near-poor families are headed by persons under age 65, while two out of five are headed by women. About half of these families had two or more earners. Three out of five heads of near-poor families were high school graduates, while three out of ten had some college education. Earners in near-poor families are disparately concentrated in lower-tier primary sector jobs, in industry, crafts, protective services, sales, and clerical occupations (Collins, 1986). These workers are overrepresented in industries with a high vulnerability to job loss due to imports, automation, and plant relocation.

The working near-poor has been virtually excluded as a key class stratum in most studies of black families. Willie (1970, 1976, 1985) is one of the few scholars to place a major emphasis on the black working class in his various research efforts. Other notable studies include Scanzoni's (1977) in-depth examination of intergenerational socialization processes among working-class two-parent black families, McAdoo's (1983) in-depth analysis of mental health patterns among employed black single mothers and their social support networks, and Malson's (1983a; 1986) research on the strategies adopted by working-class black single mothers to perform their multiple roles.

6. Middle-Income

Although the proportion of middle-income black families remained at one-fourth between 1969 and 1983, their numbers soared from 1.1 million to 1.5 million. Eight out of ten middle-income families consist of married couples, with only 13% headed by women. Four out of five middle-income couples have working wives. Two out of five heads of middle-income black families went to college, while one out of four are college graduates (Hill, 1986).

Workers in middle-income black families are disproportionately concentrated in upper-tier primary sector professional and managerial occupations. Although black women are more highly represented than black men among professionals, the former are more concentrated in lower paying jobs than the latter (Collins, 1986). Furthermore, middle-class blacks, especially women, are overrepresented in public sector jobs. Two-thirds of black female professionals work in government jobs, compared to half of black male professionals. Similarly, two-fifths of black female managers are in government positions, compared to one-third of black male managers. Thus, middle-class blacks were affected acutely by the reductions-in-force ("RIFs") in federal government jobs during the 1980s.

The black middle class has generally been "mentioned in passing" in analyses concerned mainly with the black "underclass" (Wilson, 1987). Thus, there have been relatively few in-depth studies of middle-class black families. Willie (1985) has been one of the few social scientists to focus consistently on the black middle class. McAdoo's (1981, 1983) studies of mobility patterns and informal support networks among the black middle-class have also significantly enhanced empirically-based knowledge of this group. Similarly, Landry's comparative studies of middle-class blacks and whites (1978) and his incisive analysis of the "new" black middle class (1987) have advanced markedly the nation's understanding of this growing class stratum. Many descriptive analyses (Blackwell, 1975; Cazenave, 1979; Hare, 1970; Hill, 1987a; Kronus, 1971; O'Hare, et al., 1982; Pinkney, 1984; Wilson, 1978) have also contributed to understanding of the black middle class.

7.   Upper-Income

As the proportion of upper-income black families rose from 3% to 4% between 1969 and 1983, their numbers almost doubled from 143,000 to 267,000. Upper-income black families consist overwhelmingly of married couples (96%), and there is an overrepresentation of multiple earners—two-fifths have three or more earners. Three out of five heads of upper-income families went to college, and two out of five graduated. Upper-income earners are highly represented among high-level corporation executives, bankers, entrepreneurs, college presidents, judges, political officials, physicians, lawyers, ministers, athletes, and entertainers.

Contemporary in-depth studies of upper class black families are virtually non-existent. Because of its small size, the upper class is usually combined with the middle class in most studies of social stratification in the black community. Moreover, when the black upper class is of major concern, individuals rather than families are usually the basic unit of study. Thompson's (1986) exemplary study of the black elite is one of the few in-depth contemporary empirical analyses of upper strata blacks.

Billingsley (1968) differentiates "old" and "new" upper class black families. The old upper class refers to families headed by men or women whose parents had been upper or middle class. However, the new upper class refers to family heads who achieved that status within one generation, especially athletes or entertainers. Nevertheless, as Frazier (1939) noted, because of their lesser accumulation of wealth and power, upper class blacks continue to be more comparable to middle class than to upper class whites.

VIII. IMPACT OF INDIVIDUAL FACTORS

The preceding sections focused on the impact of factors at the societal, community and family levels on the structure and functioning of black families. Yet most conventional studies of low-income blacks (Banfield, 1968; Gilder, 1981; Loury, 1984; Murray, 1984) attribute their high rates of female-headed families, unemployment, poverty and out-of-wedlock births mainly to "self-destructive" individual traits: poverty, culture norms, underclass values, welfare mentality, lack of work ethic, low achievement orientation, low self-esteem, self-hatred, and social isolation. Sweeping assertions about the importance of negative norms, values and attitudes in these studies are invariably based on inferences from behavior, since supporting psychological data are rarely provided. Moreoever, most analyses with such data usually obtain results that contradict the conventional wisdom. We will now examine the empirical evidence for popular assertions about the role of individual factors in black families.

A.   CULTURE OF POVERTY NORMS

According to some analysts (Banfield, 1968; Lemann, 1986; Loury 1984; Moynihan, 1967), conformity to "culture of poverty," "lower-class," or "underclass" norms, values, and beliefs is considered to be a major determinant of black family ills. For example, high rates of female-headed families among poor blacks have been "explained" by a higher "cultural" value on common-law relations and unwed motherhood than on legalized marriage and birth. Such casual familial values were originally attributed to slavery (Glazer & Moynihan, 1963), until pioneering historical research by Blassingame (1972), Genovese (1974), and Gutman (1976) revealed conclusively that blacks strongly valued two-parent families during and after slavery. Moreover, Geismar (1973) concluded ". . .there is no evidence from illegitimacy research or our present study that either unwed mothers or the social and cultural groups in which illegitimacy is widespread place a higher value on consensual unions or single-parent motherhood than on marriage" (p. 81).

Parker and Kleiner (1969) argued that the existence of deviant family norms among poor blacks would require evidence that they differ markedly from the norms of middle-class blacks. Yet, their empirical research revealed no significant differences between low and high socioeconomic status black men in their norms regarding the ideal and actual family roles of husbands and fathers nor in psychological stress resulting from discrepancies between ideal and actual family roles. Accordingly, Parker and Kleiner (1969) concluded:

Thus, our data do not support the idea of a "culture of poverty" as applied to lower-class Negro family life; the family ideals of the lower-status males (within the framework of the research operations employed) do not differ significantly from those of higher-status groups. (p. 504)

Numerous other research investigators (Lewis, 1967a, 1967b; Liebow, 1967; Rainwater, 1970; Valentine, 1968) found no empirical support for popular notions of distinct "cultural" norms and values among low-income blacks. Rainwater (1970) synthesizes these findings as follows:

It is important to recognize that lower class Negroes know that their particular family forms are different from those of the rest of society and that, though they often see these forms as representing the only ways of behaving, given their circumstances, they also think of the more stable forms of the working class as more desirable. That is, lower class Negroes know what the "normal American family" is supposed to be like and they consider a stable family-centered way of life superior to the conjugal and familiar situation in which they find themselves. . . .The existence of such ideas about normal family life represents a recurrent source of stress within families as individuals become aware that they are failing to measure up to the ideals. (pp. 182-183)

Nevertheless, since many low-income blacks are not able to achieve desired two-parent families because of numerous impediments (such as shortage of marriageable men, lack of jobs with livable wages, exodus of inner-city firms, racism, etc.), they are often forced to make behavioral adaptations (such as female-headed families, out-of-wedlock births, common-law unions, etc.) that are viewed as "pathological" by the wider society. As Rainwater (1970) notes, Rodman's concept of "value stretch" aptly describes those adaptations:

Perhaps the most successful attempt to deal with these issues is in Hyman Rodman's (1963) concept of the "lower-class value stretch," an adaptive mechanism by which the lower class person, without abandoning the general values of the society, develops an alternative set of values. . . [so that lower class people] have a wider range of values than others within the society. They share the general values of the society. . . but in addition they have stretched these values or developed alternative values which help them to adjust to their deprived circumstances. Rodman's formulation avoids the pitfall of implying that lower-class persons are ignorant of or indifferent to conventional norms and values or that they persist in maintaining allegiance to conventional norms despite their inability to achieve success in their terms. (pp. 365-366)

Additional proof of distinct "subcultures" among low-income blacks would require evidence of homogeneity of values, attitudes, and behavior patterns. Yet numerous empirical inquiries (Ladner, 1971; Lewis, 1967a; 1967b; Liebow, 1967; Rainwater, 1970; Stack, 1974) have revealed much heterogeneity in values, attitudes, socialization practices, and lifestyles among poor black families. In short, while low-income blacks may share a common economic status of poverty, they are not monolithic in their values, attitudes, aspirations, or lifestyles.

B. DYSFUNCTIONAL ATTITUDES

While some analysts do not point to a distinct "poverty culture" as the primary factor responsible for "self-perpetuating" the problems of black families, they identify negative psychological attitudes, such as low sense of efficacy, achievement, and future orientation. On this issue, there is widespread consensus in the research literature (Merton, 1957; Smith, et al., 1978; McAdoo, 1983): low-income persons score significantly lower on psychological measures of efficacy, achievement, and future orientation than middle-income and upper-income persons—regardless of race. However, a major shortcoming of these studies is that they are overwhelmingly based on cross-sectional surveys that obtain measurements at only one point in time. Thus, as Duncan (1984) observes, it is not possible to determine from cross-sectional data whether the dysfunctional attitudes of low-income persons are consequences of their poverty rather than causes (or vice versa):

> The idea that "good" or "bad" attitudes explain economic success or failure seems to have widespread appeal. . . but much of the evidence about the role of attitudes in determining economic success comes from cross-sectional data gathered at a single point in time. Typically, such data shows that successful people have more positive attitudes—a result that agrees with our everyday observations. But did the attitudes cause the success, or did the success cause the attitudes?. . .

> Longitudinal data are much better suited to test for causality, although they still do not give definitive results. Through repeated observations on the same individuals over time, the attitudes observed initially can be studied to determine whether they are related to subsequent economic success or failure. Do the initially poor with higher motivation have a better chance of climbing out of poverty? More generally, does economic status improve more for those who began with higher scores on the attitudinal measures? These are propositions that can be put to the test with longitudinal data. (p. 24)

In order to provide a more adequate test of such questions, Duncan and his colleagues at the University of Michigan incorporated several attitude measurements into their nationally representative Panel Study of Income Dynamics (PSID). More specifically, changes in the economic status of male- and female-headed households between 1971 and 1978 were related to three attitudinal measures: achievement motivation, orientation toward the future, and a sense of personal efficacy (e.g., control over one's life).

Extensive analysis by the University of Michigan researchers (Duncan, 1984) revealed that having "good" or "bad"attitudes was not significantly related to whether one went into or out of poverty. For example, persons with high achievement orientation and sense of efficacy were just as likely to fall into poverty (or rise out of it) as those with low achievement ethics and sense of efficacy. They concluded that negative life events (such as unemployment, illness, divorce or separation, unwanted pregnancy or birth, eviction, etc.) were more important determinants of downward economic mobility than psychological disposition.

C. WORK DISCOURAGEMENT

However, there is increasing evidence that one psychological attitude–work discouragement–is a strong determinant of success or failure in the labor market. For example, Datcher-Loury and Loury's (1986) analysis of cross-sectional National Bureau of Economic Research (NBER) data on inner-city black male youth revealed significantly more hours worked annually by youth 20 to 24 years old with high occupational aspirations and optimistic work expectations than by youth with low job aspirations and pessimistic work attitudes. These findings were reinforced by their analysis of six-year follow-up data on the cohort of males who were 17 to 19 years old in 1966 at the inception of the longitudinal NLS survey. Datcher-Loury and Loury (1986) found that black males with high job aspirations in 1966 worked significantly more hours per week in 1972 than youth with low occupational aspirations in 1966.

Moreover, Goodwin's (1983) analysis of psychological determinants of economic self-sufficiency among low-income husbands on welfare revealed the importance of work discouragement attitudes resulting from repeated past failures to obtain employment:

> [Welfare] dependency comes about in part from their inability to obtain jobs at which they can support their families. Low expectations of future employment and need for help with personal problems also depresses the achievement of independence. Expectations can be raised by positive experiences in the job market, and help with personal problems can be provided through appropriate social services. Such efforts could help increase WIN fathers' achievement of economic independence. (p. 66)

On the other hand, contrary to conventional wisdom, Goodwin's (1983) study found no relation between preferences for nonwork (or work) income and the probability of remaining welfare dependent (or achieving economic independence):

The insignificant impact of preferences on welfare recipients' achievement of economic independence, we suggest, results from recipients facing severe threats to the integrity of their families. More specifically, preferences have no statistically significant effect on welfare recipients' actions because some recipients with strong preference for non-work income go to work when they can earn more than the low level of welfare payments for which they are eligible. At the same time, other recipients who reject the idea of non-work income stay on welfare because they cannot find jobs at which they can earn as much as those low level welfare payments. (p. 132)

D. SELF-CONCEPT

Negative self-concepts have also been identified as key contributors to black community disorganization in general and black family instability in particular. The pioneering doll studies conducted by Clark and Clark (1939, 1947) are cited most frequently as providing conclusive empirical evidence of extensive "self-hatred" among blacks. According to most reviews of racial preference studies (Banks, 1976; Gordon, 1976; Cross, 1985), black racial identity shifted from "prowhite" manifestations prior to the 1960s to "problack" orientations after 1968. The surge in positive black self-concepts has been attributed to the "black pride" movement of the 1960s.

Yet Cross (1985) contends that generalizations about black "self-hatred" based on "self-concept" studies prior to the 1960s are unwarranted, since they had no direct measures of personal identity. His analysis revealed that 17 of the 18 empirical studies that are cited as documenting black self-hatred between 1939 and 1960 had measures only of group identity. Consequently, inferences about low self-esteem among blacks in these studies are not based on direct measures of self-worth, but on forced-choice measures of racial group orientations. These investigators arbitrarily assume—without empirical verification—that reference group preference is an appropriate proxy for personal identity. This assumption is strongly contradicted by the few research endeavors to provide measures of *both* self-esteem and racial group identity on the same sample.

McAdoo (1985) administered measures of self-esteem and racial group preferences to black children in 1969 when they were four and five years old, and again when they were ages nine and ten. Her sample included low-income and middle-income children from several northern cities and a black town in Mississippi. Although her first wave of data revealed high self-esteem among all of the children, they tended to have an out-group ("prowhite") orientation. Children from two-parent middle-class families were the most out-group oriented, although their self-esteem was equal to or higher than that of children from lower income families.

When McAdoo (1985) re-administered her measures in 1975, she found self-esteem to remain high among the children, although their racial group preferences

108

became more in-group oriented. Cross (1985) underscores the importance of Mc-Adoo's longitudinal study:

> McAdoo's study is significant because it also showed that black children from a variety of home environments and regions of the country had high self-esteem before and after being influenced by the Black Power Movement. The same children had a predominantly out-group orientation before the Black Power Movement and an increasingly in-group orientation as the Black Power Movement progressed. (p. 165-166)

Moreover, a reanalysis of 32 racial preference studies by Banks (1976) suggests that their forced choice techniques obscure the extent of "biculturalism" among blacks, by constraining them to select "no one group preference" as a proxy for "both group preferences." Blacks indicated no preference (i.e., a preference for cultural symbols of both racial groups) in 69% of the studies, a preference for black symbols in 25%, and a preference for white symbols in the remaining 6%. These findings are reinforced by Cross's (1982) longitudinal study of socialization practices, which revealed that black parents were much more likely than white parents to provide their children with multi-racial reference groups and world view. Consequently, Cross (1985) contends that "prowhite" preferences of blacks should not be construed as "self-hatred," but as manifesting "racial pluralism," "biculturalism," and "dualism":

> Tentative results from a longitudinal study (Cross, 1982) show black parents present both the black and white worlds to their children, while white parents tend to convey the world as being primarily white. For example, in black homes, one is as likely to find white dolls or human figures as black ones, while black dolls are seldom, if ever, found in white homes. Black children, and perhaps black people in general, have a dual reference group orientation. (p. 169)

E.   SELF-ESTEEM

Cross's (1985) reanalysis of 161 "self-concept" studies conducted between 1939 and 1977 revealed that, while only one of them had direct measures of personal identity or self-worth prior to 1968, 100 of them had such measures after 1967. Seventy-three percent of the post-1967 studies with direct personal identity measures revealed high levels of self-esteem among blacks, 15% revealed low levels, while the remaining 12% were inconclusive. Interestingly, while all (17) of the pre-1968 racial preference studies with measures of only group identity reported negative ("prowhite") orientations by blacks, only 27% of comparable studies conducted after 1967 reported negative orientations, with 68% reporting positive ("problack") orientations, and the remaining 5% mixed in pattern (Jackson, et al., 1981).

According to an in-depth examination by Cross (1985) of the 101 studies with direct measures of personal identity that were conducted between 1939 and 1977, black self-esteem was equal to or higher than that of whites in 72% of the investigations, which is comparable to the 54% derived by Gordon (1980) in her reassessment of such studies. More specifically, Cross (1985) found black self-esteem to be higher than that of whites in 21% of the studies, at the same level as whites in 51%, lower than that of whites in 16%, and inconclusive in 12%. Numerous studies (McAdoo, 1983; Gary, et al., 1983; Gary, et al., 1984; Smith, et al., 1978) have found self-esteem to be a significant factor in black social and economic mobility. Blacks with high self-esteem invariably have higher educational attainment, occupational status, and earnings than blacks with low self-esteem.

F. STRESS

Although stress significantly affects the functioning of all persons, regardless of race, it has been shown to have a disproportionate adverse impact on blacks. A major weakness of mainstream theories of family stress, according to Peters and Massey (1983), is the omission of stress resulting from racism. More specifically, they contend that two manifestations of racism must be taken into account: (a) institutionalized, i.e., Mundane Extreme Environmental Stress (MEES), and (b) individualized, i.e., chronic and unpredictable acts of discrimination. Peters and Massey (1983) illustrate how racism can be stressful to black families:

> When a black family's home is destroyed by a hurricane, for example, the stress also includes the special problems a black family may face in locating another desirable place to live. Will the housing counselor be fair? Will the family be referred to an undesirable black ghetto neighborhood for housing? Will the black family encounter hostility moving into an integrated or "White" neighborhood? (p. 201)

Teele (1970) identifies three factors that are important in determining the effects of stress on individuals and families: potentially stressful situations, perceptions of the events as stressful, and reactions to those situations. He offers the following as examples of potentially stressful situations: hostile residential or working environments, single-parent families, poverty, unemployment, and poor academic performance. Although these circumstances are likely to be stressful for all persons, regardless of race, blacks are overrepresented in each situation. Taylor (1981) contends that the resilience of "mediating" factors determines the effectiveness of one's response to stress:

> These mediating factors are of two types: those that determine the amount of *external* constraint associated with stress, and those that determine the amount of

internal constraint. The former consists of such material and social resources as money, social support from family and friends, and access to services, information and knowledge; the latter include characteristics of the individual such as intellectual ability, values, beliefs, and motives. (p. 144)

Merton's (1957) theory of social structure and deviance (or "blocked opportunity") also posits a higher rate of strain (or "anomie") among blacks than whites. Indeed, most studies have reported higher levels of stress, strain, anomie, and depression among blacks than whites. Teele (1970) summarizes Merton's thesis as follows:

According to Merton, American culture tends to indoctrinate all groups in our society in relatively high status aspirations. Success, in terms of material goods and life style, is the goal of all. Different racial, ethnic, and class groupings are unequal in their ability to realize these aspirations by legitimate means, however. Merton then deals with the solutions that result when individuals accept social goals without access to the approved means of achieving such goals. Essentially, Merton holds that when such barriers exist the individuals concerned may look for either a substitute goal, a substitute means of attaining the goal, or both. The employment of the substitute goals or means often involve delinquent or criminal behavior. (pp. 235-236)

According to Merton's theory of anomie (Cazenave, 1981), racially and economically disadvantaged low status groups are more likely than high status advantaged groups to experience stress since the former are less likely than the latter to be provided with external material resources to achieve societal goals through legitimate means. However, as many analysts note, although black men and women experience many similar forms of stress, there are significant qualitative differences by sex as well.

For example, several scholars—Ladner (1971), Rodgers-Rose (1980), Collins (1986), Malson (1983c; 1986), Pearce & McAdoo (1981)—have identified many potential and actual situations as disproportionately stressful to black women: fear of out-of-wedlock pregnancies and births, the relative shortage of marriageable black men, sole responsibility for rearing children, major or sole responsibility for providing economic support of children, sexist behavior of black and white men, and role overload in trying to fulfill multiple roles of mother, wife, and breadwinner.

Many studies (Smith, et al., 1978; Rodgers-Rose, 1980) have also documented various stressful circumstances among black women in professional positions. McAdoo's research (1983) revealed that single mothers have higher levels of stress than married mothers and never-married mothers have higher levels of stress than mothers who were formerly married. Similarly, Gary, et al.'s studies (1983, 1984) of black families yielded more stressful events and depressive symptoms for single than for married women, and for women in general than for married men.

However, other scholars (McGhee, 1984; Stewart & Scott, 1978; Taylor, 1981) have underscored numerous potential and actual situations that are disparately stressful to black men: educational tracking, suspension and expulsion practices, police arrest and detention practices, court sentencing and incarceration practices, military draft policies, the exodus of manufacturing jobs from inner-cities, unemployment and underemployment, and difficulty in fulfilling role of primary breadwinner. Although these situations have an acute adverse impact on low-income black men, Taylor (1981) also highlights stressful circumstances that have disparate effects on middle-income black men:

> On the other hand, middle-income black males may experience higher rates of other stressors than do low-income black males. Job promotions, responsibilities associated with professional or community organizations, extensive travel connected with employment, and other radical changes from the usual pattern of life, are almost exclusively middle-income stressors and are likely to be outside the experience of most low-income black males. (p. 149)

Among black men and women (Gary, et al., 1983, 1984), more stressful events and depressive symptoms were reported among individuals with low incomes, low educational attainment, and under 45 years old, than among individuals with high incomes, high educational attainment, and over 45 years old. Divorced, separated, and never-married individuals reported more stressful events and depressive symptoms than those currently married. And unemployed blacks and blacks in poor or fair health reported higher depression levels than employed blacks and blacks in good and excellent health. Among single black women, those with three or more children had more depressive symptoms than those with one or two children (Gary, et al., 1983). However, again among married black women, those with one or two children had more depressive symptoms than those with three or more children.

G. MENTAL ILLNESS

Reliable data on the incidence and prevalence of various mental disorders among blacks relative to whites are not yet available (Cannon & Locke, 1977; Sabshin, et al., 1970; Smith, et al., 1978) because of several methodological shortcomings: (a) existing statistics are based mainly on institutionalized populations, i.e., outpatients and inpatients of mental health institutions and inmates of correctional facilities for juveniles and adults; (b) racially stereotyped diagnoses of mental disorders; and (c) most instruments used to measure mental illness among blacks have only been validated for whites. Nevertheless, the disproportionate stress on black men and women, exacerbated by institutional and individual racism, suggest that rates of mental illness, however measured, are markedly higher among blacks than whites.

Blacks are twice as likely as whites to be inpatients of public mental hospitals and, regardless of race, men are twice as likely as women to be inpatients of public mental hospitals. While black men had inpatient rates (444.5) twice as high as black women (212.0) in 1975, those rates were double those of white men (214.2) and women (111.2) (U.S. Public Health Service, 1985). But white men (57.0) and women (72.5) are about one and a half times more likely to be inpatients of private mental hospitals than black men (38.1) and women (37.7). However, black men (806.9) and woman (886.3) are about one and a third times more likely to receive outpatient psychiatric services than white men (593.8) and women (678.2). Yet, when family income is held constant, whites are more likely to receive outpatient psychiatric services than blacks (Cannon & Locke, 1977).

Among blacks, the highest rates of inpatient admissions to public mental hospitals are among men 18 to 44 years old and women 25 to 64 years old. But black men 18 to 44 years old are more than twice as likely as black women 25 to 64 years old to be inpatients at public mental hospitals (Cannon & Locke, 1977). Blacks admitted to public mental hospitals are more likely than whites to be diagnosed for schizophrenia and alcohol disorders, while whites are more likely than blacks to be diagnosed for depressive disorders. Black male admissions are twice as likely as black female admissions to be diagnosed for schizophrenia and alcohol disorders. The disproportionately higher rates of mental illness among black men and women are strongly correlated with high levels of alcoholism, spousal abuse, child abuse, drug abuse, and homicides in black families (Cannon & Locke, 1977; U.S. Public Health Service, 1985).

IX. ACTION IMPLICATIONS

This report contends that the causes and nature of the current crisis among black families cannot be properly understood without incorporating a holistic perspective that systematically examines the separate and combined effects of societal trends, social policies, and factors at the community, family, and individual levels. Key societal forces with an adverse impact on black families include racism, classism, sexism, back-to-back recessions, double-digit inflation, shift from higher-paying manufacturing jobs to lower-paying service jobs, and increased job competition from legal and illegal immigrants. Black families are also adversely affected by social policies in such areas as employment, plant closings, taxes, trade, monetary supply, welfare, foster care, child support, housing, income maintenance, health, education, and criminal justice.

Major negative factors at the community, family, and individual levels include joblessness, poverty, crime, delinquency, drug abuse, alcohol abuse, AIDS, family violence, child neglect and abuse, mental illness, physical illness, homelessness, out-of-wedlock births, adolescent pregnancies, low educational attainment, lack of work skills, along with discouragement, hopelessness, and other dysfunctional attitudes. While "mediating" institutions in the black community (such as churches, social action organizations, fraternal groups, neighborhood groups, and extended family networks) help many black families to effectively counteract these negative factors, numerous other black families are acutely destabilized by them.

Thus, in order to successfully resolve this crisis, holistic strategies are required. Fortunately, comprehensive agendas for strengthening black families have been proposed by many groups in and outside the black community. Some of the most notable plans include: (a) the Congressional Black Caucus' (1982) Black Leadership Family Plan and annual counter-budgets; (b) recommendations from the Black Family Summit co-sponsored by the National Urban League and the NAACP (1983); (c) the National Urban League's annual "State of Black America" reports; (d) the Children Defense Fund's Children Survival Bill (1984) and annual children defense budgets; (e) the National Association of Black Social Workers plan for preserving black families (1986); and (f) various policy frameworks issued by the Joint Center for Political Studies (1986, 1987). Accordingly, the recommendations that follow are based largely on these comprehensive agendas. However, in order to place our proposals in proper context, it is necessary to be explicit about key guiding principles that cut across each recommendation:

A. GUIDING PRINCIPLES

1. Self-Help and Government Responsibilities

Since neither the black community nor the government–alone–can resolve all the problems afflicting black families, committed partnerships and coalitions are required that involve all segments of the public (i.e., federal, state, county, and city) and private (business, labor, nonprofit service organizations, and all institutions in the black community) sectors. This means that community-based minority organizations (such as black churches, CDCs, and neighborhood groups) with demonstrated capabilities to strengthen disadvantaged black families and individuals should be used as major conduits for aiding poor black families.

2. Combatting Racism

To insure that these proposals have enduring positive effects on black families, this nation must make a major commitment to eradicate racism in all of its forms–individual as well as institutional, and unintentional as well as intentional–in all American institutions (e.g., economic, educational, health, social welfare, housing, political, criminal justice, the military, and the media). Affirmative action mandates should be strongly enforced to remove racial barriers to adequate representation of minorities in high-level positions in all sectors.

3. Family Impact Analyses

Prior to 1987, all proposed policies were required to have an environmental impact statement that assessed their potential effects on the physical environment, but not on families and individuals. However, on September 3, 1987, President Reagan signed an executive order requiring all levels of government to systematically assess the intended and unintended consequences of current and proposed policies and regulations on American families. Thus, the black community must closely monitor government agencies to insure that the potential and actual effects of public policies on black families from various socio-economic and subcultural ethnic groups are, in fact, investigated appropriately. The Black Family Impact Analysis Program of the Baltimore Urban League should be used as a model for conducting analyses that are sensitive to black families.

4. Cost-Effective Actions

Record-level budget and trade deficits, volatile stock markets, and the probability of an impending recession suggest an austere economic climate that will require that policies for strengthening black and low-income families be cost-effective and efficiently targeted. However, blacks and other concerned groups should not allow U.S.

policymakers to use a stagnant economy as justification for neglecting the needs of the poor and racial minorities when, in fact, even greater resources should be targeted to those most in need.

B. RECOMMENDED STRATEGIES

1. Stimulating Economic Growth

Most analyses reveal that an expanding economy contributes significantly to economic progress among black families and that it is possible to reduce racial inequality while pursuing economic growth. Consequently, the black community must insist that government policies to reduce inflation no longer rely on raising unemployment by inducing recessions. Moreover, since small businesses generate the largest numbers of new jobs in the American economy, more–not less–government resources and set-asides should be targeted to enhance the effectiveness of small businesses, especially those operated by minority entrepreneurs.

2. Achieving Full Employment

This nation must rededicate itself to the goals of the Employment Act of 1946 and the Humphrey-Hawkins Act of 1978 to provide everyone willing and able to work with jobs at livable wages. Current tax credits that subsidize the exporting of American jobs abroad should be reversed to provide greater incentives for creating decent jobs at home. Moreover, livable wages will not be achieved until the federal minimum wage, which has remained at $3.35/hour since 1981, is raised to a level (about $4.65) to restore its traditional purchasing power.

3. Expanding Job Training

Evaluations of government job training programs reveal that high emphasis on quantity (i.e., numbers served) has encouraged much "creaming" of job-ready persons and an underrepresentation of "hard-core" workers with deficient work and educational skills. These analyses also reveal a sharp underrepresentation of single women heading families in these programs. Consequently, eligibility and performance criteria for job training programs should be modified to give higher priority to "long-term" jobless adults and youths, adolescent parents (male and female), and to female heads of low-income families.

4. Expanding Subsidized Jobs

Contrary to statements by the Reagan administration, analyses of the public service programs, especially those under CETA, reveal that they were highly effective in facilitating the transition of low-income and minority workers to higher-paying, unsubsidized jobs in the private sector. Consequently, funding should be restored for subsidized public service jobs and subsidized-OJT jobs in the private sector targeted to structurally unemployed workers in minority and low-income families. Moreover, more effective marketing of the Targeted Jobs Tax Credits (TJTC) to firms and procedural changes to reduce stigma among participants would increase markedly the number of disadvantaged youth and welfare recipients hired at subsidized wages through TJTC.

5.   Expanding Child Care

A major barrier to the labor force participation of many black women is the lack of affordable child care. Unfortunately, the current Dependent Care Tax Credit (DCTC) is not used by most working poor parents, since their incomes are too low to incur tax liabilities. Consequently, the DCTC should be made "refundable," similar to the Earned Income Tax Credit (EITC), to insure that working poor families receive tax rebates for child care even when they do not have to pay taxes. However, in order to deal with this issue on a more comprehensive basis, it is time for this nation to give serious consideration to implementing a children's allowance, similar to those in many European countries, so that families with young children may be lifted out of poverty.

6.   Reforming AFDC

Currently, there is increasing consensus among liberals and conservatives that fundamental changes are needed in the current AFDC program in order to facilitate greater economic self-sufficiency among welfare recipients. In addition to urging an adequate minimum benefit level nationwide, progressive welfare reform proposals in Congress appropriately emphasize: government's obligation to provide vital supportive services (such as day care, job search, transportation, housing assistance, transitional health insurance, and counseling). It should be mandated that able-bodied welfare recipients enroll in employability development programs (such as classroom and OJT job training, apprenticeships, high school equivalency, basic education, and adult literacy). Congressman Harold Ford's bill (HR 1720), which was passed by the House of Representatives in December 1987, contains several provisions that would, in the interests of redress, disproportionately benefit poor black families. For example, not only does the Ford bill mandate the AFDC-UP program for all 50 states, it also eliminates UP's restrictive eligibility criteria in order to aid poor two-parent breadwinners with limited or unstable work histories, especially adolescent parents.

7.   Enhancing Child Support

Most welfare reform proposals also include more effective enforcement of child support collections by establishing more efficient procedures for establishing paternity, locating absent parents, and withholding wages and tax refunds. Nevertheless, many inequities continue to exist in current child support policies, such as inadequate levels of child support awards ordered by courts, sharp disparities between the amount of child support payments and the ability to pay, premature termination of families from AFDC, disqualification of terminated AFDC families from child support services, and policies that discourage responsible noncustodial parents from continuing to make regular child support payments. In order to eliminate such deficiencies, more comprehensive and equitable approaches are needed, such as the Child Support Assurance program currently being tested in the State of Wisconsin (Garfinkel & Melli, 1987).

8.   Reforming Foster Care

Unfortunately, most proposals to reform the welfare system omit entirely the foster care system–despite the fact that long-term foster care youth have the highest risk of becoming welfare dependent. The number of children in foster care, especially among blacks and Hispanics, spiraled during the 1980s as a result of sharp increases in unemployment, poverty, homelessness, drug abuse, and AIDS. Innovative grass-roots efforts, such as Homes for Black Children and One Church, One Child, have found more than enough black families willing and able to take children in need of foster care or adoption. In addition to forming citizens' foster care monitoring groups, the black community should insist that minority-operated community groups with a demonstrated record of finding homes for "hard-to-place" children be designated the primary contractors for placing black special needs children and for providing preventive family preservation services. The black community should also insist that these group not be restricted, as is presently the case, to recruiting black foster care or adoptive families for nonminority agencies.

9.   Enhancing Education

Several initiatives have demonstrated effectiveness in enhancing the educational attainment of black and low-income individuals. Consequently, additional governmental resources should be targeted to preschool programs, such as Head Start; to Chapter One's compensatory educational initiatives; to scholarships for low income college students, notably Pell grants; and to historically black colleges, which continue to make it possible, in ways and to a degree not yet provided elsewhere, for disadvantaged black students to receive a college education. Moreover, in addition to providing supplemental instruction in the homes and community, groups of parents and other concerned citizens should continually monitor the public schools to insure that quality education is provided to all children, most especially those from low-income families.

10. Enhancing Physical Health

Lack of access to quality health care is another key contributor to persistent high rates of poverty, welfare dependency, and infant mortality among blacks. The lack of health benefits in low-wage jobs has acutely affected the black working poor. Consequently, there is a vital need for comprehensive health insurance (including portable coverage from job to job) targeted to economically disadvantaged families among the welfare poor, the working poor, and the working near-poor. Furthermore, aggressive society-wide action is needed to reduce the high rates of adolescent pregnancy, infant mortality, poor prenatal care, low birth weight babies, AIDS-infected parents and infants, and drug-addicted parents and infants in the black community.

11. Enchancing Mental Health

The cumulative effects of racism, classism, and sexism on blacks have contributed to extensive frustration, stress, low self-esteem, and depression, which are often manifested in disproportionate levels of mental illness, alcohol abuse, spousal abuse, child abuse, drug abuse, crime, and delinquency in black families. Black groups should insist that more community-based mental health facilities be placed in inner-cities to address more effectively such neglected problems as alcoholism and family violence.

12. Enhancing Public Housing

In several cities (e.g., Washington, D.C., St. Louis, and Jamaica Plains, Massachusetts), public housing residents have demonstrated that they can manage their housing facilities more cost-effectively than local government agencies, while reducing markedly the level of welfare dependency. For example, Kenilworth-Parkside's Resident Management Corporation has restored community pride by creating over a dozen small businesses operated by public housing residents, by sending over 500 of its youth to college, and by reducing unemployment, welfare dependency, adolescent pregnancy, and drug abuse. Public housing resident councils in other cities should be provided with appropriate technical assistance and other resources to determine the feasibility of establishing tenant management corporations.

13. Expanding Low-Income Housing

The increasing unavailability of affordable housing for low-income families has reached alarming proportions and has led to a surge in overcrowding, homelessness, foster care placements, child neglect, family violence, physical illness, and mental illness. In coalition with other advocates for the poor, blacks must mount vigorous lobbying efforts to expand the supply of low-income housing in urban and rural areas by: (a) expanding the availability of subsidized rental units; (b) restoring thousands of abandoned and boarded-up housing; (c) providing incentives for local public housing authorities to rehabilitate vacant apartments; and (d) expanding home ownership options for low-income families, such as urban homesteading, "self-help," and "sweat equity" housing.

X. APPENDIX

Assessment of the Status of Black Americans
Project Study Group Members

Project Leaders

Director: Wornie L. Reed, William Monroe Trotter Institute, University of
   Massachusetts at Boston

Co-Chair: James E. Blackwell, Department of Sociology, University of
   Massachusetts at Boston
Co-Chair: Lucius J. Barker, Department of Political Science, Washington University

Study Group on Education

Charles V. Willie (Chair), School of Education, Harvard University
Antoine M. Garibaldi (Vice-Chair), Department of Education, Xavier University
Robert A. Dentler, Department of Sociology, University of Massachusetts at Boston
Robert C. Johnson, Minority Studies Academic Program, St. Cloud State University
Meyer Weinberg, Department of Education, University of Massachusetts at Amherst

Study Group on Employment, Income and Occupations

William Darity, Jr., (Chair) Department of Economics, University of North Carolina
Barbara Jones (Vice-Chair), College of Business, Prairies View A&M University
Jeremiah P. Cotton, Department of Economics, University of Massachusetts at
   Boston
Herbert Hill, Industrial Relations Research Institute, University of Wisconsin

Study Group on Political Participation and
The Administration of Justice

Michael B. Preston (Chair), Department of Political Science, University of Southern
   California
Diane M. Pinderhughes (Vice-Chair), Department of Political Science, University of
   Illinois/Champaign
Tobe Johnson, Department of Political Science, Morehouse College

Nolan Jones, Staff Director, Committee on Criminal Justice and Public Protection,
    National Governors Association
Susan Welch, Department of Political Science, University of Nebraska
John Zipp, Department of Sociology, University of Wisconsin-Milwaukee

Study Group on Social and Cultural Change

Alphonso Pinkney (Chair), Department of Sociology, Hunter College
James Turner (Vice-Chair), Africana Studies and Research Center, Cornell
    University
John Henrik Clarke, Department of Black and Puerto Rican Studies, Hunter College
Sidney Wilhelm, Department of Sociology, State University of New York-Buffalo

Study Group on Health Status and Medical Care

William Darity, Sr. (Chair), School of Public Health, University of Massachusetts
    at Amherst
Stanford Roman (Vice-Chair), Morehouse School of Medicine, Atlanta
Claudia Baquet, National Cancer Institute, Bethesda, Maryland
Noma L. Roberson, Department of Cancer Control and Epidemiology, Rockwell Park
    Institute

Study Group on The Family

Robert B. Hill (Chair), Morgan State University, Baltimore, Maryland
Andrew Billingsley (Vice-Chair), Department of Family and Community
    Development, University of Maryland
Eleanor Engram, Engram-Miller Associates, Cleveland, Ohio
Michelene R. Malson, School of Social Work, University of North Carolina
Roger H. Rubin, Department of Family and Community Development, University of
    Maryland
Carol B. Stack, Graduate School of Education, University of California-Berkeley
James B. Stewart, Black Studies Program, Pennsylvania State University
James E. Teele, Department of Sociology, Boston University

Contributors

Carolyne Arnold, College of Public and Community Services, University of Massachusetts at Boston

James Banks, School of Education, University of Washington

Margaret Beale Spencer, College of Education, Emory University

Bob Blauner, Department of Sociology, University of California, Berkeley

Larry Carter, Department of Sociology, University of Oregon

Obie Clayton, School of Criminal Justice, University of Nebraska

James P. Comer, Department of Psychiatry, Yale Medical School

Charles Flowers, Department of Education, Fisk University

Bennett Harrison, Urban and Public Affairs, Carnegie Mellon University

Norris M. Haynes, Child Study Center, New Haven

Joseph Himes, Department of Sociology, University of North Carolina at Greensboro

Hubert E. Jones, School of Social Work, Boston University

James M. Jones, Department of Psychology, University of Delaware

Faustine C. Jones-Wilson, *Journal of Negro Education*, Howard University

Barry A. Kreisberg, National Council on Crime and Delinquency, San Francisco

Hubert G. Locke, Society of Justice Program, University of Washington

E. Yvonne Moss, William Monroe Trotter Institute, University of Massachusetts at Boston

Willie Pearson, Jr., Department of Sociology, Grambling State University

Michael L. Radelet, Department of Sociology, University of Florida

Robert Rothman, *Education Week*, Washington, DC

Diana T. Slaughter, School of Education, Northwestern University

A. Wade Smith, Department of Sociology, Arizona State University

Leonard Stevens, Compact for Educational Opportunity, Milwaukee

Wilbur Watson, Department of Sociology, Atlanta University

Warren Whatley, Department of Economics, University of Michigan

John B. Williams, Affirmative Action Office, Harvard University

Rhonda Williams, Department of Economics, University of Maryland

Reginald Wilson, American Council of Education, Washington, DC

XI. REFERENCES

Alexander, B.
1987   "The Black Church and Community Empowerment," in Woodson (ed.),
                op. cit., 45-69.

Allen, M.L., S. Miller, and J. Abbey
1987   "Teens in Foster Care: Preventing Pregnancy and Building Self-
                Sufficiency." Children's Defense Fund, September.

Allen, W.R.
1978a   "The Search for Applicable Theories of Black Family Life." *Journal of
                Marriage & the Family* 40: 1, 117-129.

Allen, W.R.
1978b   "Race, Family Setting and Adolescent Achievement Orientation."
                Journal of Negro Education 3, 230-243.

Allen, W.R.
1979   "Class, Culture and Family Organization: The Effects of Class and
                Race on Family Structure in Urban America." *Journal of Comparative
                Family Studies* 10: 301-313.

Allen, W.R.
1981   "Race and Sex Differences in the Socialization of Male Children," in
                L. Gary (ed.), *op. cit.*, 99-114.

Allen, W.R., R. A. English, and J.A. Hall (eds.)
1986   *Black American Families, 1965-1984: A Classified, Selectively
                Annotated Bibliography.* Westport, CT: Greenwood Press.

Allen, W.R. and R. Farley
1986   "The Shifting Social and Economic Tides of Black America, 1950-
                1980." *American Sociological Review* 12: 277-306.

Aschenbrenner, J.
1973   "Extended Families Among Black Americans." *Journal of
                Comparative Family Studies* 4, 257-268.

Auletta, K.
1982   *The Underclass.* New York: Vintage Books.

Austin, B.W.
1976   "White Attitudes Toward Black Discrimination." *Urban League Review* 2:1, 37-42.

Austin, B.W.
1980   "Domestic Policy Implications as They Relate to Black Ethnic Groups in America," in Bryce-Laporte (ed.), *op. cit.*, 223-229.

Bane, M.J.
1976   *Here to Stay: American Families in the Twentieth Century.* New York: Basic Books.

Bane, M.J.
1986   "Household Composition and Poverty," in Danziger & Weinberg, *op. cit.*, 209-231.

Banfield, E.C.
1968   *The Unheavenly City.* Boston: Little, Brown & Company.

Banks, J.A. and J.D. Grambs
1972   *Black Self-Concept.* New York: McGraw-Hill.

Banks, W.C.
1976   "White Preference in Blacks: A Paradigm in Search of a Phenomenon." *Psychological Bulletin* 83: 6, 1179-1186.

Baron, H.M.
1969   "The Web of Urban Racism," in Knowles & Prewitt, *op. cit.*, 134-176.

Batra, R.
1987   *The Great Depression of 1990.* New York: Simon & Schuster.

Bell, P. and J. Evans
1981   "Counseling the Black Client: Alcohol Use and Abuse in Black America." *Professional Education: 5.* Center City, MN: Hazelden Educational Materials.

Berlin, G. and A. Sum
1987   "Toward a More Perfect Union: Basic Skills, Poor Families, and Our Economic Future." September, Unpublished Paper.

Berger, B.
1970   "Black Culture or Lower-Class Culture," in L. Rainwater (ed.), *Soul.*
                New Brunswick, NJ: Transaction Books, 117-125.

Berger, P.L. and R.J. Neuhaus
1977   *To Empower People: The Role of Mediating Structures in Public Policy.*
                Washington, D.C.: American Enterprise Institute for Public Policy
                Research.

Billingsley, A.
1968   *Black Families in White America.* Englewood Cliffs, NJ: Prentice-
                Hall.

Billingsley, A.
1970   "Black Families and White Social Science." *Journal of Social Issues*
                26: 3, 127-142.

Billingsley, A.
1973   "Black Family Structure: Myths and Realities." *Studies in Public
                Welfare*, U.S. Congress, Joint Economic Committee, Paper No. 12, Part
                II, December 3, 306-319.

Billingsley, A.
1987   "Black Families in a Changing Society," in *The State of Black America,
                1987.* New York: National Urban League, 97-111.

Billingsley, A. and J.M. Giovannoni
1972   *Children of the Storm: Black Children and American Child Welfare.*
                New York: Harcourt, Brace & Jovanovich.

Blackwell, J.E.
1975   *The Black Community: Diversity and Unity.* New York: Dodd, Mead.

Blackwell, J.E. and M. Janowitz (ed.)
1974   *Black Sociologists: Historical and Contemporary Perspectives.*
                Chicago: University of Chicago Press.

Blank, R.M. and A.S. Blinder
1986   "Macroeconomics, Income Distribution and Poverty," in Danziger &
                Weinberg, *op. cit.*, 180-208.

Blauner, R.
1970   "Black Culture: Lower-Class Result or Ethnic Creation?" in Lee
                Rainwater (ed.), *Soul*. New Brunswick, NJ: Transaction Books, 129-
                166.

Blassingame, J.W.
1972   *The Slave Community: Plantation Life in the Antebellum South*. New
                York: Oxford University Press.

Block, W.E. and M.A. Walker (eds.)
1982   *Discrimination, Affirmative Action and Equal Opportunity*.
                Vancouver, B.C., Canada: The Fraser Institute.

Bluestone, B. and B. Harrison
1982   *The Deindustrialization of America*. New York: Basic Books.

Bonnett, A.W.
1980   "An Examination of Rotating Credit Associations Among Black West
                Indian Immigrants in Brooklyn," in Bryce-Laporte (ed.), *op. cit.*, 271-
                283.

Boykin, A.W. and F.D. Toms
1985   "Black Child Socialization: A Conceptual Framework," in McAdoo &
                McAdoo, *op. cit.*, 33-51.

Brenner, M.H.
1979   "Pathology and the National Economy." U.S. Congress, Joint
                Economic Committee, Task Force on Economic Priorities, October 31.

Brim, O.G., Jr.
1957   "The Parent-Child Relation as a Social System: I. Parent and Child
                Roles." *Child Development* 28:3, 345-346.

Bronfenbrenner, U.
1979   *The Ecology of Human Development*. Cambridge, MA: Harvard
                University Press.

Brown, D.R.
1982   *The Church As a Predictor of Black Social Participation in Voluntary
                Associations*. Washington, D.C.: Institute for Urban Affairs and
                Research, Howard University.

Brown, D.R. and R.W. Walters
1979   *Exploring the Role of the Black Church in the Community.*
            Washington, D.C.: Institute for Urban Affairs and Research, Howard
            University.

Brown, L.P.
1988   "Crime in the Black Community," in *The State of Black America: 1988.*
            New York: National Urban League, 95-113.

Bryce-Laporte, R.S.
1973   "Black Immigrants," in Rose, et al., *op. cit.*, 44-61.

Bryce-Laporte, R.S. (ed.)
1980   *Sourcebook on the New Immigration: Implications for the United States
            and the International Community.* New Brunswick, NJ: Transaction
            Books.

Bryce-Laporte, R.S. and D.M. Mortimer (eds.)
1976   *Caribbean Immigration to the United States.* Washington, D.C.:
            Research Institute on Immigration and Ethnic Studies, Smithsonian
            Institution.

Burbridge, L. C.
1985-86   "Black Women in Employment and Training Programs." *The Review of
            Black Political Economy* 14:2-3, 97-114.

Burbridge, L.C.
1986   "Changes in Equal Employment Enforcement." *The Review of Black
            Political Economy* 15:1, 71-80.

Butler, S. and A. Kondratas
1987   *Out of the Poverty Trap.* New York: The Free Press.

Cannon, M.S. and B.Z. Locke
1977   "Being Black Is Detrimental to One's Mental Health: Myth or
            Reality?" *Phylon* 38:4, 408-428.

Caplovitz, D.
1979   *Making Ends Meet: How Families Cope with Inflation and Recession.*
            Beverly Hills, CA: Sage Publications.

Carmichael, S. and C. Hamilton
1967   *Black Power*. New York: Vintage Books.

Cazenave, N.A.
1979   "Middle-Income Black Fathers: An Analysis of the Provider Role." *The Family Coordinator* 28: 583-593.

Cazenave, N.A.
1981   "Black Men in America: The Quest for 'Manhood'," in H.P. McAdoo, *op. cit.*, 176-185.

Cazenave, N.A.
1988   "Philadelphia's Children in Need: Black, White, Brown, Yellow and Poor." *The State of Black Philadelphia: 1988*. Urban League of Philadelphia, 47-62.

Center on Budget and Policy Priorities
1984a   "End Results: The Impact of Federal Policies Since 1980 on Low-Income Americans," Washington, D.C.: Interfaith Action for Economic Justice, September.

Center on Budget and Policy Priorities
1984b   "Falling Behind: A Report on How Blacks Have Fared Under the Reagan Policies," Washington, D.C., October.

Children's Defense Fund
1984   *A Children's Defense Budget: An Analysis of the President's FY 1985 Budget and Children*. Washington, D.C.

Children's Defense Fund
1986   *A Children's Defense Budget: An Analysis of the President's FY 1987 Federal Budget and Children*. Washington, D.C.

Children's Defense Fund
1987   *Child Care: The Time is Now*. Washington, D.C.

Christopherson, V.
1979   "Implications for Strengthening Family Life: Rural Black Families," in N. Stinnett, et al., (eds.) *Building Family Strengths: Blueprints for Action*. Lincoln: University of Nebraska Press.

Clark, K. B.
1965   *Dark Ghetto: Dilemmas of Social Power*. New York: Harper & Row.

Clark, K.B. and M.K. Clark
1939   "The Development of Consciousness of Self and the Emergence of
                Racial Identification in Negro Pre-School Children." *Journal of Social
                Psychology* 10, 591-599.

Clark, K.B. and M.K. Clark
1947   "Racial Identification and Preference in Children," in T.M. Newcomb
                and E.L. Hartley (eds.) *Readings in Social Psychology*. New York:
                Henry Holt.

Clark, R.M.
1983   *Family Life and School Achievement: Why Poor Black Children
                Succeed or Fail*. Chicago: University of Chicago Press.

Coe, R.
1978   "Dependency and Poverty in the Short and Long Run." *Five Thousand
                American Families--Patterns of Economic Progress. Vol. VI*. Ann
                Arbor: Survey Research Center, Institute for Social Research,
                University of Michigan, 273-296.

Coe, R.
1982   "Welfare Dependency: Fact or Myth?" *Challenge* September-October,
                25: 4, 43-49.

Collins, P.H.
1986   "The Afro-American Work/Family Nexus: An Exploratory Analysis."
                Western Journal of Black Studies 10: 3, 148-158.

Committee for Economic Development
1987   *Children in Need: Investment for the Educationally Disadvantaged*.
                New York.

Committee on Policy for Racial Justice
1987   *Black Initiative and Governmental Responsibility*. Washington, D.C.:
                Joint Center for Political Studies.

Congressional Black Caucus
1982   *The Black Leadership Family Plan for the Unity, Survival and Progress
                of Black People*. Washington, D.C.

Cromartie, J.B. and C.B. Stack
1987   "Who Counts? Black Homeplace Migration to the South, 1975-1980,"
                Unpublished Paper.

Cross, T.
1984   *The Black Power Imperative: Racial Inequality and the Politics of
                Nonviolence.* New York: Faulkner.

Cross, W.E.
1982   "The Ecology of Human Development of Black and White Children:
                Implications for Predicting Racial Preference Patterns," in M. Cochran
                and C. Henderson (eds.) *The Ecology of Urban Family Life.*
                Comparative Ecology of Human Development Project, Cornell
                University, Chap. 6.

Cross, W.E.
1985   "Black Identity: Rediscovering the Distinction Between Personal
                Identity and Reference Group Orientation," in Spencer, *op. cit.*, 155-
                171.

Currie, E. and J.H. Skolnick
1984   *America's Problems: Social Issues and Public Policy.* Boston: Little,
                Brown and Company.

Daniels, S. and C.B. Wilkinson
1983   "An Ecological Comparison of Male and Female Adolescents from
                Black Single Parent Female-Headed Families," Greater Kansas City
                Mental Health Foundation.

Danziger, S. and P. Gottschalk
1986   "Work, Poverty and the Working Poor: A Multifaceted Problem."
                Monthly Labor Review September, 109: 9, 17-21.

Danziger, S. and D.H. Weinberg (eds.)
1986   *Fighting Poverty: What Works and What Doesn't.* Cambridge, MA:
                Harvard University Press.

Darity, W.A. and S.L. Myers, Jr.
1984   "Does Welfare Dependency Cause Female Headship: The Case of the
                Black Family." *Journal of Marriage and the Family* November, 765-
                779.

Datcher-Loury, L. and G. Loury
1986   "The Effects of Attitudes and Aspirations on the Labor Supply of
                Young Men," in Freeman & Holzer, *op. cit.*, 377-401.

Davis, R.
1978   "Black Suicide and the Relational System: Theoretical and Empirical
                Implications of Communal and Familial Ties." Institute for Research
                on Poverty, University of Wisconsin, 481-487.

Davis, R.
1980   "Suicide Among Young Blacks: Trends and Perspectives." *Phylon*
                September, 41: 3, 223-229.

Davis, R.
1982   "Black Suicide and Support Systems: Some Implications for Mental
                Health Practitioners." *Phylon* 63: 4, 307-314.

DeAnda, D.
1984   "Bicultural Socialization: Factors Affecting the Minority Experience."
                Social Work March-April, 29: 2, 101-107.

Dill, B.T.
1980   "'The Means to Put My Children Through': Child-Rearing Goals and
                Strategies Among Black Female Domestic Servants," in Rodgers-Rose,
                (ed.), *op. cit.,* 107-123.

Dixon, V. and B. Foster (eds.)
1971   *Beyond Black or White: An Alternate America.* Boston: Little, Brown
                & Company.

Downs, A.
1970   "Racism in America and How to Combat It," in A. Downs, *Urban
                Problems and Prospects.* Chicago: Markham, 75-114.

Drake, S.C. and H.R. Cayton
1945   *Black Metropolis, Vols. 1 & 2.* New York: Harper & Row.

DuBois, W.E.B.
1896-1917   *Atlanta University Publication Series, 1896-1917: Vols 1 & 2.* New
                York: Arno Press Reprint, 1968 & 1969.

DuBois, W.E.B.
1898   "The Study of the Negro Problem." *Annals* January, 1, 1-23.

DuBois, W.E.B.
1899   *The Philadelphia Negro: A Social Study.* New York: Schocken Books.
                Reprint 1967.

DuBois, W.E.B.
1903   *The Souls of Black Folk.* New York: New American Library Reprint,
                1969.

DuBois, W.E.B.
1908   *The Negro American Family.* Atlanta University Press. Cambridge,
                MA: The MIT Press Reprint, 1970.

DuBois, W.E.B.
1915   *The Negro.* Holt & Co. New York: Oxford University Press Reprint,
                1970.

Duncan, G.J. (ed.)
1984   *Years of Poverty – Years of Plenty: The Changing Economic Fortunes of
                American Workers and Families.* Ann Arbor: Institute for Social
                Research, University of Michigan.

Edelman, M. W.
1987   *Families in Peril: An Agenda for Social Change.* Cambridge, MA:
                Harvard University Press.

Elder, G. H.
1985a   "Household, Kinship and the Life Course: Perspectives on Black
                Families and Children," in Spencer, et al., *op. cit.*, 29-43.

Elder, G.H. (ed.)
1985b   *Life Course Dynamics: Trajectories and Transitions, 1968-1980.*
                Ithaca, NY: Cornell University Press.

Ellwood, D.T. and M.J. Bane
1984   "The Impact of AFDC on Family Structure and Living Arrangements."
                U.S. Department of Health and Human Services.

Ellwood, D.T. and L.H. Summers
1986   "Poverty in America: Is Welfare the Answer or the Problem?" in
                Danziger & Weinberg, *op. cit.*, 78-105.

Engram, E.
1982   *Science, Myth, Reality: The Black Family in One-Half Century of
              Research.* Westport, CT: Greenwood Press.

Evaxx, Inc.
1981   "A Study of Black Americans' Attitudes Toward Self-Help."
              Washington, D.C.: American Enterprise Institute's Neighborhood
              Revitalization Project, August.

Everett, J.E.
1985   "An Examination of Child Support Enforcement Issues," in McAdoo &
              Parham (eds.), *op. cit.*, 75-112.

Fanshel, D. and Shinn, E.G.
1978   *Children in Foster Care: A Longitudinal Investigation.* New York:
              Columbia University Press.

Farley, R.
1984   *Blacks and Whites: Narrowing the Gap?* Cambridge, MA: Harvard
              University Press.

Farley, R. and W. R. Allen
1987   *The Color Line and the Quality of Life in America.* New York: Russell
              Sage Foundation.

Feagin, J.R.
1978   *Racial and Ethnic Relations.* Englewood Cliffs, NJ: Prentice-Hall.

Felder, H.E.
1979   *A Statistical Evaluation of the Impact of Disqualification Provisions of
              State Unemployment Insurance Laws.* Arlington, VA: SRI
              International.

Felder, H.E.
1984   *The Changing Patterns of Black Family Income, 1960-1982.*
              Washington, D.C.: Joint Center for Political Studies.

Festinger, T.
1983   *No One Asked Us.* New York: Columbia University Press.

Flaim, P. and E. Sehgal
1985   "Displaced Workers of 1979-83: How Well Have They Fared?"
              Monthly Labor Review June, 3-16.

Fogelson, R. and R.B. Hill
1968   "Who Riots? Arrest Patterns in the 1960's Riots," *Supplemental Studies for the National Advisory Commission on Civil Disorders.* Government Printing Office, 217-248.

Foster, H.J.
1983   "African Patterns in the Afro-American Family." *Journal of Black Studies* 14: 2, December, 201-232.

Franklin, A.J. and N. Boyd-Franklin
1985   "A Psychoeducational Perspective on Black Parenting," in McAdoo & McAdoo, *op. cit.*, 194-210.

Frazier, E.F.
1926   "Three Scourges of the Negro Family." *Opportunity* July, 4: 43, 210-213,234.

Frazier, E.F.
1931   "Family Disorganization Among Negroes." *Opportunity* July, 9: 7, 204-207.

Frazier, E. F.
1939   *The Negro Family in the United States.* Chicago: University of Chicago Press. Revised 1966.

Frazier, E. F.
1949   *The Negro in the United States.* New York: MacMillan. Revised 1957.

Freeman, R.B. and H.J. Holzer (eds.)
1986   *The Black Youth Employment Crisis.* Chicago: The University of Chicago Press.

Friedman, R.
1975   "Institutional Racism: How to Discriminate Without Really Trying," in T. Pettigrew (ed.), *Racial Discrimination in the U.S.* New York: Harper & Row, 384-407.

Furstenberg, F., T. Hershberg, and J. Modell
1975   "The Origins of the Female-Headed Black Family: The Impact of Urban Experience." *Journal of Interdisciplinary History* 6, 211-233.

Furstenberg, F.
1981   "Implicating the Family: Teenage Parenthood and Kinship
               Involvement," in Theodora Ooms (ed.), *Teenage Pregnancy in a Family
               Context*. Philadelphia: Temple University Press, 131-164.

Gallup Organization
1985   "Religion in America: 1935-1985," *The Gallup Report*, Report No. 236,
               May.

Garbarino, J.
1982   *Children and Families in the Social Environment*. New York: Aldine
               Publishing Company.

Garfinkel, I. and M.S. Melli
1987   *Maintenance Through the Tax System: The Proposed Wisconsin Child
               Support Assurance Program*. Madison: University of Wisconsin,
               Institute for Research on Poverty.

Gary, L. (ed.)
1981   *Black Men*. Beverly Hills, CA: Sage Publications.

Gary, L. and L.P. Brown (eds.)
1975   *Crime and Its Impact on the Black Community*. Washington, D.C.:
               Institute for Urban Affairs and Research, Howard University.

Gary, L., B. Leashore, C. Howard, and R. Buckner-Dowell
1980   *Help-Seeking Behavior Among Black Males*. Washington, D.C.:
               Institute for Urban Affairs and Research, Howard University.

Gary, L., L. Beatty, G. Berry, and M. Price
1983   *Stable Black Families: Final Report*. Washington, D.C.: Institute for
               Urban Affairs and Research, Howard University.

Gary, L., D. Brown, N. Milburn, V. Thomas, and D. Lockley
1984   *Pathways: A Study of Black Informal Support Networks*. Institute for
               Urban Affairs and Research, Howard University.

Gary, L., L. A. Beatty, and G.L. Berry
1985   "Strengthening Black Families," in Harvey, *op. cit.*, 91-125.

Geismar, L.L.
1973   *555 Families: A Social-Psychological Study of Young Families in
               Transition*. New Brunswick, NJ: Transaction Books.

Genovese, E.D.
1974   *Roll Jordan Roll: The World the Slaves Made.* New York: Random
               House.

Gibbs, J.T.
1984   "Black Adolescents and Youth: An Endangered Species." *American
               Journal of Orthopsychiatry* 54: 1, 6-21.

Gibbs, J.T. (ed.)
1988   *Young, Black, and Male in America: An Endangered Species.* Dover,
               MA: Auburn House Publishing Company.

Gilder, G.
1981   *Wealth and Poverty.* New York: Basic Books.

Glasgow, D.G.
1981   *The Black Underclass.* New York: Vintage Books.

Glazer, N.
1975   *Affirmative Discrimination.* New York: Basic Books.

Glazer, N. and D.P. Moynihan
1963   *Beyond the Melting Pot.* Cambridge, MA: MIT Press.

Goodwin, L.
1983   *Causes and Cures of Welfare: New Evidence on the Social Psychology of
               the Poor.* Lexington, MA: Lexington Books.

Gordon, V.V.
1976   "A Critique of the Methodologies for the Study of the Black Self-
               Concept." *Journal of Afro-American Issues* December.

Gordon, V.V.
1980   "A Critique of the Methodologies for the Study of the Black Self-
               Concept." *Journal of Afro-American Issues* December.

Green, D.S. and E. D. Driver (eds.)
1978   *W.E.B. DuBois: On Sociology and the Black Community.* Chicago:
               University of Chicago Press.

Gruber, M.L.
1980   "Inequality in the Social Services." *Social Service Review* March, 59-
               75.

Gurak, D.T., D. Smith, and M.F. Goldson

1982   *The Minority Foster Child: A Comparative Study of Hispanic, Black and White Children.* Bronx, NY: Hispanic Research Center, Fordham University.

Gutman, H.G.

1976   *The Black Family in Slavery and Freedom: 1750-1925.* New York: Vintage Books.

Hagen, D.Q.

1983   "The Relationship Between Job Loss and Physical and Mental Illness." *Hospital and Community Psychiatry* 34:5, 438-441.

Hale-Benson, J.E.

1982   *Black Children: Their Roots, Culture and Learning Styles.* Baltimore, MD: Johns Hopkins University Press.

Hare, B. R.

1977   "Race and Socioeconomic Variations in Preadolescent Area-Specific and General Self-Esteem." *International Journal of Intercultural Relations* 1:3, 31-59.

Hare, B.R.

1982   "The Rites of Passage: A Black Perspective." A Youth Development Discussion Paper. National Urban League.

Hare, B.R.

1988   "Black Youth at Risk," in *The State of Black America: 1988.* New York: National Urban League, 81-93.

Hare, N.

1970   *Black Anglo-Saxons.* London: Macmillan.

Hare, N.

1976   "What Black Intellectuals Misunderstand About the Black Family." *Black World* 25 (March), 4-14.

Hare, N. and J. Hare

1984   *The Endangered Black Family.* San Francisco, CA: Black Think Tank.

Harley, S. and R. Terborg-Penn (eds.)

1978   *The Afro-American Woman.* New York: Kennikat Press.

Harper, F.D.
1976   *Alcohol Abuse and Black America.* Alexandria, VA: Douglass
                Publishers.

Harper, F.D. and M.P. Dawkins
1977   "Alcohol Abuse." *The Black Scholar* April, 23-31.

Harper, H.
1985-86   "Black Women and the Job Training Partnership Act." *The Review of
                Black Political Economy* 14:2-3, 115-129.

Harvey, A.R. (ed.)
1985a   *The Black Family: An Afrocentric Perspective.* New York:
                Commission for Racial Justice, United Church of Christ.

Harvey, A.R.
1985b   "Traditional African Culture as the Basis for the Afro-American
                Church in America: The Foundation of the Black Family in America,"
                in Harvey, *op. cit.*, 1-22.

Hendricks, L.E.
1979   "Young Unwed Fathers: Problems They Encounter and the Ways They
                Deal with Them: Columbus, Ohio Sample," Institute for Urban
                Affairs & Research, Howard University, December.

Hendricks, L.E. and C.S. Howard
1979   "Young Unwed Fathers: Problems They Face and the Ways They
                Handle Them: Chicago, Illinois Sample," Institute for Urban Affairs
                & Research, Howard University, November.

Herskovits, M.J.
1941   *The Myth of the Negro Past.* Boston: Beacon Press, Beacon Paperback
                Edition, 1958.

Herzog, E.
1970   "Social Stereotypes and Social Research." *Journal of Social Issues* 26:
                3, 109-125.

Hill, R. and D.A. Hansen
1960   "The Identification of Conceptual Frameworks Utilized in Family
                Study." *Marriage of Family Living* 22: 299-311.

Hill, R.B.
1971   *The Strengths of Black Families.* New York: Emerson Hall Publishers.

Hill, R.B.
1975   *Black Families in the 1974-75 Depression.* Washington, D.C.:
              Research Department, National Urban League.

Hill, R.B.
1977   *Informal Adoption Among Black Families.* Washington, D.C.:
              Research Department, National Urban League.

Hill, R.B.
1978a   *The Illusion of Black Progress.* Washington, D.C.: Research
              Department, National Urban League.

Hill, R.B.
1978b   "A Demographic Profile of the Black Elderly." *Aging* September-
              October, 2-9.

Hill, R.B.
1980   *Merton's Role Types and Paradigm of Deviance.* New York: Arno Press
              and New York Times.

Hill, R.B.
1981   *Economic Policies and Black Progress: Myths and Realities.*
              Washington, D.C.: Research Department, National Urban League.

Hill, R.B.
1983a   "Income Maintenance Programs and the Minority Elderly," in R.L.
              McNeely & J. L. Colen (eds.) *Aging in Minority Groups.* Beverly Hills,
              CA: Sage Publications, 195-211.

Hill, R.B.
1983b   "Comparative Socio-Economic Profiles of Caribbean and Non-
              Caribbean Blacks in the United States." May.

Hill, R.B.
1984   "The Polls and Ethnic Minorities." *Annals* March, 155-166.

Hill, R.B.
1986   "The Black Middle Class: Past, Present and Future," in National
              Urban League, *State of Black America,* 43-64.

Hill, R.B.
1987a   "The Black Middle Class Defined." *Ebony* August, 30,32.

Hill, R.B.
1987b   "The Impact of the Aid to Families with Dependent Children--
Unemployed Parent (AFDC-UP) Program on Black Families," Black
Family Impact Analysis Program, Baltimore Urban League.

Hill, R.B.
1988a   "Structural Discrimination: The Unintended Consequences of
Institutional Processes," in H.J. O'Gorman (ed.), *Surveying Social Life:
Papers in Honor of Herbert Hyman.* Wesleyan University Press, 1988,
353-375.

Hill, R.B.
1988b   "Adolescent Male Responsibility in African-American Families,"
National Urban League.

Hill, R.B.
1989a   "Critical Issues for Black Families by the Year 2000," *The State of
Black America, 1989.* New York: National Urban League, 41-61.

Hill, R.B.
1989b   "Economic Forces, Structural Discrimination and Black Family
Instability." *The Review of Black Political Economy* 17:3, 5-23.

Hill, R.B. and R. Nixon
1984   *Youth Employment in American Industry.* New Brunswick, NJ:
Transaction Books.

Hines, P. and N. Boyd-Franklin
1980   "Black Families," in *The Paradigms*, 84-107.

Hofferth, S.L.
1985   "Children's Life Course: Family Structure and Living Arrangements
in Cohort Perspective," in G. Elder (ed.), *op. cit.*, 75-112.

Horvath, F.W.
1987   "The Pulse of Economic Change: Displaced Workers of 1981-85."
Monthly Labor Review June, 3-12.

Hyman, H. H. and J.S. Reed
1969   "'Black Matriarchy' Reconsidered: Evidence from Secondary Analysis
of Sample Surveys." *Public Opinion Quarterly* Fall, 33, 346-354.

Jackman, M.R.
1973   "Education and Prejudice or Education and Response Set?" *American Sociological Review* 38:3, 327-339.

Jackman, M.R. and M.J. Muha
1984   Education and Intergroup Attitudes." *American Sociological Review* 49, 751-769.

Jackson, A.W. (ed.)
1982   *Black Families and the Medium of Television.* Ann Arbor: University of Michigan, Bush Program in Child Development and Social Policy.

Jackson, J.J.
1971   "But Where Are the Men?" *The Black Scholar* December, 30-41.

Jackson, J.S., W.R. McCullough, and G. Gurin
1981   "Group Identity Development Within Black Families," in McAdoo, *Black Families*, 252-263.

Jedlicka, D., Y. Shin, and E.S. Lee
1977   "Suicide Among Blacks." *Phylon* 38: 4, 448-455.

Jeffers, C.
1967   *Living Poor: A Participant Observer Study of Choices and Priorities.* Ann Arbor, MI: Ann Arbor Publishers.

Jewell, K.S.
1988   *Survival of the Black Family: The Institutional Impact of U.S. Social Policy.* New York: Praeger.

Johnson, L.B.
1981   "Perspectives on Black Family Empirical Research: 1965-1978," in H. McAdoo (ed.), *Black Families*. Beverly Hills, CA: Sage Publications, 87-102.

Johnson,C.S.
1932   "The New Frontier of Negro Labor." *Opportunity* July, 10: 6, 168-173.

Johnson, C.S.
1934   *Shadow of the Plantation.* Chicago: University of Chicago Press.

Johnson Publishing Company
1986   "Poll Reveals Blacks Who Aid Blacks and Don't Ask for U.S. Help." *Jet* August 18.

Joint Center for Political Studies
1987   *Black Initiative and Governmental Responsibility.* Washington, D.C.

Jones, D.L.
1979   "African-American Clients: Clinical Practice Issues." *Social Work* March, 24: 2, 112-118.

Jones, F.A.
1981   "External Crosscurrents and Internal Diversity: An Assessment of Black Progress, 1960-1980." *Daedalus* 110: 2, 71-101.

Jones, J.M.
1972   *Prejudice and Racism.* Reading, MA: Addison-Wesley.

Jones, W. and M.F. Rice (ed.)
1987   *Health Care Issues in Black America: Policies, Problems and Prospects.* Westport, CT: Greenwood Press.

Kagen, S.I. , D. Powell, B. Weissbound, and E. Ziegler
1987   *America's Family Support Programs: Perspectives and Prospects.* New Haven, CT: Yale University Press.

Karenga, M.
1982   *Introduction to Black Studies.* Los Angeles, CA: Kawaida Publications.

Karenga, M.
1986   "Social Ethics and the Black Family: An Alternative Analysis." *The Black Scholar* October, 17: 5, 41-54.

Kellam, S.G., M.E. Ensminger, and R.J. Turner
1977   "Family Structure and the Mental Health of Children." *Archives of General Psychiatry* September, 34, 1012-1022.

Kenyatta, M.
1983   "In Defense of the Black Family: The Impact of Racism on the Family as a Support Sytem." *Monthly Review* March, 12-21.

Killingsworth, C.C.
1966   "Structural Unemployment in the United States," in J. Schreiber (ed.)
               Employment Problems of Automation and Advanced Technology. New
               York: St. Martin's Press, 128-156.

Kilson, M.
1981   "Black Social Classes and Intergenerational Poverty." *The Public
               Interest* Summer, 64, 58-78.

Kinder, D.R. and D.C. Sears
1981   "Prejudice and Politics: Symbolic Racism Versus Racial Threats to the
               Good Life." *Journal of Personality and Social Psychology* 40: 3, 414-
               431.

King, J.R.
1976   "African Survivals in the Black American Family: Key Factors in
               Stability." *Journal of Afro-American Issues* 4, 153-167.

Knitzer, J. and M.L. Allen
1978   *Children Without Homes: An Examination of Public Responsiblity to
               Children in Out-of-Home Care.* Washington, D.C.: Children's Defense
               Fund.

Knowles, L. and K. Prewitt (eds.)
1969   *Institutional Racism in America.* Englewood Cliffs, NJ: Prentice-Hall.

Kronus, S.
1971   *The Black Middle Class.* Columbus, OH: Charles E. Merrill
               Publishers.

Kunjufu, J.
1984   *Developing Positive Self-Images & Discipline in Black Children.*
               Chicago: African-American Images.

Kunjufu, J.
1985   *Countering the Conspiracy to Destroy Black Boys. Vol I.* Chicago:
               African-American Images.

Kunjufu, J.
1986a   *Countering the Conspiracy to Destroy Black Boys. Vol II.* Chicago:
               African-American Images.

Kunjufu, J.
1986b   *Motivating and Preparing Black Youth to Work*. Chicago: African-
               American Images.

Kuttner, R.J.
1983   "The Declining Middle." *Atlantic Monthly* July, 60-72.

Ladner, J.
1971   *Tomorrow's Tomorrow: The Black Woman*. Garden City, NY:
               Doubleday & Co.

Ladner, J.
1973   "The Urban Poor," in Rose, et al., *op. cit.*, 3-24.

Lake, R.W.
1981   *The New Suburbanites: Race & Housing in the Suburbs*. New
               Brunswick, NJ: Center for Urban Policy Research, Rutgers
               University.

Landry, B.
1978   "Growth of the Black Middle Class in the 1960s." *Urban League
               Review* 3:2 (Winter) 68-82.

Landry, B.
1987   *The New Black Middle Class*. Berkeley: University of California
               Press.

Leigh, W. and M.O. Mitchell
1980   "Public Housing and the Black Community." *The Review of Black
               Political Economy* 11:1, 53-75.

Lemann, N.
1986   "The Origins of the Underclass." *Atlantic Monthly* June: 31-55; July
               54-68.

Levitan, S.
1985   *Programs in Aid of the Poor*. Baltimore, MD: Johns Hopkins
               University Press.

Levitan, S.A. and R. Taggart
1971   *Social Experimentation and Manpower Policy: The Rhetoric and the
               Reality*. Baltimore, MD: Johns Hopkins University.

Levitan, S.A., W.B. Johnston, and R. Taggart
1975   *Still a Dream: The Changing Status of Blacks Since 1960.*
                        Cambridge, MA: Harvard University Press.

Levy, F.
1987   *Dollars and Dreams: The Changing American Income Distribution.*
                        New York: Russell Sage Foundation.

Lewis, D.K.
1975   "The Black Family: Socialization and Sex Roles." *Phylon* 36: 3, 221-
                        237.

Lewis, H.
1955   *Blackways of Kent.* Chapel Hill: University of North Carolina Press.

Lewis, H.
1967a   "Culture, Class and Poverty," Washington, D.C.: Health and
                        Welfare Council of National Capital Area--CROSS-TELL.

Lewis, H.
1967b   "Culture, Class and Family Life Among Low-Income Urban
                        Negroes," in A. Ross and H. Hill (ed.), *Employment, Race and
                        Poverty.* New York: Harcourt, Brace & World.

Lewis, H.
1967c   "Culture, Class and Child-Rearing Among Low-Income Urban
                        Negroes," in A. Ross and H. Hill (eds.) *Employment, Race and
                        Poverty.* New York: Harcourt, Brace & World.

Lewis, H.
1967d   "The Family: Resources for Change," in Rainwater & Yancey,
                        op. cit., 314-343.

Lewis, J. and J.G. Looney
1982   *The Long Struggle: Well-Functioning Working-Class Black
                        Families.* New York: Brunner-Mazel.

Lewis, O.
1959   *Five Families: Mexican Case Studies in the Culture of Poverty.*
                        New York: Basic Books.

Lieberson, S.
1980   *A Piece of the Pie: Blacks and White Immigrants Since 1880.*
                Berkeley: University of California Press.

Liebow, E.
1967   *Tally's Corner.* Boston: Little, Brown.

Lindsay, I.
1952   "The Participation of Negroes in the Establishment of Welfare
                Services, 1865-1900." Doctoral Thesis, School of Social Work,
                University of Pittsburgh.

Liwak, E.
1959-60   "The Use of Extended Family Groups in the Achievement of Social
                Goals: Some Policy Implications." *Social Problems* 177-187.

Long, L.H.
1974   "Migration and Employment Patterns of Blacks and Whites in New
                York City and Other Large Cities," May 14, Unpublished Paper.

Loury, G.
1984   "Internally Directed Action for Black Community Development:
                The Next Frontier for 'The Movement'." *Review of Black Political
                Economy* Summer-Fall, 13: 1-2, 31-46.

Malson, M.R.
1980   "A Pilot Study of the Support Systems of Urban Black Women and
                Their Families," Wellesley, MA: Wellesley College Center for
                Research on Women.

Malson, M.R.
1983a   "Black Families and Childbearing Support Networks." *Research in
                the Interweave of Social Roles* 3, 131-141.

Malson, M.R.
1983b   "The Social Support Systems of Black Families," in *The Tie That
                Binds.* Haworth Press, 37-57.

Malson, M.R.
1983c   "Black Women's Sex Roles: The Social Context for a New Ideology."
                Journal of Social Issues 39: 3, 101-113.

Malson, M.R.
1986   "Understanding Black Single-Parent Families: Stresses and
                Strengths," Wellesley, MA: Wellesley College Center for
                Developmental Services and Studies, Work in Progress, No. 25.

Malson, M.R. and B. Woody
1985   "The Work and Family Responsibilities of Black Women Single
                Parents," Wellesley, MA: Center for Research on Women,
                Wellesley College, Working Paper No. 148.

Malveaux, J.
1985   "The Economic Interests of Black and White Women: Are They
                Similar?" *Review of Black Political Economy* 14: 1, 5-27.

Manns, W.
1981   "Support Systems of Significant Others in Black Families," in
                McAdoo, H., *op. cit.*, 238-251.

Manpower Demonstration Research Committee
1980   *Summary and Findings of the National Supported Work
                Demonstration.* Cambridge, MA: Ballinger Publishers.

Marable, M.
1983   *How Capitalism Underdeveloped Black America.* Boston: South End
                Press.

Marrett, C.B. and C. Leggon (eds.)
1979   *Research in Race and Ethnic Relations.* Greenwich, CT: JAI Press.
                Vol I.

Martin, J.M. and E.P. Martin
1978a   *The Black Extended Family.* Chicago: University of Chicago Press.

Martin, J.M. and E.P. Martin
1978b   *The Helping Tradition in the Black Family and Community.* Silver
                Spring, MD: National Association of Social Workers.

Marx, K. and F. Engels
1932   *Manifesto of the Communist Party.* New York: International
                Publishers.

Massey, D.S. and N.A. Denton
1987   "Trends in the Residential Segregation of Blacks, Hispanics and
                Asians." *American Sociological Review* December, 52: 6, 802-825.

Mayhew, L.H.
1968   *Law and Equal Opportunity*. Cambridge, MA: Harvard University
                Press.

Mbiti, J.
1970   *African Religions and Philosophy*. Garden City, NY: Anchor.

McAdoo, H.P.
1978   "Factors Related to Stability in Upwardly Mobile Families."
                Journal of Marriage and the Family 40: 4.

McAdoo, H.P. (ed.)
1981   *Black Families*. Beverly Hills, CA: Sage Publications.

McAdoo, H.P.
1983   "Extended Family Support of Single Black Mothers: Final Report."
                U.S. National Institute of Mental Health, March.

McAdoo, H.P.
1985   "Racial Attitude and Self-Concept of Young Black Children Over
                Time," in McAdoo & McAdoo, *op. cit..*, 213-242.

McAdoo, H.P. and J.L. McAdoo (eds.)
1985   *Black Children: Social, Education and Parental Environments*.
                Beverly Hills, CA: Sage Publications.

McAdoo, H.P. and T.M.J. Parham (ed.)
1985   *Services to Young Families*. Washington, D.C.: American Public
                Welfare Association.

McAdoo, H.P. and R. Terborg-Penn
1985   "Historical Trends and Perspectives of Afro-American Families."
                Trends in History Winter/Spring, 97-111.

McConahay, J.B. and J.S. Hough, Jr.
1976   "Symbolic Racism." *Journal of Social Issues* 32: 2, 23-45.

McConahay, J.B., B.B. Hardee, and V. Batts
1981   "Has Racism Declined in America?" *Journal of Conflict Resolution*
                25: 4, 563-579.

McCone Commission
1965   *Violence in the City--An End or a Beginning?* A Report by the
                Governor's Commission on the Los Angeles Riot.

McGhee, J.D.
1984   "Running the Gauntlet: Black Men in America." Washington, D.C.:
                National Urban League Research Department.

Meier, A.
1963   *Negro Thought in America, 1880-1915.* Ann Arbor: University of
                Michigan.

Merton, R.K.
1936   "The Unanticipated Consequences of Purposive Social Action."
                American Sociological Review 1, 894-904.

Merton, R.K.
1957   *Social Theory and Social Structure.* Glencoe, IL: The Free Press.

Merton, R.K.
1964   "Anomie, Anomia, and Social Interaction: Contexts of Deviant
                Behavior," in M. B. Clinard (ed.), *Anomie and Deviant Behavior.*
                New York: Free Press, 213-242.

Miller, S.M.
1964   "The American Lower Classes: A Typological Approach," in A.
                Shostak & W. Gomberg (ed.), *Blue-Collar World.* Englewood Cliffs,
                NJ: Prentice-Hall, 9-23.

Millette, R.E.
1987   "West Indian Families in the United States," Unpublished.

Millette, R.E.
1988   *New Grenada in Brooklyn, Social Stratification and Adaptation
                Among First Generation Immigrants.* New York: Associated Faculty
                Press.

Mirengoff, W. and L. Rindler
1978   *CETA: Manpower Programs Under Local Control.* Washington, D.C.: National Academy of Sciences.

Moore, K., M.C. Simms, and C.L. Betsey
1986   *Choice & Circumstance: Racial Differences in Adolescent Sexuality and Fertility.* New Brunswick, NJ: Transaction Books.

Moroney, R.M.
1980   *Families, Social Services, and Social Polity: The Issue of Shared Responsibility.* U.S. National Institute of Mental Health.

Mortimer, D.M. and R.S. Bryce-Laporte (eds.)
1981   *Female Immigrants to the United States: Caribbean, Latin American and African Experiences.* Washington, D.C.: Research Institute on Immigration and Ethnic Studies, Smithsonian Institution.

Moynihan, D.P.
1967   "The Negro Family: A Case for National Action," in Rainwater & Yancey, *op. cit.*, 41-124.

Moynihan, D.P.
1987   *Family and Nation.* New York: Harcourt, Brace, Jovanovich.

Myrdal, G.
1944   *An American Dilemma. Vols. 1 & 2.* New York: Harper and Brothers.

Murray, C.
1984   *Losing Ground: American Social Policy, 1950-1980.* New York: Basic Books.

National Advisory Committee on Black Higher Education and Black Colleges and Universities, U.S. Department of Education
1980   *Still a Lifeline: The Status of Historically Black Colleges and Universities.* Washington, D.C.: Government Printing Office, November.

National Association of Black Social Workers
1986   *Preserving Black Families: Research and Action Beyond the Rhetoric.* New York.

National Center on Child Abuse and Neglect
1981   *Study Findings: National Study of the Incidence and Severity of Child Abuse and Neglect.* Washington, D.C.: U.S. Department of Health and Human Services.

National Commission for Employment Policy
1978   *Trade and Employment.* Report No. 30, November.

National Economic Association
1980   "Subsidized Progress for Low-Income People." *The Review of Black Political Economy* Fall, 11:1.

National Urban League
1980   *The Myth of Income Cushions for Blacks.* Washington, D.C.: NUL Research Department.

National Urban League
1983   *Proceedings of the Black Family Summit.* New York: National Urban League & NAACP.

National Urban League
1986   *The State of Black America, 1986.* New York.

National Urban League
1987a   *The State of Black America, 1987.* New York.

National Urban League
1987b   "1977-1987: A Decade of Double-Digit Unemployment for Blacks." *Quarterly Economic Report*, July, 16.

National Urban League
1988   *The State of Black America, 1988.* New York.

National Urban League
1989   *The State of Black America, 1989.* New York.

Nelsen, H. and A. Nelsen
1975   *Black Church in the Sixties.* Lexington: University of Kentucky Press.

Newman, D.K., N. Amidei, B. Carter, D. Day, W. Kruvant, and J. Russell.
1978   *Protest, Politics and Prosperity: Black Americans and White Institutions, 1940-75.* New York: Pantheon Books.

Nobles, W.
1974a   "African Root and American Fruit: The Black Family." *Journal of Social and Behavioral Sciences* 20:2, 52-63.

Nobles, W.
1974b   "Africanity: Its Role in Black Families." *The Black Scholar* June, 5:9, 10-17.

Nobles, W.
1978   "Toward an Empirical and Theoretical Framework for Defining Black Families." *Journal of Marriage and the Family* 40: 4, 679-688.

Nobles, W.
1981   "African-American Family Life: An Instrument of Culture," in H.P. McAdoo, *op. cit.*, 77-86.

Nobles, W. and L. L. Goddard
1985   "Black Family Life: A Theoretical and Policy Implication Literature Review," in A. Harvey, *op. cit.*, 23-89.

Norton, E.H.
1987   "Step by Step, the Court Helps Affirmative Action." *New York Times* May 13, op-ed article.

Ogbu, J.U.
1981   "Black Education: A Cultural-Ecological Perspective," in H.P. McAdoo, *op. cit.*, 139-154.

O'Hare, W.P., J. Li, R. Chatterjee, and M. Shukur
1982   *Blacks on the Move: A Decade of Demographic Change.* Washington, D.C.: Joint Center for Political Science.

Palmer, J.L. and I.V. Sawhill (eds.)
1984   *The Reagan Record.* Cambridge, MA: Ballinger Publishers.

Parker, S. and R.J. Kleiner
1969   "Social and Psychosocial Dimensions of the Family Role Performance of the Negro Male." *Journal of Marriage and the Family* 31: 3, 500-506.

Payton, I. S.
1982   "Single-Parent Households: An Alternative Approach." *Family
            Economics Review* Winter, U.S. Department. of Agriculture, 11-16.

Pearce, D., and H.P. McAdoo
1981   *Women and Children: Alone and in Poverty*. Washington, D.C.:
            National Advisory Council on Economic Opportunity.

Peters, M.F.
1974   "The Black Family: Perpetuating the Myths: An Analysis of Family
            Sociology Textbook Treatment of Black Families." *Family
            Coordinator* 23: 349-357.

Peters, M.F. and G. Massey
1983   "Mundane Extreme Environmental Stress in Family Stress
            Theories: The Case of Black Families in White America,"
            in *Social Stress and the Family*, 193-218.

Pinderhughes, E.B.
1982   "Family Functioning of Afro-Americans." *Social Work* January, 27:
            1, 91-96.

Pinkney, A.
1975   *Black Americans*. Englewood Cliffs, NJ: Prentice-Hall.

Pinkney, A.
1984   *The Myth of Black Progress*. Cambridge, MA: Cambridge
            University Press.

Piven, F.F. and R.A. Cloward
1971   *Regulating the Poor: The Functions of Public Welfare*. New York:
            Vintage Books.

Pleck, E.H.
1979   *Black Migration and Poverty*. New York: Academic Press.

Primm, B.J.
1987   "Drug Use" and "AIDS," *The State of Black America, 1987*. New
            York: National Urban League, 145-166.

Rainwater, L.
1970   *Behind Ghetto Walls: Black Family Life in a Federal Slum*. Chicago:
            Aldine Publishing Company.

Rainwater, L. and W.L. Yancey (eds.)
1967   *The Moynihan Report and the Politics of Controversy.* Cambridge,
                 MA: The MIT Press.

Randolph, A.P.
1931   "The Economic Crisis of the Negro." *Opportunity* 9:5, 145-149.

Reid, I.D.
1939   *The Negro Immigrant: His Background, Characteristics and Social
                 Adjustment, 1899-1937.* New York: Columbia University Press.

Reid, J.
1982   "Black America in the 1980s." *Population Bulletin* December, 37:4.

Rein, M.
1982   "Work in Welfare: Past Failures and Future Strategies." *Social
                 Service Review* June, 56: 2, 211-229.

Rein, M. and L. Rainwater
1977   "Patterns of Welfare Use." Boston: Joint Center for Urban Studies of
                 MIT and Harvard University, Working Paper No. 47.

Reissman, F.
1964   "Low-Income Culture: The Strengths of the Poor." *Journal of
                 Marriage and the Family* November, 25:4, 417-421.

Rodgers-Rose, L.F. (ed.)
1980   *The Black Woman.* Beverly Hills, CA: Sage Publications.

Ross, E. (ed.)
1978   *Black Heritage in Social Welfare: 1860-1930.* Metuchen, NJ: The
                 Scarecrow Press.

Rose, P.I., S. Rothman, and W. J. Wilson, (eds.)
1973   *Through Different Eyes: Black and White Perspectives on American
                 Race Relations.* New York: Oxford University Press.

Rosenthal, N.H.
1985   "The Shrinking Middle Class: Myth or Reality?" *Monthly Labor
                 Review* March, 108: 3, 3-10.

Ross, H.L. and I.V. Sawhill
1975   *Time of Transition: The Growth of Families Headed by Women.*
        Washington, D.C.: The Urban Institute.

Royce, D. and G. Turner,
1980   "Strengths of Black Families: A Black Community Perspective."
        Social Work 25: 407-409.

Rubin, R.H.
1974   "Adult Male Absence and the Self-Attitudes of Black Children."
        Child Study Journal 4: 1, 33-46.

Rubin, R.H.
1978   "Matriarchal Themes in Black Family Literature: Implications for
        Family Life Education." *The Family Coordinator* January 33-41.

Rubin, R.H.
1981   "Attitudes About Male-Female Relations Among Black
        Adolescents." *Adolescence* Spring, 16: 61, 159-174.

Sabshin, M., H. Diesenhaus, and R. Wilkerson
1970   "Dimensions of Institutional Racism in Psychiatry." *American
        Journal of Psychiatry* December 127: 6, 787-793.

Sandefur, G.D. and M. Tienda (eds.)
1988   *Divided Opportunities: Minorities, Poverty, and Social Policy.* New
        York: Plenum Press.

Sanger, M.B.
1984   "Generating Employment for AFDC Mothers." *Social Service
        Review* March 28-48.

Sasaki, M.S.,
1979   "Status Inconsistency and Religious Commitment," in R. Withnow
        (ed.) *The Religious Dimension.* New York: Academic Press.

Savage, B.D.
1987   "Child Support and Teen Parents." Washington, D.C.: Children's
        Defense Fund, November.

Scanzoni, J.H.
1971   *The Black Family in Modern Society.* Chicago: University of
        Chicago Press.

Schorr, L.B.
1988   *Within Our Reach: Breaking the Cycle of Disadvantage.* New York: Doubleday.

Schuman, H., C. Steeh, and L. Bobo
1985   *Racial Attitudes in America: Trends and Interpretations.* Cambridge, MA: Harvard University Press.

Sernett, M.C. (ed.)
1985   *Afro-American Religious History: A Documentary Witness.* Durham, NC: Duke University Press.

Shaw, C.R. and H.D. McKay
1931   *Social Factors in Juvenile Delinquency: Report on the Causes of Crime for the National Commission on Law Observance and Enforcement, Vol. II.* Washington, DC: Government Printing Office.

Shaw, C.R. and H.D. McKay
1942   *Juvenile Deliquency and Urban Areas.* Chicago: University of Chicago Press.

Shimkin, D. and V. Uchendu,
1978   "Persistence, Borrowing and Adaptive Changes in Black Kinship Systems," in D. Shimkin et al., *op. cit.*, 391-406.

Shimkin, D., E.M. Shimkin, and D.A. Frate (eds.)
1978   *The Extended Family in Black Societies.* The Hague: Mouton Publishers.

Sighall, H. and R. Page
1971   "Current Stereotypes: A Little Fading, A Little Faking." *Journal of Personality & Social Psychology* 18:2, 247-255.

Simms, M.C. (ed.)
1985-86   "Slipping Through the Cracks: The Status of Black Women." *The Review of Black Political Economy* Fall/Winter, 14: 2-3.

Sizemore, B.A.
1973   "Sexism and the Black Male." *The Black Scholar* March-April, 2-23.

Slaughter, D.T. and G.A. McWorter
1985   "Social Origins and Early Features of the Scientific Study of Black American Families and Children," in Spencer, et al, *op. cit.*, 5-18.

Smith, T. and P.B. Sheatsley
1984   "American Attitudes Toward Race Relations." *Public Opinion Quarterly* 7, 15-53.

Smith, W.A., A. Butler, M. Mosely, and W.W. Whitney
1978   *Minority Issues in Mental Health*. Reading, MA: Addison-Wesley Publishing Company.

Solomon, B.B.
1985   "The Inner-City Church: A Non-Traditional Setting for Mental Health Services, in A.R. Harvey, *op. cit.*, 129-154.

Solomon, B.B.
1987   "Social Welfare Reform," *The State of Black America, 1987*. New York: National Urban League, 113-127.

Sowell, T. (ed.)
1978   *Essays and Data on American Ethnic Groups*. Washington, D.C.: The Urban Institute.

Spencer, M.B., G.K. Brookins, and W. R. Allen (eds.)
1985   *Beginnings: The Social and Affective Development of Black Children*. Hillsdale, NJ: Lawrence Erlbaum Associates.

Stack, C.B.
1974   *All Our Kin: Strategies for Survival in a Black Community*. New York: Harper & Row.

Stack, C.B.
1987   *Calling Me Home: Black Homeplace Migration to the Rural South.* New York: Pantheon.

Stack, C.B. and H. Semmel
1973   "The Concept of Family in the Poor Black Community," *Studies in Public Welfare*. U.S. Congress, Joint Economic Committee, Paper No. 12, Part II, December 3, 275-305.

Staples, R.
1971a   "Toward a Sociology of the Black Family: A Theoretical and
             Methodological Assessment." *Journal of Marriage and the Family*
             February, 33, 19-38.

Staples, R. (ed.)
1971b   *The Black Family: Essays and Studies.* Belmont, CA: Wadsworth
             Publishing Company.

Staples, R. and A. Mirande
1980   "Racial and Cultural Variations Among American Families: A
             Decennial Review of the Literature on Minority Families." *Journal
             of Marriage and the Family* November, 42:4, 157-173.

Stembridge, B.J.
1978   *Proceedings of the Child Welfare Policy Conference: Issues and
             Answers in Region III.* Washington, D.C.: Institute for Urban
             Affairs & Research, Howard University.

Stewart, J.B.
1981a   "Some Factors Determining the Work Effort of Single Black
             Women." *Review of Social Economy* 40, 30-44.

Stewart, J.B.
1981b   "An Analysis of the Relationship Between New Household
             Formation by Young Black Females and Welfare Dependency."
             Presented at the Center for the Study of Economic Policy and
             Welfare Reform Conference, Wilberforce University, July.

Stewart, J.B.
1982   "Work Effort in Extended Black Households." Center for the
             Assessment of Economic Policy and Welfare Reform. Central State
             University, Wilberforce, Ohio. September.

Stewart, J.B.
1983   "Household Composition, Fixed Costs and Labor Supply in Black
             Female-Headed Households," Center for the Assessment of
             Economic Policy and Welfare Reform. Central State University,
             Wilberforce, Ohio. June, 1983.

Stewart, J.B. and L. Benjamin

1986   "The Influence of Household Composition and Helping Relationships
            on Values, Illness Orientation, Labor Force Participation and
            Welfare Dependency Among Black Women." Center for the
            Assessment of Economic Policy and Welfare Reform. Central State
            University, Wilberforce, Ohio. April.

Stewart, J.B. and T. J. Hyclak

1986   "The Effects of Immigrants, Women and Teenagers on the Relative
            Earnings of Black Males." *The Review of Black Political Economy*
            Summer, 15: 1, 93-101.

Stewart, J.B. and J.W. Scott

1978   "The Institutional Decimation of Black American Males." *Western
            Journal of Black Studies* Summer, 2, 82-92.

Stone, R.C. and F.T. Schlamp

1971   *Welfare and Working Fathers: Low-Income Family Life Styles.*
            Lexington, MA: Lexington Books.

Sudarkasa, N.

1975   "An Exposition on the Value Premises Underlying Black Family
            Studies." *Journal of the National Medical Association* 67:3, 235-239.

Sudarkasa, N.

1980   "African and Afro-American Family Structure: A Comparison." *The
            Black Scholar* November/ December, 11:8, 37-60.

Sudarkasa, N.

1981   "Interpreting the African Heritage in Afro-American Family
            Organization," in McAdoo, H.P., *op. cit*, 37-53.

Sussman, M. and L. Burchinal

1962   "Kin Family Network: Unheralded Structure in Current
            Conceptualization of Family Functioning." *Marriage and Family
            Living* 24, 231-240.

Swan, A.L.

1981a   *Families of Black Prisoners.* New York: G.K. Hall & Company.

Swan, A.L.

1981b   *Survival and Progress: The Afro-American Experience.* Wesport,
            CN: Greenwood Press.

Swinton, D.H.
1988   "Economic Status of Blacks: 1987," in *The State of Black America: 1988*. New York: National Urban League, 129-152.

Taylor, R.J.
1985   "The Extended Family as a Source of Support to Elderly Blacks." *The Gerontologist* 25:5, 488-495.

Taylor, R.J.
1986   "Receipt of Support from Family Among Black Americans." *Journal of Marriage and the Family* February, 48, 67-77.

Taylor, R.J.
1988   "Correlates of Religious Non-Imvolvement Among Black Americans." *Review of Religious Research* 30: 2, 126-139.

Taylor, R.L.
1981   "Psychological Modes of Adaptation," in L. Gary (ed.), *op. cit., 141-158.*

Taylor, R., M. Thornton, and L. Chatters
1987   "Black Americans' Perceptions of the Socio-Historical Role of the Church." *Journal of Black Studies* 18: 2, 123-138.

Teele, J.E.
1970   "Social Pathology and Stress," in S. Levine and N. Scotch (eds.), *Social Stress.* Chicago: Aldine, 228-256.

TenHouten, W.D.
1970   "The Black Family: Myth and Reality." *Psychiatry* May, 33: 2, 145-173.

Thomas, R.W.
1978   "Working-Class and Lower-Class Origins of Black Culture: Class Formation and the Division of Black Cultural Labor," in *Minority Voices*, 81-103.

Thompson, D.
1986   *A Black Elite.* Baton Rouge: Louisiana State University Press.

Toplin, R.B. (ed.)
1974   *Slavery and Race Relations in Latin America.* Westport, CN:
                Greenwood Press.

Turner, C.R.
1972   "Some Theoretical and Conceptual Considerations for Black Family
                Studies." *Blacklines* Winter, 2:2, 13-27.

Turner, L.D.
1949   *Africanisms in the Gullah Dialect.* Chicago: University of Chicago
                Press.

U.S. Bureau of Labor Statistics, Department of Labor
1983   *Linking Employment Problems to Economic Status.* Bulletin 2169.
                Washington, D.C.: Government Printing Office.

U.S. Bureau of Labor Statistics, Department of Labor
1984   *Linking Employment Problems to Economic Status.* Bulletin 2201.
                Washington, D.C.: Government Printing Office.

U.S. Bureau of Labor Statistics, Department of Labor
1984   *Families at Work: The Jobs and the Pay.* Bulletin 2209.
                Washington, D.C.: Government Printing Office.

U.S. Bureau of Labor Statistics, Department of Labor
1985   *Displaced Workers, 1979-1983.* Bulletin 2240. Washington, D.C.:
                Government Printing Office.

U.S. Bureau of the Census, Commerce Department
1982   "Coverage of the National Population in the 1980 Census by Age,
                Sex and Race." *Current Population Reports*, P-23: 115, February.

U.S. Bureau of the Census, Commerce Department
1983a   "Child Care Arrangements of Working Mothers: June 1982,"
                Current Population Reports: Special Studies, P-23:129.

U.S. Bureau of the Census, Commerce Department
1983b   "Labor Force Status and Other Characteristics of Persons with a
                Work Disability," *Current Population Reports; Speical Studies*,
                P-23: 127.

U.S. Bureau of the Census, Commerce Department
1985   "Characteristics of the Population Below the Poverty Level: 1983,"
                Current Population Reports, P-60:147.

U.S. Bureau of the Census, Commerce Department
1987   "Money Income and Poverty Status of Families and Persons in the
                U.S.: 1986," *Current Population Reports*, P-60: 157.

U.S. Congressional Budget Office, Congress of the United States
1985   *Reducing Poverty Among Children*, May.

U.S. Executive Office of the President, Office of Policy Development
1986   "A Self-Help Catalog," *Up from Dependency*, December.

U.S. Executive Office of the President
1987   "Compendium of Public Assistance Programs," *Up from
                Dependency*, Vol. 2, September.

U.S. Housing and Urban Development
1979   "Report on Housing Displacement." Washington, D.C.: Government
                Printing Office.

U.S. Public Health Service, Health and Human Services Department
1985   *Health Status of Minorities and Low Income Groups*. Washington,
                D.C.: Government Printing Office.

U.S. Social Security Administration
1986   "Social Security Programs in the United States." *Social Security
                Bulletin* January, 49:1, 5-59.

Valentine, C.A.
1968   *Culture and Poverty: Critique and Counter-Proposals*. Chicago:
                University of Chicago Press.

Valentine, C.A.
1971   "Deficit, Difference, and Bicultural Models of Afro-American
                Behavior. *Harvard Educational Review* May, 41:2, 137-157.

Viscusi, W.K.
1986   "Market Incentives for Criminal Behavior," in Freeman & Holzer
                (ed.) *op. cit.*, 301-351.

Weiss, H.
1982   "Neighborhoods as Contexts for Child Development," in Cochran & Henderson, *op. cit.*, Chapter 4.

Warner, W.L. and P. Lunt
1942   *The Status of a Modern Community.* New Haven: Yale University Press.

Werner, E.E. and R. S. Smith
1982   *Vulnerable but Invincible: A Longitudinal Study of Resilient Children and Youth.* New York: McGraw-Hill.

Wicker, A.W.
1969   "Attitudes Versus Action." *Journal of Social Issues* 25:4, 41-78.

Wilkinson, D.Y. and R.L. Taylor
1970   *The Black Male in America.* Chicago: Nelson Hall.

Williams, J.A. and R. Stockton
1973   "Black Family Structures and Functions: An Empirical Examination of Some Suggestions Made by Billingsley." *Journal of Marriage and The Family* February, 35: 1, 39-49.

Williams, W.E.
1982   *The State Against Blacks.* New York: McGraw-Hill.

Willie, C.V.
1970   *The Family Life of Black People.* Columbus, OH: Charles E. Merrill.

Willie, C.V.
1976   *A New Look at Black Families.* New York: General Hall.

Willie, C.V.
1983   "Dominance in the Family," in C. Willie, *Race, Ethnicity and Socioeconomic Status.* New York: General Hall, 156-162.

Willie, C.V.
1985   *Black and White Families: A Study in Complementarity.* New York: General Hall.

Wilson, W.J.
1973   *Power, Racism and Privilege.* New York: Free Press.

Wilson, W.J.
1978   *The Declining Significance of Race*. Chicago: University of Chicago
            Press.

Wilson, W.J.
1987   *The Truly Disadvantaged: The Inner City, the Underclass and
            Public Policy*. Chicago: University of Chicago Press.

Wilson, W.J. and K. Neckerman
1986   "Poverty and Family Structure," in Danziger and Weinberg (eds.),
            op. cit.

Wimberly, E.
1979   *Pastoral Care in the Black Church*. Nashville, TN: Abingdon Press.

Woodson, C.G.
1936   *The African Background Outlined or Handbook for the Study of the
            Negro*. Washington, D.C.: The Association for the Study of Negro
            Life and History.

Woodson, R.L.
1981a   *A Summons to Life: Mediating Structures and the Prevention of
            Youth Crime*. Cambridge, MA: Ballinger Publishers.

Woodson, R.L. (ed.)
1981b   *Youth Crime and Urban Policy: A View from the Inner City*.
            Washington, D.C.: American Enterprise Institute.

Woodson, R.L.
1987   *On the Road to Economic Freedom: An Agenda for Black Progress*.
            Washington, D.C.: Regnery Gateway.

Yearwood, L.S.
1980   *Black Organizations: Issues on Survival Techniques*. Landham, MD:
            University Press of America.

Young, V.H.
1970   "Family and Childhood in a Southern Negro Community."
            American Anthropologist 72, 269-288.